EMINENT TRACTARIANS

EMINENT TRACTARIANS

*How Lay Followers of the Oxford Revival
Expressed their Faith in Their
'Trivial Round and Common Task'*

John Neville Greaves

Book Guild Publishing
Sussex, England

First published in Great Britain in 2015 by
The Book Guild Ltd
The Werks
45 Church Road
Hove, BN3 2BE

Typesetting in Garamond by
Keyboard Services, Luton, Bedfordshire

Printed and bound in Great Britain by
CPI Group (UK) Ltd, Croydon, CR0 4YY

A catalogue record for this book is available from
The British Library.

ISBN 978 1 910298 36 7

To Iris

(Genesis 9:13, NIV)

Contents

Acknowledgements

The first encouragement I received for this study was from Bishop Geoffrey Rowell and from Professor Martin Daunton, of Cambridge University (via a friend), and I was greatly helped by Bishop David Jenkins of Durham, Dr John Court of the University of Kent at Canterbury, and Professor Elizabeth Schafer of the University of London. Very helpful were the Archivist of Keble College, Oxford, and Lord Aldenham, at Holwell Manor, Dorset, with access to their archives.

Important guidance was received from Professor Jeremy Gregory of Manchester University and Dr Sheridan Gilley of Durham, and I had warm co-operation from the National Trust Archive at Tyntesfield and Rachel Gibbs, and from Harvey Starey, and from Betty Payne of Bursey Farm, East Yorkshire.

The wealth of our country's archive systems, at the British Library, the Guildhall, the London Metropolitan Archive, the Mander and Mitcheson Collection at the Old Royal Naval College at Greenwich, the Bristol University Theatre Archive, and the William Salt Library in Stafford proved invaluable. The Manchester Central Library and the Library Interchange Service (especially that at Knighton, Powys) were also most helpful.

Finally, as always, Gladstone's Library at Hawarden, Flintshire, provided a unique atmosphere of resource for research and writing.

None of the above is in any way responsible for shortcomings, in conception or execution, which are entirely my own.

Preface

The history and impact of the Oxford Revival, dating from 1833, has been well written up and interpreted by scholars. However, such studies and analyses have been concerned with the importance of the influence of individual clergy leaders on the ecclesiology, doctrine and liturgy of the Church of England (this is quite in accordance with the address of the 'Tracts for the Times' as *ad clerum*).

The present study is addressed to the way in which the lay followers of the principles and convictions of the Oxford Movement expressed their loyalty in the way they conducted, day by day, their business and professional lives. The question at issue is: How did their faith affect the conduct of their worldly activities? Their faithfulness to contracts and agreements; their openness in financial matters; their honesty regarding taxation and official levies. Was their firm faith integrated, and evident to others, in their moral and ethical conduct, professionally, and in fairness, justice and compassion, in staff relationships and personal relations?

Clearly, only a selected number of individuals can be examined – those who were the most widely known – and not a comprehensive study of each and every Christian in the category. The four main subjects of this study, and their varied occupations, are:

1 The House of Antony Gibbs and Sons, merchants, with special reference to William Gibbs (1790–1875), and his nephew Henry Hucks Gibbs (1819–1907), who was also Governor of the Bank of England.

2 William Butterfield (1814–1900), architect.
3 Thomas Percival Heywood (1823–1897), Manchester banker.
4 Lilian Mary Baylis (1874–1937), theatre entrepreneur.

Introduction: The Origins and Ethos of the Oxford Movement

Moral Virtue comes about as a result of habit, whence also its name, ηθικη, *is one that is formed by a slight variation from the word* εθοσ *(habit).*

Aristotle[1]

The last decade of the eighteenth century and the first two of the nineteenth marked a period of rapid social change and religious unease. The rationalism of the Enlightenment and the French Revolution posed serious questions to both Church and State in England. There was much spiritual activity in response to the challenges, and the Evangelical Revival sought to restore the theology of the English Reformers from the neglect into which it had fallen. High Churchmen blamed the decline of the Church of England on the disregard shown for Patristic theology, after it had reached its climax of influence in the Caroline Divines.

In 1797 the evangelical William Wilberforce had sounded a warning note about the crisis in the Church of England: religion had disappeared in the higher orders of society as a guide for conduct. Some still considered it useful for keeping the common people in order, but for Wilberforce a system not supported by a real persuasion of its truth would soon collapse. The eighteenth

---

[1] *Nichomachean Ethics,* tr. Sir David Ross [Oxford: Clarendon Press, 1961], p. 28.

1

century had separated moral precepts from the doctrines of Christianity. These doctrines had almost vanished from sight, and the whole moral system was decaying, cut off from its roots and nourishment. The establishment could not survive long without a revival of vital religion, a restoration of evangelical authority.[2]

Others, too, saw an unprecedented crisis approaching, but found it difficult to see where the remedy was to come from. 'Where now is the Church of England?' exclaimed Charles Daubeny[3] in his Archidiaconal Charge in 1824, and there were not a few who lamented the 'weak and divided' Church in the face of the rising tide. Beyond orthodox Evangelical and High Churchmen there were others advocating Church reform: men like Thomas Arnold,[4] Headmaster of Rugby School from 1828 to 1842, and Professor of History at Oxford in 1841, who all agreed on the existence of a general malaise.[5]

Several groups were formed to discuss the existing crisis in both religion and politics, and to seek a clear way of resolution. Among these groups were gatherings of High Churchmen who became forerunners of the Oxford Movement itself. The largest and most enduringly influential of these 'societies' was that known as 'Nobody's Friends'. This was founded in 1800 by the Hutchinsonian William Stevens (1731 or 1732–1807), a society composed equally of clergy and laity, who were concerned about the spiritual state of the nation. They were dedicated to 'The cherishing and maintaining of those sound religious and political principles ... which under the Divine blessing have made the Church and state of England to be by God's goodness what they are, and will ... notwithstanding the dangers which now seem to threaten their peace and safety, continue to sustain the Altar and

---

[2] James Periero, *Ethos and the Oxford Movement* [Cambridge University Press, 1983], pp. 49 and 50.
[3] 1745–1827.
[4] 1795–1842.
[5] Periero, ibid., pp. 51 and 52.

throne of England for many generations.' The society derived
its name from its founder, who described himself, out of modesty
in his pseudonymous publications, as 'Nobody'. Membership, by
election, was restricted to fifty at any one time (raised to sixty
in the late 1870s).[6] When the Oxford Movement coalesced
around the issue of the Irish Bishoprics and John Keble's sermon
in 1833, many, if not most, of the members became devoted
followers of the Renewal. There was a perceived need for dogmatism
and asceticism – a relationship with a lively and personal
God, rather than with a remote and passive creator – a revolt
against the cold rationalism in the Church and in the universities.
John Henry Newman saw that in these circumstances, 'there was,
besides and above all, a higher agent promoting the spiritual
revival.'[7]

The two movements – the Evangelical and the Tractarian –
both had their part in the revitalisation of the Church of England,
and many of the prominent figures of the Oxford Revival – Robert
Wilberforce, Newman, Manning, Gladstone among them – were
strongly influenced by the Evangelical revival before becoming
Tractarians. According to Wilberforce, the first quarter of the
century was a prelude to the second of the two revivals; he claimed
that in the providence of God the second was a sort of consequence
of the first.[8]

It is not possible to understand the Oxford Movement without
a study of the character of John Keble and his perception of the

[6] 'The Club of Nobody's Friends: Biographical List of the Members Since its Foundation
on 21 June 1800 to 30 September 1885' [London: Privately Printed], p. vii. Membership
at that time, including those replaced at their death, was over 300. The club exists to
this day.
[7] Periero, ibid, pp. 62 and 64.
[8] ibid., pp. 66 and 67. Although, in long retrospect, there were seen to be too many
differences in doctrine and emphasis for this observation to be agreed by late twentieth-
century evangelicals [Periero, p. 69]. (cf. also Peter Toon, *Evangelical Theology, 1833–1856*
[London: Marshall, Morgan and Scott, 1979], pp. 209 and 210).

'participation' of God in every sphere of human development, particularly in his appreciation of the importance of the doctrine of the Incarnation. Although William Law (1686–1761) had, in his devotional writings, stressed the influence of the passions on human reasoning, it was the full-blooded expression of them in Southey and Wordsworth which inspired Keble's poetry.[9] He was a lifelong admirer of Wordsworth, but he saw nature as a sacrament, of which the Church's sacraments were a concentration of a wide manifestation of God's love and encouragement.[10] A prominent feature of Keble's legacy to the Oxford Movement, and thus arguably to the Church of England, is the concept of Reserve, and Christian resignation. He believed that emotion, blowing hot one minute and cold the next, was a danger to true religion, which was best expressed in reserve, and sacred matters should be expressed calmly and soberly. It was akin to the Church Fathers' concept of *disciplina arcana* – the discipline of the secret. Keble himself observed that he could be misinterpreted by some as supporting the Gnostic notion of knowledge accessible to only a few.[11] But 'reserve' stemmed from the saying of Jesus in Matthew, chapter 7 verse 6, about not casting precious things before the uncomprehending.[12]

It was John Keble who helped to form the moral ideal of the Movement which was essential to its theological development.[13] He saw the primary aim of education, in its broadest and truest sense, as the formation of a right *ethos*; moral uprightness was a fundamental precondition for clear intellectual perception, and so intellectual training could not be dissociated from moral formation.[14]

---

[9] Periero, ibid., p. 78. Keble was Professor of Poetry at Oxford University from 1831 to 1841.
[10] Georgina Battiscombe, *John Keble* [London: Constable and Co. Ltd, 1963], pp. 36, 50, and 44.
[11] Sermon in Winchester Cathedral, 27 September 1836.
[12] For a full study of this point, see Robin C. Selby, *The Principle of Reserve in the Writings of John Henry Cardinal Newman* [Oxford University Press, 1975].
[13] Owen Chadwick, *The Spirit of the Oxford Movement* [CUP, 1990], p. 25.
[14] Periero, ibid., p. 86.

He learned from Bishop Butler, whose purpose in his *Analogy*[15] was a practical one – 'to bring his hearers and readers to the acceptance and practice of virtue religion;'[16] an exhortation to do the right thing, not that of vice. He commended the primary and fundamental laws of civilisation, namely justice, veracity, and regard for the common good. Butler considered that 'Conduct, behaviour, abstracted from all regard to what is in fact and event the consequence of it, is itself the object of moral discernment.[17] As against Utilitarianism he said, 'The happiness of the world is the concern of him who is the Lord and Proprietor of it; nor do we know what we are about when we endeavour to promote the good of mankind in any ways but those which he has directed.'[18]

Keble learned also from Aristotle the details of virtue as set out in *The Nichomachean Ethics*: his concept of φρονησισ – understanding, practical wisdom; and αρετε – virtue: moral excellence, strengths developed towards the gradual making of a flourishing human being. 'Moral virtue comes about,' says Aristotle, 'as a result of habit, whence also its name (ηθικη) is one that is formed by a slight variation from the word εθοσ (habit).'[19] From his view of the habitual formation of virtue, it is plain that 'none of the virtues arises in us by Nature, for nothing that exists by nature can form a habit contrary to its nature ... the virtues we get first by exercising them ... Legislators make the citizens good by forming habits in them. Otherwise there would be no need of a teacher. By doing the acts that we do, in our transactions with other men, we become just or unjust... It makes all the

[15] *Analogy of Religion, Natural and Revealed, to the Constitution and Course of Nature* (1733).
[16] Terence Penelhum, *Butler* [London: Routledge and Kegan Paul, 1985]. '[Butler] gives no definition of 'virtue' or 'conscience': his cause was not philosophical but practical – refuting deism, moral laxity, indifference and scepticism, utilitarianism, frivolity, and muddled theory', pp. 4 and 5.
[17] P. Allan Carlsson, *Butler's Ethics* [London: Mouton and Co., 1964], p. 98.
[18] Carlsson, p. 104.
[19] Aristotle, *Nichomachean Ethics*, tr. Sir David Ross [Oxford: Clarendon Press, 1961], p. 28.

difference whether we form habits of one kind or another from our very youth ... [habits] of virtues or vices.'[20] Thus moral virtue can be attained only by those who are good; virtue is unattainable by those who are not habitually good. 'To act virtuously is not as Kant was later to think, to act against inclination; it is to act from inclination formed by the cultivation of the virtues.'[21] Associated with αρετη is δοκιμη – experience, character, and its cognate forms meaning testing and proving.[22] 'The concept of "ethos", in its modern and Tractarian sense, was coined by Keble as meaning the dominant moral habit or proclivity,'[23] as growing from the acquisition of sound habits through the repetition of good habits. In his *Analogy* Butler was defending Christianity against unbelief, but Keble developed him further, applying his arguments to the maintenance of orthodoxy against heresy. For Keble, moral qualities were of greater importance than intellectual ones when analysing the truth of religious propositions. His friend J.T. Coleridge, in his *Memoir of the Revd John Keble*, was a little dismissive of, and confused by, Keble's key word 'ethos'. He wrote that the concept 'imparted certainly no intellectual quality, scarcely any distinct moral one, but an habitual toning or colouring diffused over all man's moral qualities, giving the exercise of them a peculiar gentleness and grace.'[24] But Keble was quite clear, especially when he argued that the interpretation of God's works was more fruitfully arrived at through the moral sense, the sober and devout spirit, than that attempted through solely intellectual means, [which engendered], spiritually, pride and the like. The search for truth could not be separated from the pursuit of goodness. 'This was a reversal of the Enlightenment view of intellectual education as leading necessarily towards moral rectitude.'

---

[20] ibid., pp. 28, 29 and 36.
[21] Alasdair Macintyre, *After Virtue* [London: Gerald Duckworth and Co. Ltd, 1994], p. 149.
[22] As for example in Romans chapter 1 verse 28, and 12 verse 2; I Corinthians 16:3; II Corinthians 13:5; and Philippians 1:10.
[23] James Periero, in *John Keble in Context*, Ed. Kirstie Blair [London: Anthem Press, 2004], pp. 65 and 59.
[24] p. 384.

He used the term 'ethos' to refer to the moral disposition of character.[25]

Keble saw the search for truth as a spiral ascending movement: moral rectitude facilitates the discovery of truth; truth discovered should commit the person vitally; that commitment in turn would bring with it a clearer perception of revealed truth, which was there all the time, but perceived as new. Ethos *was* above intellect, but for intellect's sake. This argument is in contrast with Newman's theory of the 'Development of Christian Doctrine,' set out some years later. Keble's view is that of new, re-discovery; Newman's the theory of evolution.'[26]

The concept of 'ethos' was among those to develop further as the years went by, being conceived as a light helping men to find religious truth among a variety of possible answers, and to distinguish it from error.[27]

Developments from Keble's *Assize Sermon* of 14 July 1833

Support for the Tractarian protest against government encroachment on the Church's authority came from a movement formed in Cambridge on 21 November 1859. The objectives of the Church Defence Association were to circulate information about the position, rights, and claims of the Church, and to present petitions to parliament when appropriate. In addition it was a reply to attacks by 'The Society for the Liberation of Religion from State Patronage and Control, and Towards the Appropriation of Ecclesiastical Revenues of the Church of England for Secular Purposes'. Because 1862 was the bicentenary of the ejection of 2000 puritan clergymen, Nonconformists wanted to observe the occasion with an accusation against the Church of religious intolerance.[28]

---

[25] See Periero, in Kirstie Blair, Ed., pp. 63 and 64.
[26] Georgina Battiscombe, *John Keble* [London: Constable and Co. Ltd, 1963], p. 194.
[27] Periero, in Kirstie Blair, Ed., p. 69.
[28] *Encyclopaedia Britannica*, 1911 edition.

The Church Defence Association was initiated by the Archdeacon of Ely, in collaboration with others, and it inaugurated a series of annual Church Congresses, held in different parts of the country, from 1861 in Cambridge until the last one in Newport in 1930. The Congresses had no legislative authority, but were attended by bishops (including both the archbishops), clergy and laity, discussing key problems of vital relevance to Church life – religious, social and moral. Several lay members of 'Nobody's Friends' made important contributions to the debates.

The first half of the nineteenth century has been called The Age of Atonement, which began, as another kind of reaction, springing from the Evangelical Revival, against the effects of the French Revolution and the rise of Roman Catholic influences.[29] The Evangelical manifesto issued by William Wilberforce considered the world as 'In a state of alienation from God, lost in depravity and guilt to which the Atonement was the only hope of absolution, and the only emancipation from the power of moral corruption.'[30] But by mid-century a transition had been made from the Atonement to the Incarnation – 'The Word made flesh' – gradually from about 1840, and by 1870 Christmas was being stressed more than Easter. This was true not only of Anglicans, but also of Evangelicals: Dr Robert William Dale (1829–1895) was Minister of Carr's Lane Chapel in Birmingham in 1852. It was said of his preaching 'that it was hard-hitting and sharply-focussed'; he was one of the foremost Congregationalists of his generation and his theological writings, particularly on the Atonement, were of central importance.'[31] 'His popular influence outside the pulpit was extensive, and his works ... were widely read and recommended by different denominations. He was a public figure of significance, urging active involvement in

---

[29] Boyd Hilton, *The Age of Atonement, 1785–1865* [Oxford University Press, 1991], pp. 3–5.
[30] In *A Practical View of Christianity* [1797].
[31] E. Jane Garnett, *Aspects of the Relationship between Protestant Ethics and Economic Activity in Mid-Victorian Britain*, Unpublished D.Phil Thesis, University of Oxford, 1987, p. 279.

municipal affairs and promoting educational developments in Birmingham in co-operation with Joseph Chamberlain. He was chairman of the Congregational Union from 1869 to 1888.'[32]

In view of Dale's prominence in the evangelical community (one of his books was on 'The Evangelical Revival'), a sermon he preached at the Argyle Street Chapel in Bath on 8 October 1889 is important. 'For the first forty years of the Evangelical Revival,'[33] he said, 'the churches were distinguished for their ardour, their hopefulness, and their courage: they were confident that the evil times had passed away, that the very glory of God had broken upon the darkness of many centuries, and that the day was not remote when all nations would rejoice in the blessedness of the Christian redemption.' He pointed out that the movement had its own characteristic *ethos* – it disregarded the notion of an ideal church organisation or church polity. 'Its fellowship was of an accidental and precarious kind. It cared nothing for the idea of the Church as an august society of saints. It was the ally of individualism.'[34] 'Its leaders had very little to say about the relations of the individual Christian to the general order of society ... or the realisation of the Kingdom of God in all the various regions of human activity.'[35] 'It had no eagerness to take possession of the realms of Art, Science, Literature, Politics, Commerce, Industry, in the name of their true Sovereign and Prince ... Its ethical ideals of the individual Christian was wanting in wealth and variety; for the ethical perfection of the individual is determined by his relations to the Church and to the whole order of the world.'[36] He went on to speak of a 'great panic among English Congregationalists (about 1849), when "high authorities" were charging younger ministers with changing the *ethos* of the Evangelical Revival in caring for Truth for its own sake, and not merely as an instrument for converting the

---

[32] ibid., p. 280.
[33] Sc. to 1825. Sermon published as *The Old Evangelicalism and the New* [London: Hodder and Stoughton, 1889], p. 15.
[34] R.W. Dale, ibid., p. 17.
[35] ibid., p. 18.
[36] ibid., p. 19.

world.' They had become interested in Biblical Criticism, and discussed the nature of Inspiration. The Bible was authoritative; but they wanted a theory of its authority: what the Bible really meant, not its use as a source of proof texts.[37] 'One of Evangelicalism's deficiencies was not to surround men with a Christian society which would have educated and disciplined those we had brought to God in their personal life: the fellowship of the saints, with its ethical and spiritual traditions, with its spiritual brotherhood, and with its supernatural atmosphere, is a great means of grace.'[38] There was also confusion, he claimed, among evangelicals about redemption and the fate of those who refused the Gospel: hell and damnation, or a second chance, or even Universalism.[39] Dale goes as far as to say that the former conviction on such detailed Biblical interpretation of sin and Atonement had lost its place to a conviction that the Incarnation lies deeper than the Atonement; the way that creation and society opens up a coherent conception of all that man has learnt of the ways of God, to man is a form of 'wisdom', he says.[40]

'The two great truths of Justification by Faith and the Atonement rest on the deeper truth of the union between man and Christ.'[41] This would seem to represent, in one of evangelicalism's strongholds, the final displacement of the doctrine of the Atonement by that of the Incarnation, which was the defining doctrine of the Oxford Revival. By 1870 it was commonplace for Anglicans to assert that 'a transformation had taken place in which Christian compassion … had alleviated such stark evangelical doctrines as those of eternal and vicarious punishment, an emphasis on Jesus as a man, rather than as a lamb, Christology rather than soteriology.'[42]

The dominant theology of evangelicalism stressed conversion and grace as against the dry rationalism of the eighteenth century, but

---

[37] R.W. Dale, ibid., pp. 23–27.
[38] ibid., p. 31.
[39] ibid. pp. 38–48.
[40] ibid., p. 49.
[41] ibid. p. 51.
[42] Hilton, ibid., p. 5.

nevertheless most evangelicals stood for the rationalistic and mechanistic tradition of eighteenth-century natural theology. This was, in summary, the assumption that a 'distinct discontinuity exists between this world and the next. God transcends this world ... and his creatures are all in a state of natural depravity ... Life is an area of moral trial ... in which men are tempted, tested, and ultimately sorted into saints and sinners, in readiness for the Day of Judgement,' and dispatched to either Heaven or Hell. 'The organ of redemption is the individual conscience ... and the means are provided by Christ's Atonement on the Cross, which purchased ransom for the sins of all mankind ... Justification comes through faith in that Atonement. This all-important contractual relationship is directly between each soul and its maker: such intermediaries as priests and sacraments are of relatively little significance.'[43]

Pre-millenarianism, often of an antinomian and apocalyptic other-worldliness, alienated many moderate evangelicals, pushing them away in a High-Church direction.[44] From this individualistic viewpoint, it can be seen that the economy, which engaged so many of God's creatures, was a sphere of great spiritual trial and confusion of conscience. As God had instituted a permanent moral law on earth, a 'natural' and predictable in-built system of rewards and punishments appropriate to good and bad behaviour, society should work as closely to nature as possible by repealing interventionist laws, leaving men to work out their own salvation in peace in the course of their worldly duties. Governments should interfere in men's lives as little as possible, so that men could exercise self-help – the only means to salvation, both spiritually and economically – in a world beset with temptation. This enshrined doctrines of self-help, *laissez-faire,* and Free Trade. God runs the material world on these lines, and so men should not meddle either.[45]

---

[43] Hilton, p. 8, quoting from Henry Venn's *Complete Duty of Man* (1763), and Wilberforce's *Practical View.*
[44] ibid., p. 10.
[45] ibid., pp. 13, 16, and 17.

Several prominent Tractarians began their spiritual pilgrimage as Evangelicals, as noted above, but became followers of the Oxford Revival. However, trace elements of evangelicalism remained with them. For example, Gladstone retained a fundamental belief in the Fall – in Original Sin – and John Henry Newman had absorbed with the evangelical creed some impressions of dogma which, 'through God's mercy', have never been effaced or ignored.[46] This common inheritance has been attributed to John Wesley and the religious movement he initiated in the eighteenth century, according to Hilton (p. 28). Nevertheless the clear dividing line between them was drawn by the tendency, from mid-century, towards the doctrine of the Incarnation as God's blessing on his creation – becoming 'matter' himself – from that of Atonement, which pre-supposed a Creator at enmity with his creation, and needing a sacrifice as a propitiation. The movement from the spiritual terrorism of Hell, and the idea that God should make the innocent suffer for the sins of others, was gradually making way for the doctrine of a loving Father.[47] 'The Incarnation, and not the Atonement, is the foundation-centre of the redemption of man,' wrote Charles Edward Kennaway, Vicar of Camden, as early as 1849, following Robert Wilberforce.[48] This was a shift of ground from a static, 'natural' theology based on 'evidencies' to a more dynamic view of the natural world – God's wisdom, goodness and power being shown more and more in 'development'. 'A new concept of the stream of time, continuity, and a more linear view than the concept of stasis which preceded it.'[49]

Regarding 'Socialism', Christian or secular, the other inheritance of the Enlightenment and the French Revolution, Percy Dearmer asserted in 1908 that it was 'from Christianity alone that the world has learned the inestimable value of each human soul, the freedom, the responsibility of each separate human being. There

---

[46] *Apologia Pro Vita Sua*, p. 58. Both quoted, Hilton, p. 27.
[47] Hilton, pp. 277 and 283.
[48] ibid., pp. 288 and 289.
[49] ibid., pp. 299 and 301.

are dangers in concerted action … and entralisation … The Church is the oldest socialistic institution in existence.'[50] In this, Dearmer was echoing some words of John Keble: 'The true socialism, the true Liberty, Equality and Fraternity, was encapsulated in the teaching that Rich and Poor are one in Christ – in the One, Holy, Catholic Church.'[51] The mantle of the question of the Gospel mandate of care for the poor, and the practical demonstration of God's love for all sorts and conditions of men fell to the developing social theology of the Church itself. This doctrine was assumed by the priests and laity of the Oxford Revival, which put it into theological orthodoxy and orthopraxis at street level in the parishes throughout the land.

Such reflections led the Movement eventually to the consideration of The Christian Faith as a Philosophy. Immanuel Kant, the most influential Enlightenment thinker on the ethics of Protestant morality, formulated a rule, his 'Categorical Imperative', which stated that the moral man or woman should 'So act that you can Will the maxim of your action to be a universal law'[52] or, in an alternative formulation, 'Act always as though to treat yourself and others as an end in themselves, and not as mere means.'[53] Kant's position is that the individual person's ethical and social problems are a question of practical reason. His individualism at times almost denies an objective existence to the community, seeing it only as the harmony of individual viewpoints and actions, rather than an entity which shapes perception of a person's self-awareness and that of other people.[54]

Hegel, with his philosophical system deriving from the notion of the revelation in history of the 'Geist' or 'Idea' behind the

---

[50] In an address to the Church Congress held in October 1908 in Manchester, Official Report, pp. 96–99.
[51] In a sermon in Winchester Cathedral in 1863.
[52] Hegel commented that this formula failed to distinguish between permissible maxims and impermissible ones. [Allen W. Wood, *Hegel's Ethics*; The Cambridge Companion to Hegel, Ed. Frederick C. Beiser, Cambridge University Press, 1993], p. 223.
[53] *Dictionary of Ethics, Theology.*
[54] ibid., p. 311.

universe – a comprehensive statement of the theological principle of the Incarnation of the 'Logos' – the 'reason behind the Creation,' was thus in reaction against Kant. Hegel's influence began to be felt in the second half of the century, especially upon the English Idealist philosophers, and in particular Thomas Hill Green (1836–1882), tutor at Oriel College. 'Green, in turn, influenced certain theologians, especially those of the Lux Mundi school.'[55]

T.H. Green's concern as the nineteenth century progressed was the threat to Christian dogma posed by the doubts cast upon its origin by David Hume's empiricism and the German school of Biblical theology. Green's argument was that the Church's propositions should become a philosophy.[56] He found this in the reconciliation of opposites, the unification of reality, which is represented in German Idealism: the exposition of an all-encompassing system which posited the requirement of creation for its fulfilment. The Incarnation of the Creator (Geist) unified the Otherness with human life and history.[57] 'Human institutions are … epiphanies of God, and they stand to individuals in an almost sacramental manner.[58] He was attracted by the concept of an overall, inclusive, metaphysic – the world as 'indeed a unity, governed by a single law, animated by an undivided life, constituting a whole; … it enabled one to make sense of the whole, and fit one's self and one's actions into it.'[59] Such a foundational concept appealed to the generation of Tractarian theologians unhappy with a view of reality divided into two in various ways – Creator opposed to the creation, individual as prior to corporate, art and science as enemies of the Spirit.

Thus could a contributor to *Lux Mundi (1889)* declare that

---

[55] Ernest G. Braham, *Ourselves and Reality* [London: Epworth Press, 1929], p. 31.
[56] Andrew Vincent and Raymond Plant, *Philosophy, Politics and Citizenship: The Life and Thought of the British Idealists* [Basil Blackwell, 1984], p. 9.
[57] ibid., pp. 10 and 11, cf also Raymond Plant, *Politics Theology and History* [CUP, 2001], p. 130.
[58] Vincent and Plant, p. 10.
[59] Peter Hinchliff, *God and History: Aspects of British Theology, 1875–1914* [Oxford: Clarendon Press, 1992], p.125.

'Secular civilisation is ... in the Christian view, nothing less than the providential correlative and counterpart of the Incarnation ... which opened heaven and reconstituted earth.'[60] The doctrine of the Incarnation, in contrast to the Protestant emphasis on the Atonement – the total corruption of the world, and the concomitant rejection of the flesh (matter) as evil in itself – was to liberate the Church of England from its negativity, and restore it to a fuller exposition of the texts 'God so loved the world', and 'The Word became flesh', and 'God was in Christ, reconciling the world to himself'.

Virtue

The concept of 'Virtue' – of behaviour governed not by blind obedience to rules, but by a developed character, or informed conscience, an absorption of the tenets of attested principles, which determines action according to a comprehension of the individual and the notion of the common good – was not new. It appears in Plato and Aristotle.[61] It was incorporated into applied Christian spirituality by Thomas Aquinas (1225–1274), but was rejected by Martin Luther at the Reformation, on the grounds that to live the virtues as if we had already made the long journey to character-forming to make them part of us, was to be hypocritical.[62] This benighted the Church's thinking on the subject for a long time. But in the nineteenth century the word was retrieved to exemplify the way in which Christians could live a virtuous life without being slaves to laws and commandments, but being conscientious in 'putting on the Lord Jesus Christ', in developing Christian character.

T.H. Green said, 'Virtue is the achievement of men who have not only learnt to recognise and value the spiritual qualities to which

---

[60] J.R. Illingworth, in *Lux Mundi*, p. 155.
[61] For example, Aristotle, *The Nichomachean Ethics* [OUP, 1961. Tr. Sir David Ross], pp. 28–39, etc.
[62] N.T. Wright, *Virtue Reborn* [SPCK, 2010], p. 52.

material things serve as instruments or means of expression, but have formed the abstract conception of a universe of values.'[63] In other words, 'virtue describes a virtuous act as one that is fitting, in an appropriate setting, performed by a person who has cultivated in his or her life, wisdom, good character, and human excellence.

'The distillation of the modern, secular, search for sound principles of ethics in the business world has been characterised by raising up the concept of the failure of the Enlightenment faith in Reason as the [sole] guide for human conduct. It has, in secularised rationalism, emancipated humanity from the control of religion, [but] in its failure to establish a new moral consensus, it has brought religion into a sharper focus to the recovery of moral authority.'[64]

Lux Mundi

A group of theologians, under the leadership of Charles Gore (1853–1932), came together in 1875 with the intention of writing a comprehensive survey of the theology of the Oxford Movement, and the result of their labours was published under the above title, which Boyd Hilton described as '*The Coup de Grâce* of the doctrine of the Atonement'.[65] Their aim was 'To put the Catholic faith into its right relation to modern intellectual and moral problems ... to look afresh at what the Christian faith really means ... to find that it is as adequate as ever to interpret life and knowledge in its separate departments.'[66] 'Man has to appreciate the times he lives in ... the epoch in which we live is one of profound transformation, intellectual

---

[63] In *Prolegomena* to *Ethics*, Ed. A.C. Bradley, [Oxford: Clarendon Press, 1906], Section 243, p. 287. (It remains to be seen how in the twenty-first century the attention of the schools of Business Ethics in recommending 'virtue' as the core criterion, choose the principles by which virtue is attained.)

[64] James M. Childs, *Ethics in Business: Faith at Work* [Minneapolis: Fortress Press, 1995], p. 36.

[65] *Lux Mundi*, published in London by John Murray in 1889, running to fifteen editions.

[66] Preface (by Charles Gore) p. vii.

and social, abounding in new needs, new points of view, new questions ... Because "the truth makes her free" the Church is able to assimilate ... bringing forth out of her treasures things new and old ... showing again and again her power of witnessing ... to the capacity of her faith and life.[67] By doing so, the contributors hoped 'to help Christians perplexed by new knowledge and new problems, with which they are required to deal, ... concerned to nourish and develop what is permanent and unchanging in human life.'[68] It was such a conception of the wholeness of the Christian Faith, as distinct from piecemeal interpretations of the impact on human society and the Church, that the Oxford Renewal established itself as a key influence in the Church of England for the next three or four generations.

The core members of the *Lux Mundi* group had been meeting regularly as the so-called 'Holy Party.' One of them, Edward Stuart Talbot, was described by John Richardson Illingworth as 'the centre' of the group.[69] Walter John Forbes Robbards[70] had suggested that Leibniz could be the guide for the direction of a Christian philosophy,[71] but John Illingworth, in a letter to a friend at the time, said, 'I am coming to think more of Hegel.' In 1891 Henry Scott Holland, who had sat at the feet of Thomas Henry Green at Oriel College, had re-awakened that interest,[72] and it was Scott Holland who could write in an article after Illingworth's death that in his time as tutor at Keble, '[Illingworth] swept the hearts and imaginations of the students.' 'The power of T.H. Green was shattering the idols of empiricism, but "Green was cruelly

---

[67] ibid., p. viii.
[68] ibid., pp. x and xi (preface to the tenth edition).
[69] Agnes Louise Illingworth, *John Richardson Illingworth* [Mowbray, 1917], p. 34. John Illingworth (1861–1915) was tutor at Keble College, Oxford, Rector of Longworth in the Diocese of Oxford, 1883–1915. He was the Bampton Lecturer, 1895, and as the only contributor to write two chapters to *Lux Mundi* he was the 'philosopher' of the group, seeking a philosophical foundation for the group's theology.
[70] Later Bishop of Brechin (1904–1935), and Primus of the Scottish Episcopal Church, 1904–1934.
[71] A.L. Illingworth, p. 33.
[72] ibid., p. 81.

inarticulate, and the Hegelian jargon was teeth-breaking. Here was a man who was at home in that ... world".'

Charles Gore (1853–1932) states, in his preface to *Lux Mundi*, that 'the moral authority of ... Christian lives and characters ... exercises a determining influence on the promotion ... of faith,'[73] and Henry Scott Holland, in the opening chapter on 'Faith', declared that 'It is the personal intimacy with God in Christ which is alone our concern. We do not, in the strict sense, believe *in* the Bible or *in* the Creeds. We believe solely and absolutely in Christ Jesus. "Faith" is our living act of obedience in him, of cohesion with God. ... This adherence has a history: it has gradually been trained and perfected.'[74] This process of training and perfection lies at the root of Keble's 'virtue,' which is not a choice between ethical codes and principles, but by habit of mind and action to be acquired.

In the chapter on the Christian doctrine of God, Aubrey Moore, tutor of Magdalen and Keble Colleges, argued that 'the revelation of God in Christ is both true and complete, and yet every new truth from all the endeavours of human intelligence is designed in God's providence to make that revelation real by bringing out its hidden truths.' He quotes from St Clement: 'Truth is an ever-flowing river into which streams flow in from many sides.'[75] The argument is that all the new developments in science, politics and philosophy are to be seen as helping to deepen our faith, rather than as a threat to all that we believe. Truth is indivisible. Thus the attempted division between the realm of religion and that of scientific endeavour is to make a false dichotomy. God is one, the Creator of all things. The Incarnation had sanctified matter.[76] E.S. Talbot observed that 'The hand of God may be seen in what is marvellous, startling, exceptional, unexplained. Can it not be seen as distinctively and as persuasively in what is orderly, steadfast,

---

[73] Preface to the 10th edition (1890), p. xii.
[74] *Lux Mundi*, p. 33.
[75] ibid., p. 42.
[76] ibid., pp. 51–57.

intelligible, and where ... we can follow along in some degree the how and the why of his working?'[77]

'The Reformation ... led to a widening gulf between sacred and secular, the latter being seen as antagonistic to faith. But all things were made by the eternal λογοσ, rendering each of them as a revelation and a prophecy ... a step to higher purposes, an instrument for grander work.'[78]

Following the recovery, in the second half of the nineteenth century, of a realisation that man is a social animal, and cannot make real himself in isolation, reason, as in the 'pure' reason of the Enlightenment, came to be seen as insufficient apart from a person's background affiliations and consequent emotional development. It is in association, and under the authority of sound tradition as in the Church, that the individual achieves his or her fullness of personality and character. Gore quotes Plato and Hegel on the idea of authority, which is described as 'the function of the society by a carefully regulated education to implant right instincts, right affections and antipathies, in the growing mind of a child, at a time when he cannot know the reason of things ... and welcome truth as a friend.' In other words, virtue as the fruit of a 'truthful' moral foundation.[79]

Gore claims that the Holy Spirit consecrates the whole of nature: 'One Spirit was the original author of all that is; and all that exists is in its essence "very good." It is only sin that has produced the appearance of antagonism between the divine operation and human freedom, or between the spiritual and the material.'[80]

---

[77] ibid., p. 97.

[78] J.R. Illingworth, ibid., pp. 133, 134, and 139.

[79] C. Gore, ibid., pp. 237 and 238.

[80] ibid, p. 239. It has been argued that the Idealist philosophy paid too little attention to 'Sin', as a disruptive element in the cohesive rational system posited. For example, in evangelical literature, and in the general philosophical principle of Existentialism, as in Soren Kierkegaard (1813–1855), *Journal*, Ed. Alexander Dru [Collins, 1958], p. 187; and *Purity of Heart* [Collins, 1961], p. 162; and also in *Philosophy, The Study of Beliefs*, Ed. Klausner and Kunz [New York: Macmillan and Co, 1961], p. 89. But sin, in essence, is the expression of human free will in a denial of a person's objective status in the total reality of his or her true relationship to others and to the Creator.

The late nineteenth century was a period when theology and science became convinced of history as 'process'. The revelation of God was made in a historical sequence (see also the essay by E.S. Talbot, *The Preparation in History for Christ*, in *Lux Mundi*, Chapter 4, pp. 93–131 passim). The theory of Evolution, in its various statements, argued for a historical process of development.[81] This awareness was to prove fatal to the world-view of a rational, static construct. The assertion that the Christian faith asserts the truth as corporate, and not simply of individual, validity, receives further support from W.S. Lock, the sub-warden of Keble College, in his essay on the Church. He states that truth needs expression in a church. As long as an individual remains in isolation, it is 'dwarfed and stunted.' It is in its origin the outcome of other lives, and is at every moment of its existence dependent on others.[82] This principle applies not only to religious questions of truth, but to morality, to society, to politics … It has created the family, the tribe, the state, from nation to nation.' This truth is embodied in history – the history of the 'nation' called the people of God.[83] 'Their worship was essentially social, centred around the whole of their life. Its moral principles applied throughout every activity of their thought, word and deed. This revelation of the mind of God in Judaism received its ultimate fulfilment in the Incarnation – the Word of God made flesh and dwelling among us.[84] In the language of St Ignatius, as Christ Jesus was at once both material and spiritual, so the unity of the Church should be at once both material and spiritual. The admonition "Be perfect as your Father in heaven is perfect" means not merely spiritually and religiously perfect, but … ethically so in every corner of our lives.'[85]

In Chapter XI of *Lux Mundi*, W.J.H. Campion, tutor of Keble

---

[81] Gore, p. 258.
[82] Lock, p. 267.
[83] pp. 268 and 269.
[84] p. 271.
[85] p. 275.

College, writes on 'Christianity and Politics' – the realm of political and social life. There are two ways, he argues, in which the Church exercises a regenerative influence: one is to recoil from secularism and the power and destructiveness of sin in the lives of men, and draw a sharp distinction between things secular and things sacred; to put aside politics and business which are so imperfect and full of strife, envy and ambition, and concentrate our lives to achieve personal freedom from such temptations. The other is to recognise the sacredness of secular interests and duties, a protest against dividing the field of conscience.

The Church's call is to perpetuate whatever is pure, noble, and of good report in laws and institutions, in art, music, and poetry; in industry and in commerce, as well as in religious usages and beliefs. In other words, the creation is a whole, it is wholly under the sovereignty of God, and among other things, this means that the honesty, integrity, and redemptive love which belong of necessity to our 'religious' conscience, apply with equal force and authority to our behaviour in business and political lives. 'It is a call to spiritualize the whole of life without ceasing to be spiritual, to maintain a high morality while at the same time inter-penetrating a non-Christian or very imperfectly Christianised society with the Church's own moral habits and manners.'[86]

The final chapter in *Lux Mundi*, by R.L. Ottley, Vice-Principal of Cuddesdon College, Oxford, continues those arguments, being dedicated specifically to the subject of Christian Ethics. 'Christianity is ... a coherent system of practical ethics – a divine way of life – marked by a conception of freedom, the moral standard, the highest end of life, and the condition of human perfection.'[87] 'There is an intimate connection between dogma and worship ... truth for the intellect is also law for the will ... Christ came to liberate human thought from systems of morality having their centre or source in man.'[88] 'But he also came to liberate it from

---

[86] pp. 318, 319, and 320.
[87] p. 340.
[88] p. 341.

slavery to the sort of religion which oppresses and depresses an individual as with commands from an unreasonable taskmaster. In the Sermon on the Mount, blessedness is the true life, before it treats of "duty", and from duty passes to the means of holiness.'[89] All obedience to a truly educated conscience is of the nature of virtue. 'The Church ... is the school of human character; the nurse, therefore, of such civil and social virtues as give stability to human institutions. In her midst, Divine forces are really and manifestly at work, tending to bring about the regeneration of mankind ... the supremacy of goodness.'[90]

It is not likely, of course, that the case subjects of this study were totally cognisant of this background to their resolution to practise the Christian virtues not only in their inner lives but also in the determination of their conduct of 'good business'. But they would have absorbed the true Christ-like principles with their formation of lay discipleship from their praying, worship, and thinking in the ethos of Anglo-Catholic Revival, which we know as the Oxford Movement. The day-to-day disciplines which they exhibited may be assessed by the following summary:

1 Compassionate staff management/labour relations.
2 Fair wages.
3 Kindness and loyalty in overall commitment to the workforce.
4 Just prices and the charging of interest.
5 Profit motive/profit margins and legitimate self-interest.
6 Due share/stakeholder claims.
7 Client confidentiality.
8 Prompt payment of debts and obligations.
9 Environmental obligations (insofar as they were perceived at the time).

---

[89] p. 380.
[90] p. 381.

10 Honest presentation of goods and contracts.
11 Honesty, truthfulness and openness in transactions.
12 'Trust' as a contract in social stability.
13 Quality of goods, workmanship and service.[91]

In this study of the lives of certain lay Tractarian people I hope to find adherence to this Renewal-inspired standard, by examining four major case-studies:

1 A merchant – William Gibbs of Tyntesfield, head of the house of Antony Gibbs and Sons.
2 An architect – William Butterfield.
3 A banker – Thomas Percival Heywood of Manchester.
4 A theatre entrepreneur – Lilian Baylis, of the 'Old Vic'.

---

[91] Christopher Cowton and Roger Crisp, *Business Ethics* [Oxford University Press, 1988], pp. 3, 10ff, 27, and 28.

1

William Gibbs (1790–1875) and the House of Antony Gibbs and Sons, Merchants

According to records dating from the fourteenth century, the Gibbs family was well established in Devon by the time of the founding of the first business house bearing its name in 1778. It began with Antony Gibbs (1756-1815), son of George Abraham Gibbs (1718-1794), a surgeon of Pytte and Exeter, who established the firm in Exeter and London. The family ties and loyalties were very strong, and the very many letters and papers which have survived to posterity testify to countless instances of mutual support and co-operation in times of difficulty. This closeness is also evident in the number of times that the various branches of the family intermarried.[1]

Antony was, like his father, baptised a Presbyterian,[2] but before the end of the eighteenth century he had conformed to the Established Church.[3] He was educated at Exeter Grammar School and at the age of eighteen he was apprenticed to a Mr Brook of Exeter, who ran a considerable business with Spain in woollen

---

[1] Rachel Gibbs, Editor, *The Pedigree of the Family of Gibbs* [published privately, 4th edition, 1981], p. xvi.
[2] *Dictionary of National Biography* [Oxford University Press].
[3] James Miller, *Fertile Fortune* [The National Trust, 2006], p. 89.

cloth. On completing his apprenticeship in 1778 at the age of 22, having learned Spanish at 17, Antony set up his own business as an exporter to Spain and Italy and elsewhere; his brother Abraham (1754–1782) joined him in 1780 as his partner in a woollen mill in Exeter, having run his own business in Genoa from 1771.[4]

In 1789 Antony, with his father who had financed him substantially, became bankrupt. Antony's debt was over £18,000, and his father's was £12,000.[5] The house at Pytte had to be sold, and it was bought by his brother-in-law, Charles Crawley (1756–1849).[6] Antony had a reputation for being over sanguine, and it seems that he had over-extended his trading at a time when the French Revolution had thrown the commercial and banking world, especially as it affected the export business, into some doubt and confusion. However, he faced his misfortunes with courage, and to the end of his life worked hard to repay his creditors; he charged his sons George Henry (1785–1842) and William (1790–1875) to regard his outstanding debt as a debt of honour. In 1818 a special company account was set up, known as the 'D.S. Account' ('Deudas Sagradas' – 'Sacred Debt').

In 1784 Antony had married Dorothea Barnetta Hucks (1760–1820) of Knaresborough, Yorkshire, and after the collapse of his business he went, with the help of some family and friends, to settle in Madrid. Over the next eighteen years he worked in Spain as a commission agent for British manufacturers, but had to leave there in 1797 because of the Napoleonic War, working for four years in Lisbon. He returned to Cadiz in 1802, only to be driven out again by war. During these years England was the enemy of France or Spain, and sometimes of both, and operated a naval blockade of Cadiz, but Antony's capacity for winning friends and inspiring confidence and trust helped him through all these privations and frustrations. His integrity and high principles,

---

[4] Wilfred Maude, *Antony Gibbs and Sons, 1808–1958* [London, 1958], p. 11.
[5] Elizabeth Neill, *Fragile Fortunes* [Rylands/Halsgrove House, 2008], p. 119.
[6] Rachel Gibbs, ibid., p. xvii.

qualities which were to characterise his family for over 100 years, ensured that businesses and leading families in Spain were able to deposit money and securities with the firm in complete confidence.[7]

In 1805 England was at war with Spain, and Antony had to explore the possibility of alternative markets – exporting his goods to Spanish South American colonies. The difficulty with that idea was that the stocks were nominally Spanish and shipment had to be by Spanish ships. Antony would have to obtain a licence from the British government, as England commanded the high seas. This was fraught with difficulties, but he returned to London – surviving the capture of his ship by a privateer, and the capture of the privateer itself by an English ship – and sought the help of his brother, Sir Vicary Gibbs (1751–1820), Solicitor General in Pitt's last parliament, who was successful in obtaining the licence in 1806.

In 1808, in London, the firm of Antony Gibbs and Son was founded, and in 1813 it became 'Sons' plural, when William, who had been removed from school at the age of twelve to be trained in the business, was taken into partnership. Cadiz was still their access to the Spanish trade, and for the export trade to South America, most importantly to Peru, and although France occupied the rest of Spain, the British army and navy prevented the conquest of Cadiz. However, smuggling, both into and out of Spain, took place on a vast scale. George Henry wrote to his father to say that he and William had 'decidedly agreed that smuggling in any shape whatsoever was dishonorable,' and that 'it was settled as a rule for our conduct in business that we should always avoid doing anything on the propriety of which there rested the least doubt.'[8]

After eighteen years of trading in the Iberian Peninsula, Antony had established a wide network of importers and retailers who

---

[7] Maude, ibid., p. 20.
[8] ibid.

had learned that his word was his bond, and his goods were of the highest quality. Although his commission and agency business had been laid on solid foundations and sound policies, and integrity and trust in all his personal dealings, the political and economic crises of the Napoleonic era still made life very difficult.[9] However, from these declared principles it can be seen that the society of laity and clergy in equal numbers, known as 'Nobody's Friends' and formed in 1800, should attract to itself several members of the Gibbs family, the first being George Henry Gibbs in 1832.[10] The society was dedicated to 'the cherishing and maintaining of those sound religious and ethical principles ... which under the Divine blessing have made the Church and State of England to be what they are, and which will ... notwithstanding the dangers which now seem to threaten their peace and safety, continue to sustain the Altar and Throne of England for many generations.'[11]

The Gibbs business survived considerable losses in Peru (where it had opened in 1822), and Chile (1826), and in a financial panic in London in 1825/6, but the trade climate settled down in 1832. 'It is to Antony's sons George Henry and William that the rise of Antony Gibbs and Sons was due. Conscious of the pitfalls which had engulfed Antony, they steered brilliantly the fortunes of the firm.'[12] In 1840 they discharged finally the last debts of their grandfather's and father's bankruptcy of 1789. The two brothers took into partnership in 1820 their cousin Charles Crawley (1788–1871),[13] who had entered the office six years before.[14]

From August 1833 onwards, George Henry was spending much of his time developing other projects, one of which was a railway

---

[9] ibid., p. 21.
[10] As member No. 11.
[11] Preface to the 'List of Members of the Club', privately printed, London, 1885.
[12] Rachel Gibbs, p. viii.
[13] Nobody's Friend No. 58. His brother, George Abraham Crawley, was No. 75.
[14] Maude, p. 23.

between London and Bristol. The two committees of Antony Gibbs and Sons, one in Bristol and one in London, with six London directors (including George Henry) and four from the Bristol board,[15] came together on 19 August 1833 to consider in earnest an idea first floated in 1824 for the connection of the two cities by a railway. George Henry was in the chair at the meeting of March 1834, and on 15 September 1835 the directors were merged. They appointed the secretary (Charles Saunders), the engineer (Isambard Kingdom Brunel, George Henry's constant companion),[16] and the standing counsel (the Hon. I.C. Talbot), with George Carr Glyn as treasurer.[17] This was the genesis of what was to become the Great Western Railway Company in 1835. On 5 March 1836 Gibbs wrote in his journal, 'The affairs and prospects of the Gt Wn Railway have very much engrossed my mind for the last fortnight ... I regard it as a great national work, calculated to effect an important change in our internal relations and to produce a great balance of good.' He went on to list some of the shareholders in the new venture, well over one-fifth of the shares issued so far being bought by the Gibbs family, friends, and close associates. George Henry Gibbs died in 1842, and in his will he left £300[18] for the provision of 'schools and places of worship at the new Swindon Works' of the company. The first church and school were completed in 1845, the church being designed by Sir George Gilbert Scott (1811–1878), and dedicated to St Mark.[19]

Charles Crawley retired from the House of Antony Gibbs and Sons in 1838 to Littlemore in Oxfordshire, where his friend John Henry Newman was to live, and devoted himself to furthering the Tractarian Movement. By 1842 William Gibbs was the sole

---

[15] National Archives, GWR 250/1, pp. 1 and 4.
[16] Rachel Gibbs, p. xviii.
[17] ibid., p. 20. GWR 250/2, pp. 2, 3, and 25.
[18] Which was, at the appeal of the directors to the proprietors, supplemented to £500. Minutes of meeting held on 1 December 1842, GWR250/3, p. 3.
[19] It became the parish church of Swindon New Town. After a refurbishment and an extension, it still serves that function, *Backtrack Magazine* [August 2008], p. 493.

partner and 'Prior'[20] of the company and was also a prominent supporter of the Movement. Henry Hucks Gibbs (1819–1907) was William's nephew, the eldest son of George Henry and Caroline, née Crawley (1794–1850).[21] He started work in the office in 1843 as a clerk, was made a partner in 1848, and 'Prior' on William's death in 1875. After Rugby School and Exeter College, Oxford, Henry Hucks became a director of the Bank of England (1853–1901), and Governor from 1876 to 1877. He was elected MP for the City of London at the age of 72, and appointed Sheriff of Hertfordshire in 1884. In 1879 he participated in the preparation of 'A new English Dictionary on Historical Principles', later known as *The Oxford English Dictionary*, acting as sub-editor to Dr James Murray. When the project was in danger of being suspended because of financial problems, he generously gave sufficient assistance. He was created Baron Aldenham in 1896. In 1887 he was elected as one of the governors forming the Council of the Church House,[22] the other members being the Duke of Westminster, the Dean of Windsor, George Spottiswoode,[23] Lord Justice (Henry) Cotton,[24] the Bishop of Carlisle,[25] George Cubit, Mr Blakiston, and Mr Thesiger.[26] Henry Hucks was responsible for the consolidation of the guano trade, and for its eventual substitution by nitrates.[27] In accordance with the family tradition, he gave generously to the funding of churches, notably in his partial endowment of the deanery and canons, and the restoration of the high altar screen, of the newly founded Cathedral of St Albans, and also for the complete rebuilding of the organ

---

[20] This title for the head of the House passed on to his successors, and was probably adopted in the style of the ecclesiastical title. *The Oxford English Dictionary* cites the use of it in an 1853 company circular as the first in commerce in England.
[21] They were first cousins.
[22] The National Administrative Headquarters of the Church of England, London.
[23] Nobody's Friend Club No. 266.
[24] ibid., No. 250.
[25] ibid., No. 249 – Dr Harvey Goodwin.
[26] ibid., No. 317.
[27] *Dictionary of Business Biography*, Vol. 2, p. 549.

there at his own expense.[28] He was a member of the Club of Nobody's Friends (No. 156), was its president from 1895 to 1907, and was also on the Council of Keble College, Oxford.

The Gibbs company enjoyed a 'remarkable' period of prosperity and rapid development from 1843 to 1907,[29] the main source of which was their having gone into the gathering and marketing of Peruvian guano. The company, through the Lima office, had bid for the first guano contract offered by the Peruvian government in November 1841, but the bid failed. This failure was so small a disappointment as to elicit the comment from the London office, 'We have ... little confidence in it,' and William Gibbs wrote to Lima 'Congratulations on your failure.' In fact the South American partners had caused much consternation by their initiative. William felt it was a development contrary to the firm's traditions of circumspection and caution – of steady development rather than such great and dangerously speculative jumps. In 1842 he reminded them of the company's sound, prudent and cautious maxims.[30]

However, Gibbs, Crawley and Company in Lima felt they were justified, on the grounds that the natives there had successfully used guano as manure for hundreds of years, and therefore it could not fail to be effective elsewhere, and a second attempt in 1842 was successful. The government of Peru had appreciated that they had on their doorstep a mine of possible wealth, and interested parties tried to make viable contracts. However, because of their reputation, in April 1842 the Gibbs House secured a government agreement for 126,900 tons, and this was the first of many. Any sense of imperial exploitation by the British company was dispelled by the strict terms imposed, quite legitimately as it was a national asset, by the Peruvian government. The contracts

---

[28] Rosemary Heale, 'New Status, Old Structures: Problems and Progress at St Albans Cathedral, 1877–1914', unpublished M.Theol. dissertation, University of Wales, Lampeter, 2006, pp. 6, 7, and 52.

[29] Maude, p. 26.

[30] W.M. Mathew, *The House of Gibbs and the Peruvian Monopoly* [London: Royal Historical Society, 1981], pp. 34 and 39.

required that Gibbs pay a loan to the government in advance of sales: there is a record in the Gibbs archives, from around the early 1860s, of an advance of four million pesos.[31] In the mid-1850s Gibbs received 8s 4d per ton of guano, and the government took £4 16s per ton; 11.5 times as much.

Guano was a commodity which only required collecting, transporting and marketing. Birds deposited it, and a few hundred Chinese labourers, indented by the Peruvian authorities, dug it. No processing was needed, and its situation on small islands meant that transporting it away involved no significant costs. Peru had a virtual world monopoly in nitrogenous guano, and its contribution to the government's finances was enormously important. In 1858 the Finance Minister said, 'So great is this branch of the national riches that without exaggeration it may be asserted that on its estimation and good handling depend the substance of the State, and the preservation of public order.'[32] Guano came to dominate the Peruvian export structure, and to provide the state with the great bulk of its revenues, giving Peru for a time a position of prominence in exchanges of international commodity and capital. Between 1861 and 1875 the Peruvian government floated more on the London market than any other South American state: £41.7 million, compared with the £14.4 million of Brazil, its closest rival.[33] By the late 1850s, Gibbs controlled almost the entire European market for guano, and held monopoly rights for Africa, Australia, and the West Indies as well.[34]

Not everyone saw this state of affairs as wholly moral or beneficent. Frederick B. Pike, in his *Modern History of Peru*, argued that 'By the late 1840s Peru's economy was largely at the mercy of Antony Gibbs and Sons of London.'[35] In the view of José Casimiro Ulloa,

---

[31] W.M. Mathew, in D.C.M. Platt, Ed., *Business Imperialism*, 1840–1930 [Oxford: Clarendon Press, 1977], p. 352.
[32] ibid., p. 240.
[33] W.M. Mathew, *The House of Gibbs...*, pp. 1 and 2.
[34] ibid., p.4
[35] Pike [New York and London], p. 4.

writing in Lima in 1859, the English House wielded 'the greatest despotism that a person or family could exercise over a nation.' Another Peruvian argued that Gibbs' participation in the trade had been a complete disaster for Peru, and a public calamity.'[36] Set against the company's claim to have acted always according to the principles of justice, integrity, honesty and fair dealing, and the Christian insights of the 'Oxford Renewal', there has been no shortage of critics of Antony Gibbs and their relationship with the government of Peru. As early as 1881 A.J. Duffield could say, 'It was a good thing for Peru that the accursed Age of Guano has been brought to a close.'[37] There was the consideration of the damage done to an undeveloped economy when it formed close ties with the most powerful metropolitan economies of burgeoning Western capitalism. Similarly, E.J. Hobsbawm saw Peru and the other relatively backward economies in the world as 'victims' and 'losers': societies at the mercy of the West.[38] Peru did get drawn, through its guano exports, into a world economy shaped and dominated by advancing capitalism, and its opportunity for borrowing in the markets in London and elsewhere – opportunities which proved highly destructive in the long run and the cause of much of the trouble generated at that time. However, Mathew draws attention to the independently conceived follies of the Peruvian government 'as a corrective to the interpretation that presents Peru as exclusively the passive innocent victim of economic imperialism'; and he observed that 'Governments are not normally compelled to borrow against their will.'

A rival contractor for the guano trade, Carlos Barroilhet, had some very harsh words to address to the Gibbs firm, as part of a 'Pamphlet War' in 1856. Much of the contumely was 'ill-conceived and badly reasoned' and the timing of the attack – towards the end of the Gibbs contract – suggests that the motives

---

[36] ibid., p. 6.
[37] In *The Prospects of Peru* [London, 1881], p.91.
[38] In *The Age of Capital, 1848–1875* [London, 1977].

of the pamphleteers were not wholly disinterested. Barroilhet went so far as to accuse William Gibbs of being 'close to monomania' in his prudential management of the trade in co-operation with the Peruvian government.[39] Henry Hucks Gibbs, in his journal, records his view of this incident:

> I have received a copy of a scandalous pamphlet by one Barroilhet imputing to us all manner of Malversation in the conduct of the guano business. This man came to us some years ago, supposing that we did as most of his countrymen and too many others would do, that is, make other incidental profits not contemplated by our contract, and offered not to expose us if we would give him a round sum! Of course we treated it with the contempt it deserved and he is now agitating the matter in Lima. It is fortunate that we have never allowed ourselves to make these incidental profits which many consider legitimate. Among other things he lays to our charge is that we have maliciously sold guano at a price lower than it would bear – in other words, that we have defrauded ourselves of thousands of pounds of commissions!![40]

On Thursday 5 June, on p. 126 of his journal, Henry notes the receipt of 'disagreeable letters' from Lima: 'Poor Stubbs[41] must be having a hard time of it to counteract Barroilhet's machinations, which seem to be telling on the ignorant members of the Congress.' He had further occasion to refer to these machinations when he wrote on 20 August to William, asking for advice because Barroilhet had 'turned up again, largely to extort money.' More letters on the same subject followed on 22 and 23 August, with another spate on 9, 13, and 24 October 1857, seeking further guidance. In the last he expressed concern for his uncle's health, exhorting

---

[39] Mathew, p. 199.
[40] Henry Hucks Gibbs, Journal, Monday 19 May 1856, p. 121. [Lord Aldenham Collection, Holwell Manor, Dorset].
[41] Gibbs' agent in the Lima Office.

him 'not to let this disagreeable business worry you', suggesting that 'the only answer we can give to the accusations is "You know by experience that the principles of this House is to charge just what it pays. No doubt [this House] will show you their invoices if you desire them".'[42] The President of Peru (1845–51 and 1855–62), Gran Mariscal Ramon Castilla, although he had occasionally in the 1840s expressed some dissatisfaction with the Gibbs contract, dismissed Barroilhet in 1856 'with angry remarks about charlatans wasting his time and trying his patience' when the latter came bearing tales.[43]

An objective overview of the management by the Peruvian government of the country's financial and social economy would have to begin with Peru's attempts at independence from the Spanish Empire. The Napoleonic invasion of Spain in 1808 sparked off a struggle between 1810 and 1821 in the South American colonies. At first the concentration of Spanish military power in Lima, and many Spaniards in administrative positions, thwarted any attempts, Upper and Lower Peru being the political and economic heart of Spain's South American empire. After sea attacks by Chile in 1821, Peru declared its independence from Spain and secured it militarily in 1824. Bolivia's independence came in 1825 – the two countries, administered as 'Upper and lower Peru' by Spain, were of roughly equal population – but for some years it was uncertain whether they would survive as two separate entities. Peru, conscious of its former imperial glory, wanted to extend its authority into the new neighbouring states of Bolivia (to the south) and Ecuador (to the north), and in 1828 it initiated thirteen years of warfare which resulted in no lasting gain to either side. Peru was economically unstable and politically bankrupt, and transport and communications were poor or non-existent. The years between 1826 and 1845 may be described as a time when military questions absorbed completely the attention of the

---

[42] London Metropolitan Archives 11036, Vol. 2, ff. 16–89.
[43] Mathew, ibid., p. 244.

people. Peru's was a government of soldiers. The post-Spanish Empire government had not developed organically or representatively out of the country's heterogeneous social composition.[44]

The economic exploitation of Peru's guano deposit, owned by the state but managed by Antony Gibbs and Sons, rapidly became the mainstay of Peru's economy. This was in sharp contrast to the experience of Bolivia, whose own guano resources were soon exploited by Chile.[45] The economic windfall for Peru created a new capitalist class and banking interests and, during the first twenty years, twenty-three million dollars were spent on social benefits. More could have been so used, but the military diversions were very costly. In the early 1860s the Gibbs contract with the government was not renewed, and in 1864 Spain sent a naval force to the Pacific to re-establish domination over its former colony. The conflict lasted until 1869 when, in the face of stubborn opposition from Peru and Chile, Spain withdrew and recognised for the first time Peruvian independence. The War of the Pacific (1879–1883) between Peru and Chile, over the rich nitrate beds in the Atacama desert in Peru, ended in the overwhelming defeat of Peru and Bolivia, and greatly depleted the economic resources of both. General Roman Castilla (1797–1867) had seized power as President of Peru in 1845 and during his years in office he abolished black slavery and the tax on native Indians and established a system of state education at primary and secondary levels, while his administration adopted a constitution in 1860 which lasted until 1920.[46] However, Peruvian government finances were scarcely sufficient to secure the simplest administrative functions. As late as 1840 the total revenue was only 3 million pesos, of which 1.6 million came from customs duties and the rest almost all from the Poll Tax. The various military regimes operated according to a rationale not of liberalism or *étatisme*, but of short-term financial expediency, with the funding of the army and navy

---

[44] C.A. McQueen, *Peruvian Public Finance* [Washington, 1926], p. 3.
[45] *Encyclopaedia Britannica*, 2002, pp. 524 and 525. *The Cambridge Encyclopaedia of Latin America* [CUP, 1985], pp. 239–241.
[46] *Encyclopaedia of Latin America*, Ed. Helen Delpar [McGraw-Hill, 1947], p. 471.

their primary concern. Internal turmoil was incessant, and wars were fought regularly with Peru's neighbours.[47]

Traders like Gibbs usually operated in a political environment which was variously illiberal, unstable, hostile and violent. The only way to raise extra money was by forced loan, or agreement with individuals. The people with the largest amounts of cash were usually merchants, and the most attractive of these were European traders with their access to metropolitan credit. Peru received larger and larger sums from the sale of its guano overseas, and its debts assumed quite gigantic dimensions. For all the criticisms which were levelled from time to time at the Gibbs company, both from within the Peruvian establishment (who were always keen, most often from slender calculation, to increase the share of profits from the national resource) and from competitors (who quite naturally wanted a larger share for themselves), it was a fact that Gibbs had the managerial and financial expertise to conduct the business better than any alternative competitors. 'The system yielded most generous returns to the government, and Gibbs' behaviour, in relation to what the government had asked of them, was quite beyond reproach.'[48] Gibbs' decision to make this unstable, impoverished and private corner of South America the main base of their mercantile operations must have seemed a sign of a very limited ambition. What no one knew, Gibbs least of all, was that they had, with their financial reserves, contacts and experience, entered into one of the great trades of the nineteenth century. It was further proof of the modesty of the firm that it became involved in the guano business with the greatest reluctance and with the most profound misgivings.[49]

It is necessary to look briefly, in view of the explicit or lurking accusations over the years, at the charge that Britain's military and economic power simply pursued its own financial interests irrespective of other considerations, particularly as it affects the

---

[47] Columbia, 1826–29; Bolivia, 1828, 1835 and 1841; Chile and Argentina, 1836–39.
[48] Mathew, pp. 16, 17, and 209.
[49] ibid., pp. 4 and 5.

history of the Gibbs dynasty, bearing in mind that Business Imperialism is an elusive concept in which emotion substitutes for reason, theories for facts, politics for history.[50] Elegance of abstract economic theory is quite implausible when the records of a particular business, and the correspondence of the individuals involved, their long-term interests and actual strategy, are examined with care. All businesses aim to make a profit, but the majority enter and conduct their enterprises in the expectation of reasonable return on their capital and effort over a period of years, rather than a swift exit after an exploitative windfall gain. Platt cites as his examples the Baring brothers in Argentina, the Rothschilds in Brazil, and Antony Gibbs and Sons in Peru.[51] British businessmen and investors learned early on in the world-wide establishment of Adam Smith's capitalism not to depend on their own government for the pursuit of their interest, but also that in any operation with a national government, that government has the last word. Platt says of Antony Gibbs and Sons that over the twenty years in which they acted as government contractors, they simply learned to live with a government chronically indebted, arbitrary in its acts and politically unstable, and to accept its decisions as a necessary condition of doing business. When Gibbs was dropped by the Peruvian government from its guano operation in 1861, the company did not seem to be particularly upset.[52]

At the start, Peru had needed the expertise and experience to sell and promote the use of guano in the principal market, Great Britain; but after twenty years there had arisen a great feeling in favour of running it themselves. In a world of a large number of competitors, it would have been surprising if Britons had been able, consistently, to extract an uncompetitively high profit from their labours. The charge against such a monopoly contract could

---

[50] D.C.M. Platt, Ed., in *Business Imperialism, 1840–1930* [Oxford: 1977], p. 1.
[51] ibid., pp. 4 and 5.
[52] Henry Hucks Gibbs wrote to George Gibbs on 1 November 1860 to say that if the business did go from them he would be quite satisfied that it 'would have brought more kicks than halfpence.' Quoted in Platt, p. 10.

be that the Gibbs' management of the guano trade, efficient as it was and at no more than conventional cost, could have contributed inadvertently to damaging the Peruvian economy by tempting it, unwittingly, to sink ever more into indebtedness. In their operation, British banks lent a semblance of stability to what were inherently unstable economic processes.[53] As it was, the government claimed a vast amount of the returns from the guano trade; it was an extraordinarily advantageous arrangement for the Peruvian administration. And this was, of course, perfectly proper: the government represented a nation; the merchants represented only themselves and their financial backers.[54]

However, suspicions of commercial exploitation and shady dealing were, in the circumstances of virtual monopoly, to be expected. 'Every Peruvian minister who had recently served in London,' wrote one of their number, Francisco de Rivero in 1860, 'arrived there naturally prejudiced against the House of Antony Gibbs and Sons, cherishing, if not the most vulgar notions bred among us, at least some doubts as to their management of the business as honest men. After observing the consignees at close quarters, however, they had been delighted to do full justice to the energy, integrity and probity with which the trade is run. Only ill-informed and mean-spirited had taken a different view.' Gibbs had been 'vilely, unjustly and crudely attacked by certain individuals full of rancour and envy,' by 'communists of a new sort, envious of their wealth.' Gibbs, in short, were blameless of all sin. Their affairs were organised with an uncompromised 'purity'.[55]

This was praise indeed, coming from one who started from a naturally prejudiced position. Henry Hucks wrote to his uncle William on 9 October 1857, *a propos* charges of sharp dealing, 'We have got to tell the truth which ... will always prevail with those who understand the subject matter, and I may say with

[53] Platt, ibid., pp. 12 to 14.
[54] Mathew, in Platt, ibid., p. 350.
[55] Quoted, Mathew, in Platt, p. 364.

honest men.'[56] He wrote again to William on 3 February 1860, claiming that the House was justified in taking 'whatever hard-earned advantages our contract gives us'. He received a sharp answer from his uncle, disapproving of this attitude, and Henry was obliged to agree that he had been in contravention, not of usually acceptable business conduct, but of the strict basic tenor of the company. Platt includes the record that they were honest, liberal, and patient men, working long hours, whose wives saw little of them, and whose record of philanthropy was creditable.[57] Their success, not always easily explained, excited jealousy.

As recorded earlier, because of George Henry's interests outside the company William Gibbs ran the business from the mid-1830s virtually by himself, and it would appear, judging from the correspondence voluminously preserved in the London Metropolitan Archives, that he kept a very tight ship in this responsibility. In a long letter dated 14 February 1852, from the London office to the company's offices in Lima, Arequipa, Tacna (in Peru) and Valparaiso (Chile), he advocates keeping private correspondence separate from that pertaining to past and present accounts: 'Hitherto there has been a great deal too much jumbled together, so that issues dealt with in the "private" letters have not been addressed properly in your replies, and they have had to be repeated constantly year after year. The system we have been recommending will in every way be useful, and we will thank you to begin to act upon it.'[58] He warns about dealing with certain (named) people, the necessity for security in backing any transactions,[59] and the exercise of providence before engaging in any deals in any product. Advocating open discussion and plain speaking before any conditions are agreed to, he insists that a close check be kept on all transactions, and on rigorous attention to detail in all contracts – a very strict control by the

---

[56] ibid.
[57] Robert Greenhill, in Platt, p. 188.
[58] London Metropolitan Archives (ex Guildhall Library Archive), Mss 11471, Vol. 1, ref 2806144, ff. 1 and 5.
[59] ibid., f. 6.

company in all its offices. He criticises strongly the paying of £1000 on the balance owed to a certain company, 'When we should have received from them the whole or part of the still larger amount they owe us.'[60] It seems from this letter that the agents had been charging the Peruvian government more for the bags for the shipping of guano than they had actually paid in the purchase of them. In response William wrote, 'It appears clear to us that you ought not to charge the government more than you actually pay. Your legitimate gains over their guano business are already sufficiently remunerative, and we cannot tell you how much we dislike and disapprove any underhand proceedings or any profits or charges which cannot be defended on those strict principles of honesty and integrity which ought to be the undeviating guide of every merchant's conduct.' He goes on to concede that 'We are quite sure that the standard of propriety is very different in Peru [from] what it is in England, and that many things which would be considered discreditable in this country would be quite allowable in the former. It is impossible also but that *to a certain extent* this low standard should affect the conduct of everyone, however honourable, when such a standard prevails, but this need not, nor should not, confound his well-defined distinctions of right and wrong.'[61] He continues with an example:

To illustrate our meaning, we will refer to the well-known custom which prevails in Peru of bribing public men and officials, and to the impossibility of carrying on the most current and regular business conducted in a smooth and proper manner and without all manner of difficulties being placed in the way of progress, unless this custom is complied with. Now though such a practice would be decidedly wrong in this country, we should not consider it to be so in Peru, *provided* the object to be obtained was fair and honest, and

---

[60] ibid., ff. 11, 12, and 14.
[61] ibid., f. 15.

here is the grand distinction which ought never to be lost sight of. If what a man wishes to accomplish is justifiable and straightforward, and what he would have no objection to proclaim to the world, we can see no objection to his obtaining his lawful wishes by giving a fee to those in authority, if the custom of the country does not allow him to obtain his object in any other way.[62]

In the same letter William says, 'We have thought it necessary to explain at some length our views on this subject because we think it very important that you should be thoroughly imbued with them, and that they should be your invisible and undeviating guide in all your dealings and transactions. Now if we apply the straightforward and honest principles to which we have just referred, to the bag charge, you will see how utterly indefensible it would be, unless the government, with its eyes open have sanctioned your making this profit.'[63] 'Pray look into this affair at once and don't let the example of others or any other consideration prevent your immediately taking measures for putting it on a correct and proper footing with the least possible delay.'

This same letter then raises another question of business ethics: 'We will thank you to explain to us how your profit of $1,497 on Port Agency has arisen. If it proceeds from a charge made to vessels, it is a perfectly legitimate gain, but we suspect that this is not the case, and fear it may result from your adding something to what Conroy charges you on the goods. If so, we consider it exceedingly objectionable and must beg you to discontinue it.' William, speaking corporately for the company and not solely for himself, goes on to ask his agent to prevail on 'Conroy' to reduce his rates, 'for [his] Port Agency Charge is very much complained of,' and it is his 'duty as well as his interest to practice every possible economy.'[64]

---

[62] ibid., ff. 15 and 16.
[63] ibid., ff. 16 and 17.
[64] ibid., f. 17.

The 'Prior' must have had a reply to this letter of strong and detailed admonition, for he writes on 16 March 1852 (again marked 'Private') commenting on the reason for the larger profit on the Transport Charge Account than he thought proper or justified or necessary. 'We are perfectly astonished,' he complains, that 'it proceeded from Customs House Rent ... due to the Government but which had not been demanded. Either the rent is due, or it is not. If it is due surely the circumstances of the debt having been carelessly overlooked by the proper authorities [there is no reason] for passing the amount to profit. If we have understood the transaction correctly, you will know the proper way [of putting it right] without unnecessarily compromising the employees responsible for the error.'[65]

Writing on 30 October 1852, William refers to the Annual Account ending 30 April 1851. After stern rebukes for delays in replying, and warm praise for actual achievements, he brings up again the affair of the Customs House Rent for the warehouse at Tacna, replying to the agent's excuse for withholding the government's rental charge. 'However vexatious,' he writes, 'and even unjust may have been the conduct of the Customs House authorities, towards yourselves in the settlement of duties and government dues, it could never justify your withholding from them of a regular charge which they by accident had overlooked.'[66]

His letter of December 1852 refers to a lack of clarity in accounting procedures, and draws attention to 'The proper rendering of yearly accounts in accordance with the system which has been laid down.' On 9 May 1853 he gives approval for several measures undertaken by the agent to facilitate business, for example, 'loans, providing they are temporary and not permanent.'[67] The question of the payment of duty appears yet again in a letter of 9 March 1857: 'We cannot trace through this Account the source of the loss of $2,508 on the Duty Account. When you answer this letter

[65] ibid., letter numbered 207, f. 3.
[66] ibid., letter numbered 208, ff. 1 and 2.
[67] ibid., letter numbered 210, f. 5.

43

be so good as to tell us how it came about; for while we do not wish to make a profit on this account, we do not equally insist on your making a loss!'[68]

In November 1857 the Peruvian government instituted a Commission to enquire into the Gibbs Company's conduct of the guano business, a move which was regarded by Henry Hucks Gibbs as 'A most ungrateful and misproper proceeding.' He was sure that there was 'not a single blot in the whole of our transactions from first to last – not even anything that we cannot justify to ourselves though we might justify it easily by recognised and almost universal mercantile practice. The Commissioners,' he wrote, 'had the means of satisfying themselves from the accounts, of the scrupulousness with which we had always managed their business.' He was pleased to record that 'eventually they did speak most handsomely of us.'[69] Such apparent self-congratulation could be criticised as self-righteous, but objective judgement according to the facts would seem to bear out the justice of the pride in the company's record.

In 1873 William made enquiries of the Lima office in connection with the credit-worthiness of certain recipients of advances by the company: 'For our guidance ... we should be obliged by your affording us all information in your power regarding the capital position and state of credit of the different parties on whom we have remitted drafts for recovery ... We should be glad to learn anything you may be able to ascertain as to their connections with the parties here who are in the habit of drawing on them.'[70]

It is clear that William Gibbs had a highly developed doctrine of the application of Christian principles to the conduct of business. Not for nothing was the family motto *Tenax Propositi* – 'Strength of Purpose' – and his own personal motto, embossed on a crest bookplate in many of the books in his library *En Dios Mi Amporo y Esparanza* – 'God my Protector and Hope'.

---

[68] Letter not numbered, f. 14.
[69] Henry Hucks Gibbs, Journal for November 185 [Lord Aldenham Archives, Holwell Manor, Dorset].
[70] 28 June 1873. London Metropolitan Archives, 11121.

The main expression of William's Tractarian spirituality was in his beneficence. Although he had expressed some initial dismay at the initiative displayed by his agents in Peru in entering into the trade in guano, that trade was to be the ultimate making of Antony Gibbs and Sons, and mainly of its head, William Gibbs. He was to become the chief recipient of the enormous wealth that accrued from that source. From 1842 to 1875, the partners' profits could be as much as £100,000 per annum. William remained the sole partner until 1847, and after that he held a stockholding of between 50 and 70 per cent. By the 1860s he had £1,500,000 of his own capital in the business. According to *The Times* he was the richest commoner in England.[71] During his formative years in Spain he had moved from his family's Protestant background to a love of ceremonial, and through his admiration for the Tractarians he developed a love for the beauty of holiness. Matilda Blanche Crawley-Boevey (1813–1887) whom he married in 1839, was also an ardent supporter of the Tractarian Movement. Eventually they had seven children and eighteen grandchildren.[72]

William had acquired Tyntesfield Place in Somerset from the Revd George Turner Seymour in April 1844.[73] After years of planning and building he transformed the house, in 1865, to the designs of the architect John Norton (1823–1904),[74] and it was renamed 'Tyntesfield'. After 1850 he records in his diary his meetings with architects and artists, particularly John Gregory Crace (1809–1889). The firm of J.G. Crace had formed a working relationship with Augustus Welby Northmore Pugin (1812–1852), and Tyntesfield became 'a powerful and bristling Gothic House.'[75]

---

[71] James Miller, *Fertile Fortune: A History of Tyntesfield* [National Trust, 2006], p. 34.
[72] Mark Girouard, *The Victorian Country House* [New Haven and London: Yale University Press, 1979].
[73] Rachel Gibbs, ibid., p. xviii. The Seymour family had owned it since 1813, and built the original house, called *Tyntes Place*, c.1820.
[74] Pupil of Benjamin Ferrey (1810–1880), who had studied with A.W.N. Pugin. Roger Dixon and Stefan Muthesius. *Victorian Architecture* [London: Thames and Hudson Ltd, 1978], p. 258.
[75] James Miller, p. 59.

'Norton's creation was quite extraordinary. He had combined the Gothic beauty of holiness with a reverence for nature ... the tenets of Ruskin and Pugin have become transfixed in stone ... Gibbs, Norton and Cubit [the builder] had built a masterpiece.'[76] Charlotte Yonge commented, 'That beautiful house is like a church in spirit.'[77]

Each day at Tyntesfield, breakfast was followed by prayers in the oratory for the family, guests and servants, led by the resident chaplain the Revd John Hardie (1811–1894), quondam Archdeacon of the Cape, who was followed by the Revd John Medley (died 1907) who lived in the chaplain's house on the North Drive. The oratory was a room in the house used for services before the building of the chapel; Morning and Evening Prayer were said daily, the lessons being read by William.[78] The chapel, designed by Sir Arthur William Blomfield (1822–1899),[79] was consecrated only just before William died, in April 1875.[80]

The nineteenth century was studded with mansions, castles and follies built by Victorian merchants, manufacturers, and professional men, once they had made a sufficient fortune. They had to decide whether or not to establish themselves and their family as landed gentry, and the prestige and power of the country house ownership tempted the *arriviste* industrial rich to emulate the worst faults of some of the aristocracy. 'There were worldly families, frivolous families, families who took advantage of the fact that the circumstances of their life made work unnecessary, and the pursuit of enjoyment easy, living in disregard of local custom and ancient rights'.[81] William Gibbs built a large country house, and a large chapel towering above it,[82] symbolising the centre of his life and

[76] James Miller, pp. 68 and 87.
[77] Charlotte Yonge the novelist, a follower of John Keble, and a friend of the Gibbs family. Quoted in Mark Girouard, ibid., p. 244.
[78] John Lomax Gibbs, ibid., pp. 105 and 125.
[79] Son of the Bishop of London.
[80] James Miller, p. 107.
[81] Girouard, ibid., p. 15.
[82] W.J. Robinson, *West Country Houses* [published by the author, 1930], p. 170.

his enormous generosity in furthering the Kingdom of God, and not his own position in this world.

As an indication of the wider concerns of the company, William wrote to his nephew Henry Hucks Gibbs on 24 November 1862 to say, 'I am glad you have begun subscribing to the Lancashire Distress...'[83] This was a reference to the distress of the Lancashire Cotton Operatives whose products, from raw cotton imported from the USA, were exported as finished garments to that country. A blockade had been set up to intercept the importing of goods from Lancashire, and the mill owners had either suspended work and closed their mills, or had reduced the number of 'hands' to a small fraction of the workforce. This had caused great hardship, and many in England and in the USA had rallied in support of the workers. But even in their own near-starvation condition the cotton operatives were nevertheless mindful of the circumstances – slavery – in which the raw material was produced. A meeting of working men in Manchester's Free Trade Hall on 31 December 1862 chaired by the Mayor, Abel Heywood, adopted the Resolution 'That this meeting recognizing the common brotherhood of mankind and the sacred and undeniable right of every human being to personal freedom and equal protection, records its detestation of negro slavery in America.' A further Resolution from a packed public meeting in the Free Trade Hall in February 1863 affirmed that 'no amount of privation will induce the people of the cotton districts [of Lancashire] to sanction any recognition of a Confederacy based upon the doctrine that it is right for man to hold property in man.' They threatened to strike in support of this declaration, despite being maintained on Poor Law benefit, and threatened to withhold their children from school.[84] Both William and Henry Hucks contributed to the Distress Fund.

Throughout his life William Gibbs was a substantial and beneficent subscriber to good works, the most prominent of which, suggested

---

[83] London Metropolitan Archives, 11038.
[84] PDF/Adobe Acrobat, Internet.

to him by his friend Sir John Taylor Coleridge,[85] was the endowment of the chapel and library of the newly founded Keble College, Oxford. On 18 July 1872 J.A. Shaw Stewart, a member of Keble College Council, wrote to the Warden, 'Have you heard the glorious news – the result of correspondence between Mr Butterfield, Sir John Coleridge [also a member of the College Council], and Mr W. Gibbs is this – the latter proposes to build our chapel at a cost of from £25,000 to £30,000. I have seen Mr H.H. Gibbs, nephew of the noble donor (who is, I believe, aet 82) and he is to communicate at once with Mr Butterfield. It is a great cause of joy and thankfulness, and may the good work redound to the glory of God'.[86] William had written to Coleridge on 14 November 1870 to say, 'What a great blessing it was to have secured so admirable a man as Warden (the Revd Edward Stuart Talbot), and there is every occasion to hope that under his guidance the college will prosper, and bring forth many, many men devoted to the service of our dear Church. I trust that many admirers of Keble will be anxious to show their respect for his message by making this college worthy of his name.'[87] In 1872 the College Minute Book[88] recorded his offer to build the chapel at a cost of £25,000 to £30,000. Henry Hucks Gibbs noted in his Journal[89] that he attended a conclave about Keble College Chapel at Tyntesfield, 'To settle all preliminary matters about size and general form.' There he met Edward Talbot and Charlotte Yonge, and attending the actual meeting were 'Uncle William, Old Sir John Coleridge, Talbot, Butterfield, Hardie, and myself, among others.'

Work began in 1873 with William's laying of the foundation stone on St Mark's Day, 25 April. It was completed on St Mark's Day 1876,[90] when William's son Antony formally presented the

[85] Rachel Gibbs, ibid., p. xviii.
[86] Keble College Archives, 1–38, 1872 and 1873.
[87] ibid., 1870.
[88] College Minute Book, p. 53.
[89] Thursday 5 September 1872.
[90] College Benefactions Book, p. 8.

chapel, and the Archbishop of Canterbury conducted the service.[91] On the same day Lord Salisbury, Chancellor of the University, laid the foundation stone for the rest of the buildings at the college. The hall and library range, the kitchen and the common room (1872–1878) marked the completion of the main quadrangle of the college, apart from a small block added later. The south quadrangle was never completely enclosed, for after most of the east side had been built in 1875, it was decided to use the end site for the warden's house, which was built in 1877. The bursary block was added to the buildings on the west side of the south quadrangle. The total cost was about £150,000, of which £80,000 was accounted for by the chapel, hall, and library.[92]

Exhibitions and organ scholarships were endowed to £20,000 in April 1878[93] and the 'Gibbs Scholarships and Exhibitions Fund' was established by William's widow, Matilda Blanche Gibbs (who continued after his death to disburse their funds in accordance with his express wishes) on 18 June 1881.[94] The amount in this fund was £16,000 which was invested in Great Western Railway 5 per cent Debenture Stock and 5 per cent Preference Stock, at 50 per cent each. Certain scholarships and exhibitions were specified: two scholarships of equal amounts of £160 'For worthy candidates',[95] and an additional benefaction of £1000 was granted by Henry Hucks Gibbs in 1890. A marble bust of John Keble, by George Richmond RA (1809–1896), was commissioned in January 1892 by Henry Martin Gibbs (1850–1928), son of William and Matilda Blanche. William maintained a theological interest in the details of the design of the chapel throughout its construction, especially when disputes arose between the interested parties who were critical of Butterfield's design: he remained steadfast in his support for the architect's intentions.[96]

---

[91] Rachel Gibbs, ibid., p. xviii.
[92] Paul Thompson, *William Butterfield* [London: Routledge and Kegan Paul, 1971], p. 394.
[93] Keble College Council Minute Book, p. 8.
[94] Fund Book, p. 13.
[95] Ibid., p. 14.
[96] Keble College Archives, Letters between August 1872 and December 1873.

Other substantial benefactions were bestowed by him in the building, restoring, or enhancing of various churches, vicarages, and ancillary structures, building six churches and contributing towards thirteen others. In approximate date order, these included:

1 St George, Clyst St George: Restoration, 1856.
2 The parish church of Flaxley, near Gloucester (architect, George Gilbert Scott), 1856.
3 The parish church of St Michael and All Angels, Paddington, and Vicarage, London. Architect, Major Rhode Hawkins (1831–1884); plus adjoining houses (Town Terrace, Star Street), by William Butterfield, 1861.
4 Bishopton, Bristol, St Michael and All Angels, 1862.
5 Exeter, St Michael and All Angels and Vicarage (Rhode Hawkins), £21,000, 1868.
6 St Leonard, Cowley, Gloucester (formerly the Chapel of Ease of St Antony), Rhode Hawkins, 1868.
7 Exeter Cathedral, Reredos (George Gilbert Scott), 1870.
8 St Andrew's, Exwick, Devon: Enlargement of church, 1872, and new vicarage, 1874, by John Hayward (1808–1891), local architect, builder of the original church in 1842.
9 Keble College Chapel, William Butterfield, 1873.
10 St Andrew, Blackwell, Somerset: Restoration, 1873.
11 St John the Evangelist, Ivybridge, Devon: Restored, c.1875, £5000.
12 St Martin, Brighton, 1875, George Somers Clarke (1841–1926).
13 St Paul's Cathedral, London: Renovations, £1000.
14 Bristol Cathedral: Reredos (George Edmund Street), £2000, 1877.
15 Ely Cathedral: Restoration of the floor of the nave, 1878. (There is a memorial tablet there to William Gibbs.)

16 St Michael and All Angels, Flaxburton, Somerset: Restoration, 1881.
17 The English Church in Rome.
18 The Anglican Church in Madrid (where William was baptised).
19 All Saints, Wraxall, Somerset: Restoration, by Antony Gibbs, 1841/2–1907, eldest son, in accordance with his father's plans.[97]

William gave his nephew, the Revd John Lomax Gibbs (1832–1914), £10,000 to relieve his clerical impecuniousness as incumbent of Clifton Hampden, near Dorchester, and a further £5000 when he was forced to retire early in 1874, due to ill-health. William purchased the endowments for stipend of the parishes of Exwick, St Michael's Exeter, and St Michael's Paddington (for both vicar and curates; more than £50,000 expended on this parish in total) and he acquired the patronages of Clyst St George, Exwick, Paddington, Stowe Nine Churches, North Newton, Somerset, and Otterbourne, Hampshire (the latter because of the connection with John Keble).

In addition to the above ecclesiastical benefactions, he also built almshouses in north Somerset, the primary school at St David's Exeter, and Wraxall Primary School, founded the Mission to Seamen in Brixham, Devon, in 1859, and in 1860 the British Seamen Orphan Boys' Home. (His interest in Brixham was due to his temporary residence there at that time in Berryhead House, the home of the Revd John Hogg.) William's wife, Matilda, continued her husband's wishes after his death and made substantial benefactions to several institutions, in addition to the further development of Keble College. She gave 33 beds to the new sanatorium at Weston-super-Mare, and built St Michael's Sanatorium at Axbridge, Cheddar Gorge, to the designs of William Butterfield. This latter opened in 1878, complete with a chapel

[97] Information by courtesy of Rachel Gibbs and John Hogg.

and a chaplain, and managed by the Sisterhood of St Peter's, Kilburn, for whom she also gave the site for the Convalescent and Incurable Home at Woking, Surrey. In the village of Wraxall Matilda built a cottage convalescent home, St John's Lodge, in 1885, and the large clubhouse in the village; in 1887 seven almshouses ('The Jubilee Cottages'), and the Battle Axes Inn, founded on the principle of temperance as distinct from teetotalism. In addition to the inn itself, she provided the coach houses, the inn sign, the bar, the tap room and wine cellar – all to the designs of Butterfield. She also made contributions to Wraxall church and churchyard, and to windows at the chapel of Barrow Court, Barrow Gurney, Somerset – where in 1888 Henry Woodyer (a pupil, and later a friend, of Butterfield) restored the house and rebuilt the adjacent parish church. Matilda also rebuilt the organ at Flaxley church.[98] The family also financed much of Lancing and Hurstpierpoint colleges for the Woodard Foundation.[99]

William Gibbs' spiritual formation received testimony from a speaker at the Church Congress held in Stoke on Trent in 1875. Canon Edward King, Principal of Cuddesdon College, Oxford, and Professor of Pastoral Theology (1873–1885),[100] read a paper on 'Religious and Devotional Books'. After referring to the works of the truly holy, truly English saint of Hursley, he widened his recommendation to whatever is truly Catholic, as belonging to the English Church – authors like Thomas a Kempis, Francis de Sales, Richard Baxter, Jeremy Taylor and Lancelot Andrewes. He concluded by saying that 'such works of grave simplicity, wholesome sobriety, soundness of teaching, and riches of scriptural instruction and exhortation were seldom out of the hands, and never off the library table, of the munificent donor of Keble Chapel; [they] enabled him by God's grace to bear the burden of that princely fortune, and yet

---

[98] All the above information conflated from the Gibbs' family records, primarily from the 'Pedigree' by Rachel Gibbs and David J. Hogg.
[99] John Elliott and John Pritchard, *Henry Woodyer, Gentleman Architect* [Oxford: Alden Press, 2002], p. 76, Footnote 7.
[100] Later Bishop of Lincoln, 1885–1910.

retain in the primitive and apostolic sense poor in spirit.'[101]

An examination of the enormous list of books on a wide range of subjects in William Gibbs' library at Tyntesfield House shows how he nurtured his Tractarian faith over the years. His devotional and doctrinal reading (among the 225 listed as 'religious'), included the following:

Holy Living, Jeremy Taylor. [National Trust Inventory Number] 3143718

Holy Living, Jeremy Taylor. 314719

William Law, Non-Juror and Mystic, J.H. Overton. 3143602

Characteristics of Christian Morality (Bampton Lectures, 1873), J. Gregory Smith. 3143605

Companions for the Devout Life – 7 Lectures, 1876, J.E. Kempe (Ed.). 3143608[102]

Companions for the Devout Life – 6 Lectures, 1875, J.E. Kempe (Ed.). 3143634

Christ and the Christian Life (Boyle Lectures, 1866), E.H. Plumtre. 3143601

Sermons Doctrinal and Practical, W.A. Butler. 3143604

The Works of Joseph Butler (1692–1752), Bishop of Durham. 3143633

The One Mediator ... In Nature and Grace (Bampton Lectures, 1882), Peter Goldsmith. Medd. 3143630

The Holy Spirit in the Body of Christ (Bampton Lectures, 1868), George Moberly. 3143631

The Victory of Faith, Julian Charles Hare. 3143637

By John Keble:
On Eucharistic Doctrine. 3143641
Studia Sacra. 3143651
Occasional Papers and Reviews. 3143654
Village Sermons on Baptism. 3143660

---

[101] Church Congress, Stoke on Trent, Official Report, pp. 523–528.
[102] John Edward Kempe, 'Nobody's Friend' No. 179. Chaplain to the Club, 1871–1884.

Thoughts on the Study of the Holy Gospels, Isaac Williams. 3143538
Sermons on the Characters of the Old Testament, Isaac Williams. 3143539
Sermons on the Epistles and Gospels for each Sunday and Holy Days, Isaac Williams. 3143540

By J.H. Newman:
  Oxford Sermons and Writings. 3143557
  Parochial and Plain Sermons. 3143574
  Two Essays on Scripture Miracles. 3143576
  Lectures on the Doctrine of Justification. 3143577
  Fifteen Oxford Sermons. 3143578
  Sermons on Various Occasions. 3143586
  The Arians of the Fourth Century. 3143579
  The Church of the Fathers. 3143581
  Apologia Pro Vita Sua. 3143580
  Parochial Sermons (two volumes). 3143667 and 3143668
  Oxford Sermons. 3143669
  Tracts Theological and Ecclesiastical. 3143670
  Essays on the Development of Christian Doctrine. 3143672
  The Anglican Church. 3143584
  The Grammar of Assent. 3143585

Memoir of John Keble, Sir John Taylor Coleridge.[103] 3143587
The Discipline of the Christian Character, R.W. Church.[104] 3143592
A Companion to the Altar, William Vickery. 3143569
Christ the Bread of Life, John MacLeod Campbell. 3143589
Lectures on the Sacrament of the Lord's Supper, R.L. Cotton. 3143691
The 39 Articles – An Exposition, Edward Harold Browne (Bishop of Ely/Winchester).[105]
Faith and Philosophy, J. Gregory Smith. 3143606
The Divinity of our Lord and Saviour Jesus Christ (Bampton Lectures, 1866), Henry Parry Liddon. 3143609

---

[103] 'Nobody's Friend' No. 80.
[104] 'Nobody's Friend' No. 230.
[105] 'Nobody's Friend' No. 195.

By Frederick Denison Maurice:
  Theological Essays. 3143549
  Lectures on Christian Ethics. 3143550
  The Claims of the Bible and of Science. 3143551
  The Wisdom of Christ. 3143552
  Philosophy – Ancient. 3143547. *Medieval*. 3143546 and 3143548.
    Modern. 3143543
  Moral and Metaphysical Philosophy. 3143546 and 3143547
  Sermons. 3143545

By Edward Manning:[106]
  Sermons. 3143658
  Sermons. 3143659
  The Unity of the Church. 3143661

The Theological Works of William van Mildert[107] (six volumes),
  3143663
Essays and Letters, E.B. Pusey. 3143693 to 3143696
Worship in the Church of England, A.J.B. Beresford Hope.[108]
The Ancient Liturgy of the Church of England, William Maskell.
  3143710
Apostolic Succession in the Church of England, E.C. Harrington.
  3143689
*Lectures to Assist the Practice of Domestic Instruction and Devotion
  (four volumes)*, John Bird Sumner.[109] 3143728–3143731

There were also many Bibles and Greek New Testaments, Studies
of the Early Church and the Eastern Orthodox Churches,
and study copies of the Book of Common Prayer.[110] He carried
with him constantly a *Manual of Devotion* by Richard Hele,[111]
'An invaluable assistance to a life of continual prayer ... It

---

[106] 'Nobody's Friend' No. 143.
[107] 'Nobody's Friend' No. 33.
[108] 'Nobody's Friend' No. 212.
[109] Archbishop of Canterbury, 1848–1862.
[110] Library Lists by courtesy of the Collector's Office, Tyntesfield House.
[111] Published in 1825 and still in print in 2013.

was seldom out of his hands; never off his library table.'[112]

William Gibbs died on 3 April 1875, 'Leaving a fortune amassed by diligence and foresight, trading by strict moral and ethical principles, his money dispersed quietly for the betterment of his family, the building of a great house and chapel, and above all for the promotion of the Kingdom of God.'[113] On 9 April 1875 his friends and colleagues produced a book, *A Memoir of William Gibbs*, in his memory, printed for private publication. It contained reproductions from the obituaries in the *Guardian* and *John Bull* newspapers and the published *In Memoriam* sermon by the Vicar of St Michael and All Angels, Paddington, together with appreciations, one in verse, from 15 others. A selection of their encomia reveals the character of the man as they knew him:

'He was a man of simplicity, truthfulness, affectionateness, true greatness of heart and [of a] true valuation of God's gifts to him in money. I regard his memory ... with feelings amounting to veneration.'[114]

'A man with so much of both worlds about him, so wise and prudent, yet so pure and guileless ... so utterly unspoiled.'[115]

'A strong brave spirit that faced sorrow after sorrow, stooping reverently to bear it as each came.'[116]

'He walked the path of love and faith and obedience.'[117]

'He was proof of the power of Christianity to Christianise wealth ... An example of a life lived in, and yet above, the world ... which proves the truth and power of the Gospel promises. What a magnificent proof of all this is daily rising before our eyes in this university [Oxford, Keble College].'[118]

---

[112] Obituary, the *Guardian*.
[113] Miller, p. 107.
[114] 'J.T.C.' Without much doubt, Sir John Taylor Coleridge.
[115] Page 21, 'C.'
[116] Pages 21, 22, 'J.P.N.'
[117] Page 22, 'A.M.'
[118] Page 24, 'E.K.' Without much doubt, Canon Edward King.

'He was a true child of the English Church; just such a character, with all its simplicity and beauty, as the English Church can form.'[119]

'One whose equal for piety, honour, and liberality has rarely been found in any age of Christianity, and preserved all these, and many other virtues, under ... a weight of domestic affliction as might have tended rather to deaden and kill all such things.'[120]

'He was a partner in the house of Antony Gibbs and Sons for 62 years, and for 33 its chief, and during all that time he kept before him as a guide [the] principles of honour and integrity. Those principles have been the foundation and maintenance of all our past prosperity.'[121]

'Underlying all his qualities, the sense of responsibility – his faith deep and unaffected, and his love for God and all that referred to him.'[122]

The Revd G.F. Prescott, Vicar of St Michael and All Angels, Paddington, in his sermon at his *In Memoriam* service, said of William Gibbs:

> Those who met him could take knowledge that 'He had been with Jesus.' His chief aim in life was to do all for the glory of God. It pleased God to give him wealth, and when we remember the amazing temptations of wealth and how hard it is for a rich man to enter the Kingdom of God we are obliged to own that in his case, the thing which is impossible with men was made possible only by God. He held himself to be a steward, not an owner, but what was good and right he supported with free liberality. He had a

[119] Pages 24 and 25, 'F.M.'
[120] Page 25, 'J.W.M.'
[121] Pages 26 and 27, 'H.H.G.', Henry Hucks Gibbs.
[122] Page 28, 'R.F.W.'

deep sympathy for the suffering, and for widows of all classes, and always made excuses for [those] whose actions had been very distasteful and galling to him. He loved the Church of his fathers ... with the deepest affection and strongest conviction ... He abhorred bigotry and religious intolerance ... [but] could give honour to others who differed from him and credit them with perfect conscientiousness.[123]

Prescott went on to relate that on one occasion he had to write to William, at the request of the Bishop [London], to furnish a return, in order to make up a statement required by the House of Lords, and in his reply he said, that if it was for the good of the Church he did not object, 'and but for this accident it would never have come to my knowledge'. He felt that the Anglican Church had a distinct and trustworthy foundation of her own, and had a capacity for extending her usefulness, for converting and edifying souls on a sober and real basis, without having recourse on the one hand to ceremonies and doctrines savouring of Roman theology, nor on the other to unrestrained licence in opinion and practice. This was the view taken by Bishop Ken, Bishop Wilson, Bishop Andrewes, by Hooker, Isaac Williams, Bishop Armstrong, Bishop Gray, and Bishop Patteson. It is consistent with the most fervent devotion, the soundest and deepest learning, and the genuine missionary and apostolic spirit.' He was moved to put within the reach of the poorest part of the parish of St John Paddington to build the church of St Michael, to provide for them the privilege of daily Prayer and weekly Communion, a church they might call their own.[124] He once said to me that 'the pleasure of doing good to others and of promoting God's glory was so great that he could not help mistrusting his own motives.'[125]

---

[123] Sermon, pp. 5 and 6.
[124] ibid., pp. 6 and 7.
[125] ibid., p. 8.

John Lomax Gibbs, eighth son of George Henry Gibbs (1785–1842), wrote of his 'Uncle William' that 'It was one of the great objects of his life to make others share in the blessings with which God had blessed him … Business and money-making may sometimes make people unable to cherish the higher qualities but it was not so with him. His piety, humility and generosity, and his loving affection were most striking.'[126]

---

[126] The Revd John Lomax Gibbs (1832–1914), privately typed and unpublished Reminiscences, pp. 52 and 60.

2

William Butterfield (1814–1900), Architect

William Butterfield was born on 7 September 1814 in London, the eldest son of nine children of William and Anne Butterfield. They had a chemist's shop opposite St Clement Danes at 173 The Strand. Anne's father, Robert Steven, was a leather broker, a very pious man and a director of the Congregationalist London Missionary Society. Butterfield's parents were married in their parish church in February 1811, but were also Nonconformists. Anne's sister Mary married a similarly strict non-Anglican, William Day Wills, a Bristol tobacconist, whose patronage was nevertheless important to Butterfield at the start of his architectural career.

In 1838 Butterfield's eldest sister Anne (1813–1891) married Benjamin Starey (1807–1874) of Milton Ernest, a wholesale linen draper whom she had met when she was a governess in London. Anne and her children were to be the only persons to whom Butterfield could show any open affection, and he wrote many letters to her; he seems to have led a very lonely and quiet life, 'self-reliant, independent of criticism, and with the self-confidence of an eldest son'.[1] By enterprise and industry his father had prospered, and in 1821 purchased his Freedom of the City of London.

---

[1] Paul Thompson, *William Butterfield* [London: Routledge and Kegan Paul, 1971], p. 3.

Butterfield himself, having completed his formal education in his early teens, after being apprenticed to a builder – Thomas Archer – in Pimlico in 1831, decided to become an architect and in 1833 was indentured under E.M. Blackburne, a restorer of ancient churches and an antiquarian scholar. From there he went to the office of William and Henry Inwood, who specialised in the design of Classical buildings; but the Classical style did not suit him, and after six months he became an articled assistant in the office of a Worcester architect, Harvey Eginton,[2] continuing to live close to his parents. In 1840 he set up his own office, overcoming a relatively modest education and professional formation, at 38 Lincoln's Inn Fields, moving two years later to 4 Adam Street, The Adelphi, London, where he stayed for the rest of his professional life.

From his connection with the Wills family, through his mother's sister, he received a commission in 1841 to build Highbury Congregational Church[3] in Bristol. His first Anglican commission, in 1844, was the building of a vicarage and church at Coalpit Heath, Gloucestershire, a mining district near Bristol with a reputation for vice and irreligion. In the following year he was charged with his first schools – Jedburgh and Wilmcote and East Farleigh in 1846. In May 1846 William Henry Dawnay (1812–1900), of Cowick, Snaith, six miles south of Selby, Yorkshire, who was MP for Rutland from 1841 to 1846, succeeded to the title of the Seventh Viscount Downe and began eleven years of vigorous church-building activity, the first at Cautley on the extensive Dawnay estates in Rutland and Yorkshire, and paying for many Yorkshire churches designed by Butterfield.[4] Occasionally Butterfield, to whom devotion to the cause was an important element in a commission, designed without charging a fee,[5] as

---

[2] C.M. Smart Jnr, *Muscular Churches* [London: University of Arkansas Press, 1989], p. 26.
[3] Later known as 'Cotham Church'.
[4] Roger Dixon and Stefan Muthesius, *Victorian Architecture* [London: Thames and Hudson, 1978], p. 204.
[5] ibid, p. 204.

with St Dunstan's Abbey Convent in Plymouth in October 1850.[6] In 1847 and the two subsequent years there were four new churches, three churches to complete, three houses, two schools, a college, a workhouse chapel, and four designs for cathedrals.[7] 1849 brought alterations to Llangorwen Church and three small chapels – two without charging a fee – at Wantage, Oxford. In 1850, besides the Plymouth commission mentioned above, he designed the Convent in Osnaburgh Street, London, for the Sisters of the Holy Cross.[8]

In 1842 Butterfield had become involved with the Cambridge Camden Society, being elected a member in 1844. The society had been founded in 1839 on the initiative of two undergraduates, Benjamin Webb (1819–1895) and John Mason Neale (1818–1866), assisted by their tutor, Archdeacon Thomas Thorp. Webb had read Oxford Tracts at the age of seventeen, and moved gradually from an Evangelical position to one of a more sacramental, sacerdotal, and Catholic commitment. Neale had also come from a 'very evangelical and very stiff' background, and the society caught securely 'a mood of the time.'[9] Their magazine (to which Butterfield contributed articles from time to time), *The Ecclesiologist*, in its Volume 3 (1844) had an index which listed 'Architects Approved' and 'Architects Condemned.'[10] In the former category were Butterfield and Richard Cromwell Carpenter (1812–1855), and in the latter were Charles Barry, Edward Blore, and Robert Carver.

Alongside this commitment, Butterfield was drawing inspiration

---

[6] Built for The Society of the Most Holy Trinity. At the request of Lord Nelson, several of the nuns were sent to the Crimea to help Florence Nightingale. Two of them received special mention, one being awarded the Red Cross by Queen Victoria in 1899.
[7] Adelaide, Australia; Fredericton, Canada; and Cape Town, South Africa, and St Ninian's, Perth, Scotland.
[8] Thompson, ibid, pp. 390 and 391.
[9] Geoffrey K. Brandwood in *A Church as it Should Be, The Cambridge Camden Society and its Influence*, Christopher Webster and John Elliott, Eds. [Shawn Tyas, 2000], pp. 45, 46, and 47.
[10] ibid., p. 54.

from the Oxford Movement, having been a member of the 'ginger group' *Nobody's Friends*, of which he was member No. 200. He became a committed 'Gothic Revival' architect, interpreting the medieval style in a Victorian idiom. However, Butterfield and the Camden society parted company, mutually, and his membership had ended by 1854, though his friendship with Webb continued for many years.[11] Butterfield was reputed to be an obstinate and rather unfriendly character, but there is ample evidence that he and Webb were on visiting terms: in a letter dated 27 November 1869 Webb wrote to him to say, 'You were quite wrong in supposing I should not like the buildings [of Keble College]. I like them very much indeed [particularly] the skill you have shewn in putting together the requisite little boxes of rooms and yet that the building should not look small.'[12] A letter to Webb from C.J. Faulkner, dated 24 May 1873, in respect of his designs for New Examination Schools in Oxford which were rejected ungraciously, said it was the second time the university had 'treated architects with contumely,' adding that 'Street and Waterhouses declined to send in any design, on the grounds that they did not choose to subject themselves to the chance of being snubbed.' Webb, in his reply,[13] said, 'there is only one architect living who I think could do something which would not seriously hurt Oxford and who would yet be capable of carrying with him some opinion more extensive than that of himself ... and that is Butterfield.'[14] Webb's opinion of Butterfield, and his warm appreciation of his work, was part of the evidence for the latter's increasing reputation.

'In 1844 Benjamin Webb recorded in his diary that A.W.N. Pugin met William Butterfield in a party of Camdenian and Tractarian friends,' wrote Rosemary Hill in her book on Pugin,

---

[11] Chris Brooks, in *A Church as it Should Be...*, p. 147.
[12] John Brandon-Jones, 'Philip Webb and his Contemporaries', in *Architectural History*, Vol. 8 (1965), p. 54.
[13] 26 May 1873.
[14] Brandon-Jones, ibid., p. 61.

God's Architect.[15] She supposed that 'Pugin would have expounded his latest ideas about domestic and vernacular buildings and the value of humble barns and gates.' Butterfield's house, church, and lychgate at Coalpit Heath in Gloucestershire have generally been considered by historians as marking the High Victorian age and a sign of the end of Puginism. 'The parsonage house at Peper Harow [has] been seen as the great breakthrough into modern domestic planning.' But Butterfield was soon being held as the 'Anglican Pugin'. Benjamin Ferrey (1810–1870), a pupil of A.W.N. Pugin, could say that 'many churches and schools built later by the Anglican Church will bear comparison with anything [Pugin] did'.[16]

The term 'Gothic' was coined in Renaissance Italy to denote architecture which departed from Classical norms. It was intended as a pejorative term, the equivalent of 'barbaric'. In eighteenth-century England the word was still being used in this sense, to mean 'bizarre' or 'tasteless'.[17] Charles Eastlake[18] traced the influence of Gothic architecture during the eighteenth century, from the Picturesque, or Mixed, style of the late eighteenth and early nineteenth centuries up to the Pugin-inspired revival of the true form. He was very complimentary about Butterfield's work at St Augustine's College, Canterbury, especially for its 'extreme simplicity',[19] having steered in 'a middle course between a reverence for the past and the necessities of the present age, he succeeded admirably'.[20] Eastlake was not entirely uncritical: he was aware of dissatisfaction with the architect's so-called eccentricities in certain

---

[15] [London: Allen Lane, Penguin Books], 2007, pp. 298 and 299.
[16] A. Benjamin Ferrey, *Recollections of A. Welby Pugin and his Father Augustin Pugin* [London: Edwin Stamford, 1861], p. 114.
[17] Stephen Halliday, *Making the Metropolis: Creators of Victoria's London* [Derby: Breedon Books, 2003], pp. 172 and 173.
[18] Charles Lock Eastlake (1793–1863), *A History of the Gothic Revival* [Leicester University Press 1872, reprinted 1970], Ed. J. Mordaunt Crook, pp. 145 ff.
[19] ibid., p. 226. He applied the term 'studied simplicity' to Butterfield's additions to Merton College, Oxford (p. 287).
[20] ibid., p. 227.

unprecedented ways,[21] but his overall opinion was warmly of praise: 'Butterfield's Middle Period Gothic carefully avoided incongruities of style and that restless striving after effect, or the sacrifice of dignity [and of 'truth', Pugin would have added], which had been the bane of modern Gothic ... his works, in short, were thoughtful, wise, and scholarly.'[22]

In 1844 a letter in the *English Churchman* inspired Alexander J.B. Beresford Hope to arrange the purchase of the ruins of St Augustine's Abbey, Canterbury, to restore the site and chapel. He chose Butterfield as the architect, thus establishing him in the vanguard of ecclesiastical Gothic – and thus of Gothic Revival architecture as a whole. Other commissions followed, including a Tractarian College on the Isle of Cumbrae in the Firth of Clyde.[23] The missionary nature of St Augustine's Abbey[24] brought Butterfield into contact with Anglicanism's outreach in the Empire, well supported by the Cambridge Camden Society. His proposal for Adelaide Cathedral in Australia was eventually built, to the revised scheme he prepared, in 1868–69. Also via the Canterbury Abbey work he was introduced to the Coleridges, who were to become close friends. Sir John Taylor Coleridge (1790–1876)[25] seconded Butterfield for membership of the Athenaeum Club in 1858, and in 1867 for his election to *Nobody's Friends*. John Duke Lord Coleridge (1821–1882) wrote to his father[26] of travelling with Lord Eversley:[27] 'he was (for him), quite enthusiastic over

[21] ibid., p. 257.

[22] ibid., p. 250. Eastlake was the originator of the term 'Muscular Gothic', meaning 'Where forms had been round or polygonal in the 1850s they were now square, and where piers had been clustered they were now massively cylindrical' [Dixon and Muthesius, ibid., p. 214].

[23] At the request of George Frederick Boyle (1825–1890), the future (1869) Earl of Glasgow, former secretary of the Oxford Architectural Society [Chris Brooks in *The Church as it Should be...*, pp. 132 and 134].

[24] Which Butterfield hoped to be as 'something of a restoration of the old monastery, rather than a mere college.' (Paul Thompson, ibid., p. 31).

[25] *Nobody's Friends*, No. 80.

[26] 8 January 1866.

[27] Lord Eversley of Heckfield: Lefevre Shaw Charles, Viscount Eversley, Ecclesiastical Commissioner, Barrister, Speaker of the House of Commons.

Butterfield's merits and the glories he had created.'[28] To Sir William Heathcote,[29] on 14 August 1868, he wrote, 'Regarding the House in Sussex Square, London [which Butterfield was restoring], I feel sure that we shall all exceedingly like what is being done.' To his father (from 1 Sussex Square),[30] he said, 'We went to see Salisbury's new house ... interesting and ingenious, though I can see that Butterfield would have made a finer thing of it.'[31]

The architect restored the South Transept of Ottery St Mary Church, Coleridge's parish church, in 1879.[32] Coleridge's father recorded, 'In the restoration of Hursley Church in 1858, Mr Keble received advice from Mr Dyce, Mr Copley Fielding, and Mr Richmond, but eventually he had the good fortune to secure the direction and inspection of Mr Butterfield, a cordial but severe judge, who, I remember, was not satisfied in respect of the East Window, until the third essay had been made; two which were finished and placed were moved to make way for it. It is but justice to Mr Wailes,[33] who, I think, executed all the windows, to say that he submitted to all Butterfield's judgements with perfect good temper.'[34]

To Lord Chief Justice Lindley, on Easter Monday 1894, Coleridge wrote that 'Architects and contractors are an unstable set of fellows in general, though I have been spoiled by old Butterfield, who kept his time to an hour, never exceeded his estimates by a shilling, and whose work, some of which I have known for forty years, seems as if it would last for ages.'[35] In 1851 he had written of Butterfield as a great architect. From boyhood Coleridge had

---

[28] Ernest Hartley Coleridge, *Life and Correspondence of John Duke Lord Coleridge, Lord Chief Justice of England, Vol. 2* [London: William Heinemann, 1904], p. 136.
[29] *Nobody's Friends*, No. 175.
[30] 30 May 1875.
[31] ibid., p. 158.
[32] ibid., p. 270.
[33] William Wailes (1808–1881), one of the leading stained glass designers in the country.
[34] Sir John Taylor Coleridge, *Memories of the Revd John Keble* [Oxford and London, Parker and Company, 1869] p. 335.
[35] ibid., p. 381.

known church architecture, and one of his earliest publications was 'On the Restoration of the Chancel of St Mary the Virgin, Ottery St Mary',[36] 'To commemorate the piety, perseverance and munificence of the restorers ... and to extol the designer, William Butterfield.' The restoration was described as 'a famous victory – overcoming both passive and active opposition, because the restoration involved not a little alteration.'[37] Butterfield was becoming known for his exceptional qualities: professionalism, honesty, reliability, courtesy, and flexibility.

In 1849 Beresford Hope went on to fund the building to Butterfield's design of the parish church of All Saints Margaret Street, London. The site had been occupied since 1760 by what was originally a Deist chapel, but by the late 1830s, under the ministry of the Revd Frederick Oakley, it had become a thriving church on Tractarian principles, with a congregation including William Ewart Gladstone and William Butterfield. The first incumbent of All Saints, William Upton Richards (1811–1873), was determined to develop a much more suitable building. The site was no more than 100 feet square and had to accommodate the church, the clergy house and the choir school. The result was 'A fascinating blend of ancient and modern – the windows of the choir school and clergy house were modern – double-hung sash instead of Gothic casements, and iron beams for the structural frames forming these units, and there is not much that is Gothic about the street facades. No historic precedent can be found for the total composition.'[38] Although All Saints Margaret Street was intended by Beresford Hope to be the 'model church of the Tractarian Revival,' the contrast between ancient and modern, tradition and progress, produced a very mixed reaction. The first surprise was the use of brick instead of stone, following prominent examples in Italy and Germany. The impact of this feature was compounded by the use of different coloured bricks –

---

[36] 1851.
[37] Ernest Hartley Coleridge, ibid., Vol. I, pp. 217 and 219.
[38] C.M. Smart Jnr, *Muscular Churches* [London: University of Arkansas, 1989], p. 34.

polychromaticism – which constituted an offence to the eye for many contemporaries. Butterfield attracted much criticism for his use of colour in church design. Keble College Chapel, which he had intended to be 'gay'[39] was at once dubbed 'holy zebra style, in which the startlingly contrasted colours … destroyed all breadth and repose.'[40] By 1889, however, a contributor to *The British Architect* was to write of the warmth and glow of colour to ennoble architecture. 'Some saw that the intention of the High Victorian revival of colour as the very reverse of Puritanical austerity: we would have every inch glowing; Puritans would have every inch colourless.' John Francis Bentley (1839–1902), architect of Westminster Cathedral, asked 'if Italy and all her sunny beauty and azure backgrounds requires nature's dyes, how much more cold and cheerless England?'[41] Sir John Summerson wrote of 'The innocence, the lack of assumed sophistication which Butterfield brought to All Saints, Margaret Street, which tended to obscure that noble elegance, which makes it, in some ways, the most moving building of the century.'[42] Paul Thompson observes that the element of wildness, of abandon, was needed right in the heart of joyless London.[43]

Butterfield absorbed from A.W.N. Pugin the conception of 'moral integrity' in architecture: that the design of a building ought to reflect its inner purpose and function. Pugin argued strongly that to build churches in the Classical style of architecture which had been the norm in the seventeenth and eighteenth centuries was 'untruthful': Classicism was in thrall to the paganism of Greece and Rome. It could not possibly witness to the Christian God. A church built according to Classical principles, both in its exterior design and in its detailed interior, did not present its inner purpose and function: doctrines of the Church and its

---

[39] 'Cheerful, joyful, merry' – OED.
[40] *Building News*, 1869 (17), p. 284. Also *The Builder*, 1870 (28), p. 260.
[41] Quoted in Paul Thompson, p. 229.
[42] *Heavenly Mansions* [Cresset Press, 1949], pp. 174–176.
[43] ibid., p. 236.

worship of God, which was its *raison d'être*. Pugin quoted the Dominican preacher, Savonarola (1452–1498), who warned, in his first sermon in Florence, of the desolation about to fall on the Church, the terrible danger in the new age for classic and pagan styles that were beginning to usurp the place of Christian art and feeling: 'By your continued study of these things, and your neglect of the sublime truths of the Catholic faith, you will become ashamed of the Cross of Christ, and imbibe the proud and luxurious spirit and feelings of Paganism; till, weak both in faith and good works, you will fall into heresies, or infidelity itself.'[44] 'The great test of architectural beauty is the fitness of the design to the purpose for which it is intended, and the style of a building should so correspond with its use that the spectator may at once perceive the purpose for which it was erected.'[45] In this he embraced all aspects of design, down to detail: 'Schools of painting, national museums and collections, have only tended to corrupt taste and poison the intellect, by setting forth classic art as the summit of excellence, and substituting mere natural and sensuous productions in place of the mystical and divine.'[46]

Charles Robert Cockerell (1788–1863), Professor of Architecture at the Royal Academy of Art from September 1839, architect to St Paul's Cathedral and the Bank of England in London, Manchester, and Liverpool, was described by George Gilbert Scott as 'A pure Classicist.'[47] His references to Gothic in his earliest lectures to the Royal Society were brief and hostile, but around 1845 his view changed dramatically, when he discovered that Gothic architecture might be governed by a series of proportional relationships as sophisticated as those found in Greek temples.[48] Like Ruskin and Pugin, he came to recognise a connection between art and morals:

---

[44] Quoted, A.W.N. Pugin, in *Contrasts* [London: Charles Dolman, 1836 and second edition, 1841; reprinted Leicester University Press, 1969], Preface, p. v.
[45] Pugin, Contrasts, p. 1.
[46] ibid., p. 16.
[47] Quoted by David Watkin in his *The Life and Work of C.R. Cockerell* [London: A. Zemmer, 1974], p. 245.
[48] ibid., p. 125.

'A work of architecture should strike us as a moral deed,' he said in a lecture.[49] The notion of architecture as being capable of immorality was first declared by Pugin: 'The charge against the architecture of the eighteenth century is that it is utterly false. Every feature of a building should be essential to its construction; facades and blind windows are part of a system of sham. A church is designed for the worship of God ... and should symbolise Christianity in all its details, not the principles of a pagan religion'.[50] One commentator described Butterfield's work thus: 'To drag the Gothic Revival from its pedestal and scholarship and gentility and re-create it in a builder's yard.'[51] To Butterfield the 'truthfulness' of his architectural principles was a reflection of his commitment to the theology of the Tractarian Revival. Summerson goes on to write, 'The first glory of Butterfield is ... his utter ruthlessness. Late Georgian London – smooth, dull or facetious, an unbearable repressiveness ... filthy streets, flaccid stucco, flimsy railings, six or seven million chimney pots – in which he saw the vision of an architecture ... full of everything which the architecture around him negates.' 'All Saints, Margaret Street,' he continues, '[emerged] as something ... very like taste, but on quite a new plane. From the hardness and ruthlessness emerges [a] noble elegance.[52] Summerson claims that 'The second glory of Butterfield is his wonderful childish inventiveness ... an innocent. The eighteenth century rule of *taste* was finally broken in the years 1864–65 ... he is the great symbol of that sense of revelation and liberation which permeated English art and letters in those years. Out of this context he is difficult to estimate. Within it he is conspicuous as one of its most remarkable witnesses.'[53] He concludes his assessment by observing, 'Taste is the smiling surface of a lake whose depths are great, impenetrable, and cold. At unpredictable moments the waters

---

[49] ibid., p. 131.
[50] Kenneth Clark, *The Gothic Revival* [London: John Murray Publishers Ltd, 1995 edn.], pp. 148 and 149.
[51] Sir John Summerson, *Heavenly Mansions*, p. 173 (in a chapter, number vii, entitled 'The Glory of Ugliness').
[52] ibid., pp. 173 and 174.
[53] ibid., p. 171.

divide, the smooth surface vanishes and the depths are revealed. But only for a moment and the storm leaves nothing but ripples on the fresh icy surface. Butterfield reminds us of this.'[54] The simile captures Butterfield's incarnational and sacramental approach to architecture, with its perception of reality in its down-to-earth *chunkiness,* as being an outward and visible sign of an inward and spiritual grace.

Two other eminent testimonies to the overall conception of All Saints Margaret Street were, first, from George Edmund Street, who was quoted as saying, 'I cannot hesitate for an instance [sic] in allowing that this church is not only the most beautiful but the most vigorous, thoughtful and original among them all.' The other is from John Ruskin,[55] who said, 'It is the first piece of architecture which I have seen, built in modern days, which is free from all signs of timidity and incapacity. In general proportion of parts, in refinement and piquancy of mouldings, above all in force, vitality and grace of ornament, worked in a broad and muscular manner, it challenges fearless comparison with the noblest work of any time.'[56]

Throughout his planning of commissions Butterfield was morally conscious of social conscience and propriety which underlay the design of buildings and their ornaments. This was a concern for 'reality', which for him, as for Pugin, meant the reality of God's purpose in creation – a gospel of compassion for people and therefore an incarnational expression of man's true fulfilment and contentment. Thus Butterfield conceived his designs for churches, chapels, colleges, schools and houses as fitting and enhancing their setting, whether urban or rural. St Thomas's church in Leeds, which he built in 1850–52, was in an impoverished area of the city, and it was recognised as from the hand of a master, standing in a squalid waste, strewn with heaps of rubbish. St Thomas's

---

[54] ibid., p. 176.
[55] Butterfield had 'almost certainly read Ruskin's admiration for polychromatic architectural styles in his *The Seven Lamps of Architecture* of 1849' [Chris Brooks in *A Church as it Should Be...*, p. 141].
[56] Quoted by Summerson, ibid., pp. 37 and 38.

stands out unmistakably as a town church. 'Mr Butterfield always seems to build *con amore* where there are extraordinary difficulties.'[57] 'Butterfield's town churches dominate their settings, not for reasons of destroying the unity of the existing townscape, but because he believed that churches should be its focus; a constant reminder to the people of God's presence among them: the importance of the spiritual at the heart of the commercial.'[58]

The two masterpieces of the 1870s – the chapels of Rugby School and Keble College – show Butterfield's polychromaticism at its most audacious and controversial. At Rugby the colours of the interior 'add ...vitality, and impart a glow and a warmth.' Keble College chapel 'was conceived as a statement of faith; as a Te Deum, strictly ordered, but manifestly triumphant.'[59] Reactions differed, however. Academic Oxford, custodians of 600 years of unbroken tradition,[60] did not see Keble chapel in quite the same way. Butterfield's work was described variously as 'uncouth', 'coarse', 'unharmonious', 'deficient in dignity and unpleasing in form, with a dread of beauty, indeed a preference for ugliness.'[61] But his overall style, indifferent to changes in architectural fashion and with disregard for the commercial mass market, was never anything other than aesthetically radical; both fulsome praise and bitter denigration were his lot throughout his career.[62] 'He made Gothic's vocabulary a dynamic influence across the whole marvellously varied range of High Victorian Gothic: here was the architecture of the vanguard – its potential for meaning and expression.'[63] His very introversion and perceived unsociableness were a safeguard both to his inner convictions and his disinclination to accept commissions other than those for the promotion of the Kingdom of God, to the exclusion of potentially lucrative invitations for

[57] *The Ecclesiologist*, 1854 (15), p. 59.
[58] Paul Thompson, p. 320.
[59] C.M. Smart Jnr, ibid., pp. 62 and 66.
[60] 'Oxford, once the headquarters of medieval taste' [C.L. Eastlake, ibid.]
[61] Chris Brooks, ibid., p. 145.
[62] ibid., p. 130.
[63] ibid., pp. 130, 141 and 147.

'civic' and 'private' designs. He accepted his RIBA medal only reluctantly, and refused to attend the ceremony.

Many of his clients respected his conscientiousness. Frederick Temple (1821–1902)[64] at Rugby School refused to submit to the distaste of the school governors and the boys for Butterfield's brick patterns, and continued to use him later – 'obstinately faithful' – for the chapel, New Big School, the gymnasium, the Temple Reading Room, and Art Museum, and also when he was Bishop of Exeter, and then of London.[65] If Butterfield could not rely on support from his clients, he would resign the commission. But he was not dictatorial: he had firm standards of openness in design, and a willingness to explain it, and of loyalty to agreements and absorption of his clients' wishes. It was only when his architectural and theological principles were opposed that he would resign. He expected criticism from his patrons and he expected them to listen to his own arguments and explanations. Sir Arthur Elton of Clevedon Court, Somerset[66] had been warned of Butterfield's strong-mindedness – that he was reputed to be used to having entirely his own way. But he found him very congenial company: 'A very interesting, religious-minded and ... a truly honest man. He was very pleasing and kind and quite ready to change materials – stone for brick, for instance ... I do like him.' The forbidding architect had become an intellectual companion. 'For Butterfield, such intellectual exchange, combined with personal trust, was the heart of a professional relationship.'[67]

---

[64] Headmaster, Rugby School, 1858–1869; Bishop of Exeter, 1869–1882; Bishop of London, 1885–1896; and Archbishop of Canterbury, 1896–1902.
[65] J.B. Hope Simpson, *Rugby Since Arnold* [London: Macmillan, 1867], pp. 47 and 48.
[66] Arthur Hallam Elton (1814–1883), 7th Baronet, MP for Bath, 1857–1859; Deputy Lieutenant of Somerset, 1852, High Sheriff 1857. After inheriting the title, he spent his life improving the town of Clevedon – libraries, allotments, a cottage hospital, Hallam Hall on Dial Hill, and orphanage (later a children's home, a Gothic listed building). [*Dictionary of National Biography*, OUP]
[67] Thompson, ibid., pp. 54 and 55.

Professional Standards

Butterfield's specifications – to the excavator, mason, bricklayer, carpenter, plumber, smith, glazier and tiler or slater – running usually to more than 5000 words of detailed instruction, always ended with a clear assertion of where lay the overall authority and finality of decision on each part of the work. He was not, however, in over-attendance of the processes, being content with superintending the crucial stages: setting out the foundation, completing the roof, securing the right tones and colours in the wood or plastering, and clearing up on completion. Three or four visits usually sufficed. The attention to every detail was delegated to loyal and reliable assistants, six or more on each site, who were never irritated with frequent changes of plan – every small detail of which was already thought through by the architect, and its implementation clearly described in his specification. It was through this trust and integration that he was able to maintain such accuracy for his buildings. Bursea Chapel in East Yorkshire affords a good case-study in this respect.

In 1849, in the course of his exploration of the development of dual-purpose buildings, Butterfield designed two chapels/schools, which could be used as places of worship on Sundays and schools during the week. *The Ecclesiologist* described the concept as 'New in idea and practice.'[68] But by 1869, when Thomas Henry Sutton Sotheron Estcourt (1801–1876), of Estcourt, Tetbury, Gloucestershire,[69] whose wife's ancestors had inherited land at Holme in East Yorkshire, responded favourably to the proposal for a chapel at Bursea,[70] a hamlet of some 200 people, Butterfield had lost faith in the idea of dual-function buildings. He said in a letter to the vicar, the Revd George Gorham Holmes (1822–1900) that school chapels were a failure: 'They obtain no reverence and

---

[68] 1849 (9), p. 321.
[69] MP for Devizes and North Wiltshire from 1874 to 1875.
[70] 'What is needed at Bursea is a chapel, a school, and a permanent clergyman' – Estcourt to the vicar, 4 June 1869.

can never inspire people with any notion of worship. They make neither school nor chapel.'[71] The commission went ahead purely as a chapel of ease in the parish of Holme upon Spalding Moor. In the early sixteenth century there had been a thatched chapel on the site, adjacent to Bursea farm house, but by the nineteenth century only the name Chapel Field survived.

In 1869, Butterfield sent out a drawing for estimates from suitable builders, and he accepted one tender which he considered very reasonable. However, when Estcourt's local agent, Mr A. Meek, intervened with a still lower tender from a builder in Goole, the architect accepted it with great reluctance and from that time was faced with a tiresome correspondence – '... run to a most ridiculous length'[72] – over every detail of the construction. Because the builder consistently failed to understand why Butterfield should be so persistent in doing each stage of the work to such a high standard, the work went on, despite the smallness of the building, for three years. When Estcourt's family had declined to offer Butterfield further commissions, 'because of his having made difficulties at Bursea,' the architect confided philosophically to the vicar that this added insult to injury, but 'One lives to learn.'[73] Escourt, all along, trusted the judgements of his agent rather than the vicar's interpretation of the architect's frustrations, but at the end he summed up the business as a builder 'quite unaccustomed to work under a suspicious Chief ... a first rate Architect who will not tolerate the least infringement upon his directions.'[74]

On 31 July Butterfield wrote to the vicar to say, 'I am truly glad to receive the welcome news that the chapel at Bursea is fit for use.' It was opened on 6 August 1872, and the vicar recorded in a letter to Estcourt that there were large congregations at both Morning Eucharist and Evensong. Services continued until 1883, when parochial

---

[71] Bursea Chest, 5 September 1871. Holmes, a Tractarian, was a nephew of the Revd G.C. Gorham, the subject of a heresy trial in 1850.
[72] Butterfield to the vicar, 28 July 1871.
[73] 19 March 1873.
[74] Sotheron Estcourt to the vicar, 10 July 1872.

income could not maintain a curate, and it was closed, until re-opening in 1903.[75] The chapel had cost £350 to build, and when the ownership was transferred to the parish in 1926 the secretary of the York Diocesan Trust expressed great surprise at the smallness of the amount, having assessed the charge, for conveyance, at £500.[76]

In a sermon at the chapel on the 100th anniversary, in August 1972, the preacher[77] said of Butterfield, 'His art was very definitely inspired by his keen churchmanship, which was based on something far deeper than ceremonial ... You might imagine that Butterfield, and other church architects, were very prosperous; but he died a great deal worse off than many a tradesman. But he did not make money his main object. First and foremost, he was a devout churchman, and secondly a dedicated architect. He would ... approve of [my] text, from Psalm 127: "Except the Lord build the house, their labour is but lost that build it".'

Butterfield's contracts took him far and wide, and he was constantly on the move, using the railway network from London to Winchester, York, Oxford, Wales and Cornwall. His absences from his office in London were possible because he had a dependable staff there. They served him for many years, not so much on account of their rates of pay, which were moderate, but because of paid holidays, alternate Saturdays off, and the security of his respect for them as individuals. These conditions might not seem remarkable by the Trades Union standards of the next centuries, but they were very good by the conditions of mid- and late-Victorian terms of employment. His considerateness was also applied to 'employees' on the sites: Halsey Richards, a pupil at Rugby School, recalled that in the course of Butterfield's contract[78] 'There were no sudden changes of plan inspired by site visits ...

---

[75] Centenary Booklet, 1972, Ed. David Neave, privately printed and circulated, pp. 1 and 2.

[76] Letter to the then incumbent, the Revd G. Robinson, 6 December 1926 [Bursea Chest].

[77] Full five-page in text in the Bursea Chest, but the name of the preacher is not now remembered.

[78] For the New Quad and the Chapel.

no accidents of construction, no growth that came during erection; there was nothing permitted but what had been foreseen.'[79]

As noted earlier, Butterfield was not slavishly dedicated to medieval precedent. This was exemplified by his modern innovations at the clergy house and choir school of All Saints, Margaret Street. In Keble College chapel he required that joints of roofs and rafters to be cut 'to reasonable modern sizes instead of the necessarily extravagant scandlings of medieval carpentry.' In Oxford he wrote that he had 'taken the freedom to disregard the fact that unwilling dons were reluctant to accept anything without local precedent, and to use in the buildings at Keble College materials such as the nineteenth century and modern Oxford provides.'[80] In his use of nails and bolts in roofing he followed the best contemporary practice rather than medieval precedent. Precedent was no bar to convenient service of the present day; this was a principle which he followed from the beginning of his career. Gilbert Scott thought that Butterfield's use of cast iron girders and brackets at All Saints Margaret Street 'The only successful instance I have seen of architecturalizing of cast iron beams.' Thompson comments that the spectacular use of girders at the St Pancras Hotel owes something to Butterfield's influence.[81] 'His early work at St Augustine's Library and Student Range at Canterbury are not only a little earlier than Pugin's designs at Maynooth, but a far bolder demonstration of the New Principles. Butterfield's practice had become a High Victorian doctrine.'[82]

Butterfield's application of his beliefs in the sphere of labour relations was also ahead of his time. He had respect for the Trade Union movement, even though he was of the opinion that the regulation of the trades by the medieval guilds had been more satisfactory.[83] At the time of the great London Building Strike of 1859 he was one of the architects nominated by the workmen as

---

[79] Thompson, ibid., pp. 64 and 66.
[80] ibid., p. 74.
[81] ibid., p. 179.
[82] ibid., pp. 206 and 207.
[83] Butterfield to William Starey, 15 November 1867 [The Starey Chest].

'arbitrator.'[84] This was a testimony to his reputation for fairness, sympathy, justice and concept of social cohesion. He was convinced that architecture was made for man, and not man for architecture.[85] His theological principle was clear, and may be summarised as: God was supreme in all considerations; man was the crown of creation; the Church was the continuation of the Incarnation, and responsible for God's will on earth; therefore all art and philosophy and creativity were subject to the fulfilment of people, and not to the rational, political and abstract ideas arising from man's hubris.

One of his rare non-ecclesiastical contracts was for the Royal County Hampshire Hospital at Winchester, 1863–1868. He prepared well in advance of presenting his drawings by frequent consultations with experts at the War Office, including Captain Dalton, RE, who had designed the Woolwich Hospital (1860);[86] in discussions on many occasions with the Winchester doctors; and in reading both Florence Nightingale's *Notes on Hospitals*, a copy of which she had sent him, and the long letters she wrote from her sickbed. She expressed herself 'Quite delighted' with the final scheme. The plans included a hospital chapel, funded by private subscription, to which the architect himself contributed £500 (a quarter of his income in 1866). His arrangements for wards and amenities, heating and ventilation installations, were well up to the level of current best practice, and his separation of sewage, rainwater, and bathwater was far in advance of the practice of the time.[87] He combined beauty of form with practical need, and in doing so exemplified the century's progression from utilitarian simplicity to architectural splendour, as argued by Owen Jones, whose conviction was that 'Ornament must necessarily increase with all peoples in the ratio of the progress of civilisation.'[88]

---

[84] Thompson, ibid., 75.
[85] Letter to *The Times*, 2 August 1884.
[86] Roger Dixon and Stefan Muthesius, ibid., p. 112.
[87] Thompson, ibid., pp. 112, 116, and 127.
[88] Owen Jones, 1809–1874, in *Grammar of Ornament* [London: Day and Son Ltd, 1856; reprinted 1868, 1910, and 1986].

Town Planning

In 1866, Butterfield was involved in applying his theological ideas, of architecture in its context, to the realm of town planning. The developers of Hunstanton in Norfolk were concerned to expand the old town to accommodate the new influx of dwellers and tourists, caused by the spread of the railway system and the desire for access to coastal holiday resorts. The impetus for this vision came from Henry Styleman Le Strange (1815–1862), of the ancestral family for 1000 years of Hunstanton Hall, who was an amateur architect, and who invited Butterfield to draw up plans for the new development. The old town, centred on the parish church of St Mary the Virgin,[89] was hardly more than a hamlet, and the new town, planned in the vicinity of the site chosen for the railway terminus, was to grow to a full township called St Edmund, with a new parish church of that dedication.[90] The development, based around the substantially-built Royal Hotel, included accommodation for seaside visitors, and a block plan with Butterfield's irregular forms and masses, interspersed with gardens and open spaces. 'The bizarre and often hideous forms of buildings often seen in the new developing seaside resorts were avoided by the enforcement of a general similarity of style and material, the former approaching in character the domestic architecture of the middle ages, and the latter involving the liberal use of the warm-coloured carrstone of the locality.'[91]

In the same year, Butterfield wrote to *The Times*[92] on the proposed link road from the Strand to the Embankment in London. He objected to the idea, claiming that 'The Adelphi [threatened with demolition] is a systematically-planned block of

---

[89] Fifteenth century, on an old site; massively restored by Le Strange in 1860.
[90] To the design of a local architect (a cousin of Le Strange), Frederick Preedy, closely influenced by Butterfield's Gothic.
[91] *Hunstanton and its Neighbourhood* (5th Ed.), George Webster [London: Simpkin, Marshall and Co, 1878], pp. 47 and 50.
[92] 16 January 1866.

buildings, including several streets, raised upon arches to a great elevation at great cost. We have nothing else in London of the same character.' He objected to the proposed crescent-shaped road – 'Always a collection of uncomfortable houses without a square corner in any one of them.' He castigated as 'unusually unfortunate an idea' such a formation connecting to an embankment: 'Buildings along a river's edge should follow the line of the river and help to lead the eye along so as to assist the perspective view. The Houses of Parliament, the new St Thomas's Hospital, Somerset House, all do this.' The scheme was not adopted.

Honours and Competitions

Despite the opposition of Classicists and counter-lobbying and heated speeches at the Council of the Royal Institute of British Architects when Butterfield was, on two separate occasions, proposed for the award of its Gold Medal, he was awarded it in 1884. He insisted, however, that he should not be obliged to receive it in public.[93] He was highly critical of competitions for commissions, partly because they were a distraction from 'quiet, steady work, provoking rivalry and hostility in the profession,' but also, 'if they were not tied to a sum there could be no competition, as some of the submitted designs were two or three times the cost of others.' He entered only one competition, at the very outset of his career, at the persuasion of his uncle, W.D. Wills: he submitted a design in 1845 for the Great Western Railway works village and chapel at Swindon.[94]

Keble College, Oxford

In 1870 Butterfield was commissioned to design the chapel and the college buildings of Keble College. The benefactor, William

---

[93] Thompson, ibid., p. 61.
[94] The competition was won by George Gilbert Scott.

Gibbs, was closely involved with the concept and design of this commission. During the discussion period a series of letters was exchanged on subjects of contention which arose over matters concerning Butterfield's plans. Those of Gibbs, of the architect himself, and of the Warden[95] and Dr Henry Parry Liddon[96] are especially of interest, primarily to appreciate the theological grasp and an enhancement of Butterfield's vision of the design, which was composed throughout in theological detail.

Several questions were asked of some features of the chapel by certain members of the College Council: the choir stalls – traditionally inward-facing but why not facing east?; the pitch of the roof – not high-pointed enough; the use of polychromatic bricks instead of the Oxford norm of sandstone; an objection to the proposed use of chimney stacks on the chapel. But the main two sources of dissent were the depiction of a cross in the east end mosaics instead of a crucifix; and the placing in the chapel of Holman Hunt's picture *The Light of the World* as requested by the donor. Dr Liddon was the spokesman for most of these points, with contributions by Dr Edward Pusey,[97] and Lord Beauchamp.[98]

Liddon's letters are marked by a stubborn and persistent advocacy of his views in the context of great courtesy. Concerning the cross/crucifix dispute, he quoted St Paul, 'I determined to know

---

[95] The Revd Edward Stuart Talbot (1844–1934), appointed as first Warden in 1869, where he served until 1888.
[96] 1829–1890, Vice-Principal of Cuddesdon Theological College (1854–1859) and of St Edmund's Hall, Oxford; defender of Tractarianism against liberal reaction, and an unbounded admirer of Dr Pusey. He was Canon of St Paul's Cathedral from 1870.
[97] Although Pusey later (22 October 1873) bowed to the wishes of William Gibbs and agreed firmly with the architect's views.
[98] Frederick Lygon (1830–1891), 6th Earl Beauchamp, of Madresfield Court, Malvern. MP for Tewkesbury, 1857–1863, and for West Worcestershire, 1863–1866. He was appointed as Privy Councillor in 1874, and served as Lord Steward of the Household under Disraeli from 1874 to 1880, and as Paymaster General under Lord Salisbury between 1885 and 1887. He inherited the title in 1866. Beauchamp was one of the originators of the Keble Memorial Fund, and served as a Trustee until it was wound up in 1873. He was one of the most active members of the Keble College Council from 1870 to his death in 1891 [letter from the College Archivist, 13 October 2006].

nothing among you but Jesus and him Crucified.'[99] Butterfield, in his reply,[100] continued the quotation: ' " ... who died, yea, rather that is risen again." In the Acts of the Apostles – the preaching of the Resurrection, and the Book of Revelation – Jesus is represented as a divine presence in the midst of his Church on earth: "I am alive for evermore, and have the keys of heaven and of earth." Ephesians describes him as "sitting at God's right hand in the heavenly places, far above all principalities and power, and made ... head over all things to the Church, which is his body, the fullness of him that filleth all in all." I want the complete work in this spirit.' Liddon's point regarding his preference for a crucifix in the mosaic tiles had been forcibly expressed: 'As we are, most of us, sinners, we dare not approach the sanctity and justice of God except with our eyes fixed upon the one great and enduring Propitiation. Especially ... would this hold good of young men, who have to maintain a daily struggle against many serious and strong temptations, and who are generally little able to enter into ... large and balanced appreciation of revealed truth which comes with later years.'[101]

Butterfield answered to the effect that it was wrong to underestimate the ability of young people to grasp large issues, and it was important to put them all before them in early life, and not to limit it to individuals thinking entirely of themselves. He had in mind, he said, that John Keble would have approved of his conception, being based on the sequential construction of *The Christian Year*, to 'give as comprehensive a course of religious subjects as the space and circumstances will allow, to begin as far as possible at the beginning, and to end with the end.'[102] He argued for the 'inclusion of Old Testament depictions, for we lose greatly in the understanding of things if we ignore it. These are followed by the Passion, Crucifixion, and Resurrection of our Lord (the Nativity and the Ascension are

---

[99] Liddon to the Warden, 31 December 1872 [Keble College Archives ('KC')/14, 10].
[100] 7 January 1873 [KC/14, 13].
[101] KC/14, 1 January 1873, f.12.
[102] 14 January 1873, KC/14, f.16.

in the stained glass). The figure of the Lord as seen by St John in *Revelation* is as a living presence in his Church on earth.' His point was that if all these things were an expression of the whole Catholic faith, a crucifix would be anomalous in such a historical presentation. 'It would be a mistake,' he said, 'it is not a final subject.' He claimed that the latter part of the Middle Ages put forward the Passion of our Lord with undue prominence, out of proportion with other things – it was death rather than life that men were expected to meditate upon, the past rather than the future, instead of the two in their proper relationship. This gave the Christianity of Western Europe a strong Puritan and melancholy tinge. 'Early Christian art told a different story because of a more complete one. The whole faith is laid out in sequence [in my plan], from beginning to end, that is, the Last Judgement.'[103] There seems to have been an antipathy between Liddon's advocacy of a Catholic symbol – a crucifix – with an adherence to a near-Calvinistic doctrine of innate sinfulness and the Atonement. Butterfield's view of an empty cross as part of a catholic comprehensiveness was more faithful to the doctrine of the Incarnation.

Butterfield summarised the dispute, in a letter to the Warden of the same date: 'Distortion and disorder for supposed good ends must have no permanent part in a building erected [for public worship] which is to last for generations ... We must endeavour to stamp upon it what is divine, rather than what is human ... To give the restfulness and strength, and sense of communion that come of quiet order, completeness and proportion, must be our aim.'[104] Butterfield's *Credo* in the discussion of his interior design of Keble Chapel was set out in a letter to William Gibbs's nephew, Henry Hucks Gibbs, dated 11 October 1874:

I believe that our Lord is in the midst of his Church, as he promised ... His relationship to his Church must be all-

---

[103] Butterfield to Liddon, with a copy to the Warden, 20 January 1873 [KC/14, f.19].
[104] 20 January 1873, KC/14, f.19.

important. It crowns his whole work. He came to purchase for himself a glorious Church. And the more we see that Church divided and at a variance in Christendom, so much more is it necessary to go back to St John's vision of her at Unity, with our Lord in the midst.

Thus he made clear his view, based on the full biblical conspectus of Creation, Incarnation, and, via the Redemption, the church as Christ's continuing body on earth empowered by the Spirit of God, to the final unification and consummation of matter.

The second major dispute was over the proposed inclusion of Holman Hunt's painting of *The Light of the World* in the chapel. Butterfield's view was that it did not accord with the overall plan of the chapel's interior design; the main proponent pressing in favour of its inclusion, in accordance with the wishes of Mrs Combe, the widow of the former printer of the University Press, was Dr Liddon, who seemed to have espoused her cause personally on behalf of the College Council.[105] Writing to the Warden, Liddon asserted that 'the picture, if in the Chapel, would excite devotion, rather than the admiration or criticism if it were hung in the Library or Hall.'[106]

William Gibbs, in his letter of 31 December to Coleridge, wrote that 'A ... difficulty has occurred, with regard to a beautiful picture of Holman Hunt ... which was given some time ago to Keble College on condition that it should be placed in the Chapel, by Mrs Combe.' He believed that 'a fancy picture, which this is, would not be an appropriate Church Ornament,[107] and would not harmonize at all with Butterfield's design; and in addition Holman Hunt himself says there would be no sufficient light for it. It is quite clear that it must not be placed there.' On his behalf his nephew, Henry Hucks Gibbs, sent 'a very proper letter to the Warden, asking him to explain the matter to Mrs Combe, persuading her to allow the picture to be reserved for the Library,

---

[105] KC/14, 31 December 1873, William Gibbs to John Taylor Coleridge.
[106] 16 March 1873, KC/14, f.22.
[107] pp. 3 and 4.

when it is built, where it would be quite in its proper place.' William Gibbs could not doubt 'that she would view the matter in a proper light, and would at once accede to our request.' However, Liddon thought it right to intervene again, and pledged himself to Mrs Combe that the picture would be placed in the chapel. 'Though in many ways a good man,' Gibbs continued, '[Liddon] has, I hear, a most imperious disposition, and cannot bear any opposition ... However, until Butterfield has finished the Chapel, I and/or my Executors have made a formal gift of it to the College, I shall not introduce anything into it which Butterfield may not approve, and consider to harmonize entirely with his own plans; for I assure you that the more I see of Butterfield the more I like him.' It would appear that William Gibbs had a higher regard for the theology of the lay architect than for that of a highly respected priest/theologian.

Melbourne Cathedral, 1877–1891

One of the projects – at once high in prestige, and the most frustrating in view of the distance involved – was the commission to build a cathedral in Melbourne, Australia. The history of such a conception dated back to 1853, and when the architect Leonard Terry[108] became diocesan architect in 1860 he was in partnership with Percy Oakden,[109] both acting as local architects for Butterfield, when the latter was appointed, until 1884. The first diocesan bishop, Charles Perry,[110] on his arrival in Melbourne, presided over much debate between parishioners as to what kind of design of cathedral should be adopted. Ideas ranged over a wide field of possibilities, from a temporary

---

[108] 1825–1884.
[109] 1845–1917. A local architect, he was born in Launceston, Van Diemen's land [Tasmania]. He was a Methodist, and his work was largely with Presbyterian, Congregational, and Methodist churches, although his style was characterised by the use of polychromatic brick.
[110] Born in London in 1807, consecrated at Westminster in 1847.

building (Melbourne being in its first stages of development as a city) in order to leave the way for a permanent structure later, to a definitely 'Gothicky' cathedral. However, a fear that the government might reclaim the allotted land compelled the Diocesan Church Assembly, on 21 January 1864, to make a decision.[111]

Many thought automatically of an English architect, and only a few suggested that invitations should be issued to one of colonial origin. It had been noted in a local newspaper that the new cathedral for Christchurch New Zealand had been awarded to Gilbert Scott, 'Who stands foremost among the architects of England.' A Bill to authorise the building of a cathedral was passed in 1869, and a member of the committee advocated an open competition for the design, an idea that was abandoned in 1878.[112] Bishop Perry left the Diocese in 1874 to return to England, although he resigned formally only in 1876.[113] The supervision of the plans for the cathedral fell to his successor, James Moorhouse, who served from 1876 to 1886.[114]

Expectations of the cathedral design in the local church press were expressed in terms of visual fancy and romantic reveries which overrode the practical realities – an attitude which was to prove a serious irritant to Butterfield when he was eventually appointed, deploring as he did such ill-informed romanticism.[115]

---

[111] Canon Albert Bayne McPherson (1929?–2011), *That Uncomfortable Genius*, Unpublished MA Dissertation, University of Melbourne, 1980, pp. 19–21.

[112] ibid., pp. 31 and 76.

[113] He was made a Canon of Llandaff Cathedral, Wales, in 1878, and was one of the founders of Wycliffe Hall, Oxford, and Ridley Hall, Cambridge.

[114] Moorhouse was born in Sheffield in 1826, and ordained in 1853. As a curate he established a People's Institute, where all kinds of opinion could be discussed by working men. He left in 1859 to become Vicar of St John's Fitzroy Square, London, where his congregation ranged sociologically from Lord Robert Cecil (later Marquess of Salisbury) (*Nobody's Friend*, No. 202), and Sir Charles Eastlake, to the inhabitants of dirty and squalid housing, and he established again a Working Men's Institute. In 1867 he moved to be Vicar of St James's, Paddington, and Rural Dean of St Pancras Deanery. He has come down in history as a scholar with an acute knowledge of how working people lived, and of the development of cities. He was consecrated as Bishop of Melbourne on 22 October 1876.

[115] MacPherson, ibid., p. 41.

The arrival of Bishop Moorhouse, with his vision of a cathedral which had a ministry to a developing city, and to the whole spectrum of people there, filled the finance sub-committee with renewed enthusiasm, and in 1877 they made four resolutions. The first of these was 'That application be made to one of the best architects in England for plans for a cathedral ... The Bishop proposed the best-known architect in the world for the purpose,' and on 17 December 1877, 'It was moved that in the first instance an application be made to Mr Butterfield for designs for a cathedral.' By 1877 there would be few people with any acquaintance with architecture who would not have known the name of William Butterfield.[116] MacPherson quotes the view of Butterfield 'as the pioneer and central figure of the High Victorian phase of the Gothic Revival, as well as the first architect to experiment with constructional colour. His achievement is now being viewed as a triumphant expression of that style, more deeply representative of the power, confidence, and fear of his age than any other architect. After the decision, there was no more official wavering from the conviction that an English architect would be superior to a colonial one.'[117] Butterfield's cathedral commissions had all been much earlier in his career than this one: at Perth, Scotland, in 1847–50, the completion of Frederickton, Canada, in 1848, and the two designs for Adelaide in 1847 and 1868, the second of which, being designed in brick, was rejected by the Bishop,[118] who was determined to have the building in stone.

Butterfield's reply to the invitation from Melbourne of 22 January 1878 was not received until 28 September; a circumstance which was observed to be very unlike him, as he was well known for his courtesy and strict observance of social norms. Whatever the reason for the delay, the Cathedral Board was delighted with the plans, which were perceived as 'A return to simplicity by the architect.' They were approved by the Board and submitted to

---

[116] ibid., p. 72.
[117] ibid., p. 74 and 76.
[118] Augustus Short (1802–1883), who was Bishop of Adelaide from 1847 to 1882.

the Church Assembly in 1878. Nevertheless there was still much murmuring against the choice of an overseas architect, and criticism of Bishop Moorhouse for that decision; it had been seen as an implication that colonial skill was inadequate to the task.[119] Some violent criticisms were voiced against the plans, but these were all too often founded on ignorance and blind prejudice. Making a good impression, wrote McPherson, was part of a romantic notion of a cathedral, 'A strain of romanticism that had influenced many of Melbourne's public buildings, where elaborate decoration and grandiose effects were used to create an impression. "Making a good impression" was not [totally] objectionable to Butterfield, provided it was based on sound ideas,'[120] following as he did the Pugin doctrine of honesty and truthfulness to the central conception. McPherson[121] records that colonial and imperial tensions were complex. Although the majority of the population was Australian-born by the 1870s, they were not a dominant force in the social structure until the 1890s. The members of the Cathedral Board were almost entirely born in Great Britain.

Encountering problems with the traditional east-west orientation of the building, because of the constriction of the site, Butterfield proved himself not irreversibly committed to such a tradition: in 1879 he sent out new plans, laying out the building north-south as requested. This episode, observes McPherson, disproved a popular notion that the architect was not aware that the cathedral was being built in a different direction from his original plans, and also modifies considerably the judgement that he was totally implacable in what he had designed. 'He was anxious to give his patrons what they wanted, unless their desires were ... at a variance with his principles. The current Australian fashion in taste was a prominent principle in selecting the style of a building they desired. But fashion in taste had nothing to do with Butterfield's approach: there was an uncompromising practicality about his work which

---

[119] McPherson, ibid., pp. 79 and 82.
[120] ibid., p. 85.
[121] The Canon Precentor at Melbourne Cathedral.

was far removed from any romantic, literary, or sentimental notions of Gothic architecture.'[122] Basil Clarke wrote of Butterfield that he was 'A solitary, austere, ascetic man, and his churches express exactly the spirit of the Tractarian leaders,'[123] including the spirit of Keble's doctrine of 'Reserve'.[124]

The foundation stone was laid in 1880, but the project ran into the difficulty of raising the appropriate funding, one of the problems being that despite the nexus between Church and State no longer existing, the Church of England still enjoyed a historical prestige. It was inevitable that the Queen's representative in the nineteenth century would always be an Anglican, and it was also a fact that, rich or poor, Anglicans were notoriously niggardly givers to the cost of ministry and maintenance.[125]

Butterfield was visited in London by Leonard Terry between August 1879 and June 1880, and was in close conversation with him, grateful for being able to talk to someone who could give him first-hand information about the details of the building programme, and conditions and local matters concerning Melbourne. In a letter to Bishop Moorhouse[126] Butterfield expressed an enthusiasm for a colleague, which was rare. However, difficulties arose later over clashes with stubborn personalities with firm ideas, the conflict between new and old architectural methods (a conflict which occurred also between the English-born[127] Terry and his Tasmanian colleague, Percy Oakden), and the inevitable clash of misunderstanding between imperial convictions and colonial brashness. There was disagreement over such details as the use of cement or mortar for the foundations, in which Butterfield preferred mortar because it was more flexible and, in any case, less expensive. The slowness and infrequency of correspondence with the site gave Butterfield much concern, and

---

[122] ibid., pp. 88–89.
[123] Basil F.C. Clarke, *Anglican Cathedrals Outside the British Isles* [London: SPCK, 1958], p. 99.
[124] See Introduction, supra.
[125] McPherson, ibid., pp. 92–96.
[126] 5 November 1879.
[127] In Scarborough, Yorkshire.

decisions were taken on the spot before his instructions had been received.[128] The demand for skilled manual labour, outrunning the supply, was another source of anxiety for Butterfield, committed as he was to the highest standards of building. Such finely-tuned considerations, and the decisions having to be made on the spot to build the cathedral in stages, with a series of contracts instead of with a single contract, led to the local purchase of plant and the choice of materials, and the supervision of local labour, all of which gave rise to considerable disagreement with the architect. The Board ordered Terry and Oakden to adhere strictly to Butterfield's instructions and details of construction but, in the absence of communication from them, Butterfield was in regular touch with the Clerk of Works, William Harrison, a circumstance which was a source of annoyance to Terry and Oakden who, as architects, felt diminished by the process. Butterfield wrote both to Bishop Moorhouse and to Terry,[129] acquainting the bishop with the difficulties he was encountering, and to Terry to say that he had hoped for his steady judgement but had not had it. He had been disappointed; having reckoned on minutely detailed and practical letters, he had not received any.[130]

A few weeks later, Butterfield sent his first letter of resignation,[131] after receiving what he considered to be an unsatisfactory letter regarding his requests and complaints. The Board was alarmed at all the friction, and the confusion and delay it was causing to the building. But the departures from his plans by Terry and Oakden were irretrievable. The Board regretted his resignation, feeling that if the building were to be completed under the direction of a local architect, the result would be discreditable to all parties concerned. They begged him to reconsider his resignation.

Butterfield, in reply, made conditions: Oakden and Terry were

---

[128] McPherson, ibid., pp. 114 and 115.
[129] 16 November 1882.
[130] McPherson, ibid., pp. 121 to 123.
[131] Dated 23 January 1883, although he continued to correspond as the official architect (McPherson, ibid., p. 158).

to be dismissed from the project, and it emerged, despite their protests, that they had never completely understood the architect's designs, particularly in the areas of construction and the use of colour. McPherson comments, 'Butterfield dragged Gothic from the pedestal of scholarship and gentility and re-created it in the builder's yard.'[132]

An allegation was brought before the Board that the work superintended by Terry and Oakden was unsatisfactory, and the Board's relationship with them began to deteriorate. Butterfield wrote to the Board on 10 January 1883, regretting that the initial harmony between Terry and himself seemed to have been corrupted by his partnership with Oakley. After Terry's untimely death, he said in a letter[133] to a member of the Board that he was sorry to hear of it, and again laid the blame for the misunderstandings on Oakley.[134] 'Remote control of such a vast project as the cathedral did not work in colonial Melbourne,' commented McPherson. 'Terry and Oakley were unable to cope with a highly original genius of the architectural profession, or be in sympathy with his plans and ideals ... [they] refused to regard themselves as subordinate ... or in any way inferior to Butterfield. Distance was the chief enemy ... it delayed correspondence and replies, until utter confusion reigned in the matter of instructions and directions. But there was a gap between two different societies, one old and established, assured and confident, the other young and experimenting – confident, but really very insecure.'[135] It was the dismissal as Clerk of Works of William Harrison the builder, by the Board, as their having lost confidence in him, that caused Butterfield's final resignation. The architect had had his differences with Harrison, but regarded him as reliable, and had shown an increasing sympathy and understanding

---

[132] ibid., pp. 126 and 127. He quotes from John Summerson, 'Christian Gothic', in *Architectural Review*, Vol. XCVIII, p. 172. Similarly, another writer claimed that 'He tried to treat Gothic as a living language' [Mark Girouard, in 'Milton Ernest Hall', in *Country Life* magazine, 23 October 1969].

[133] 8 August 1884.

[134] McPherson, ibid., pp. 126 to 130.

[135] ibid., p. 131.

of his wishes. His final resignation was accepted by the Board on 26 September 1884.[136] He had supplied a large number of drawings for the completion of the building, for the architect given responsibility after his departure, Joseph Reed (1823?–1890),[137] who was able to take the project to a fairly authentic conclusion, so that it might rightly be called 'Butterfield's building.'[138] The completion of the spires and towers of Butterfield's design could not be attempted until 1924, due to lack of funds, but although the saddle-back towers were abandoned for spires, and the central spire changed for a more massive and highly decorated design, these alterations did not detract from the overall effect (and Butterfield might have reconsidered them himself),[139] so that Paul Thompson could declare it 'Butterfield's final masterpiece.'[140]

McPherson concluded his study by affirming Kenneth Clark's description of the architect as 'An uncomfortable Genius' as apt, but 'a genius nevertheless'. Over-riding all the difficulties and misunderstandings, and the punctiliousness of every detail of his designs, is the ultimate triumph. And this is attributable, by almost all commentators on his work, to the glory of his religious faith and the principles he came to apply.'[141]

Family Sentiments

Butterfield seems to have led a very solitary life; rigorously disciplined, reserved, unemotional and undemonstrative. There are, however, occasional glimpses of his personal depth of feeling, in the correspondence to his sister Anne, and her son, the Revd William Starey. Also revealing are the anonymous letters he wrote

---

[136] Shortly afterwards Bishop Moorhouse, who had been the chief motivating force of efforts to build the cathedral, resigned, on his acceptance of the See of Manchester, UK.
[137] Born in Cornwall; he became Melbourne's most influential architect.
[138] McPherson, ibid., p. 201.
[139] ibid., p. 195.
[140] Thompson, *William Butterfield* [London: Routledge and Kegan Paul, 1971], p. 250.
[141] McPherson, ibid., pp. 205 and 200.

to the press, notably *The Guardian*, a prominent church newspaper of the day, *The Times*, and to various journals. His sister Anne was closer to him than anyone else, and he took a keen interest in the upbringing of her children, as their godfather. Early in 1848[142] he began to write with stern admonitions on child training, and in a continuation of the same theme[143] a few days later, he wrote, 'I have been taking the responsibility on my help in part ... of your children. I view children as very sacred things. Our Lord says "Be converted and become as little children" – the most beautiful thing to think of: the devil and the world and the flesh have as yet little power in them, and God in their Baptism has done very much for them.' He goes on to argue that we 'must guide and train them, to prevent their being stained by adverse habits,' although he admits there is a question of '"How is this to be done?" The responsibilities of a godfather are fearful to contemplate.' Clearly he brought to that subject the minute attention to detail and overall effect that he applied to his own life and to his profession. He became quite critical at times of how his sister was behaving as a parent, citing the children's manners – asking questions, and speaking when they were not spoken to. He went into great detail about what he saw as misbehaviour, and urged her to satisfy herself as to the state of the discipline in the nursery and the schoolroom, and especially to change her nurse if she is unsatisfactory, 'So as not to risk the children.' And so on for fifteen pages.

In a subsequent letter[144] he exhorted his sister to 'Be careful in the way Elizabeth [her daughter] is more attentive to Scripture reading ... The various sects can draw wrong conclusions; she needs guidance to know which of the many characters in Scripture are worthy of example.' He enquires of Anne if she 'won't mind my asking you privately to ensure that children are brought up with the Christian virtues.' These are listed by him as 'Being

---

[142] 29 January: Starey File Reference SY 78/3.
[143] 2 February, ibid., SY 78/4.
[144] 3 March 1848, ibid., SY 78/5.

obedient, alive to duty (their own and not other people's), unselfish, punctual, at all times deferential to their elders, with honest and true hearts in which the Holy Spirit can work.'

Anne's replies to her brother's admonitions have not come down to us, but Butterfield's next letter began, 'I am sorry to hear of your determination, but as it is I shall say no more about it.' He goes on, however, to observe that she has the most indistinct views of [Elizabeth's] relationship with, and position in, the family, and to give her his further opinions on the correct disciplining of children. They are those which might be expected of a Victorian bachelor godfather, but also of a mature, thoughtful observer of how the next generation changes the traditions, and the problem of how parents accommodate themselves to it. These seemed to Butterfield as a threat to what had been found wise and practical and prudent to the preceding generation. His principles are sound enough, but the rational insistence on them in teaching children would not occur to him as in danger of being intrusive or unwise. In the September of that year[145] he wrote to express a hope that he would see Anne 'on Sunday week' unless he is in Scotland,[146] and on the Monday following he would be visiting Archdeacon Manning in Lavington. Butterfield had written to the Vicar of Wantage, Oxfordshire, William J. Butler, to persuade him to take on his nephew William Starey as a curate, successfully as it happened, although the recipient had replied that he was 'rather overstocked with curates'. Butler was in touch with the Revd Henry Manning[147] (1808–1892), the Vicar of Lavington[148] (ostensibly an Evangelical but with daily Morning Prayers in church, the tolling of the bell, and many villagers attending). Butler had asked for guidance on hearing Confession from a

---

[145] 5 September 1848, ibid., SY 78/7.
[146] He was in the process of preparing his design for St Ninian's Cathedral, Perth.
[147] Manning was *Nobody's Friends*, No. 143.
[148] Later Archdeacon of Chichester (1841) and as a result of the Gorham Judgement of 1850, and the institution of the Roman Catholic Hierarchy in 1850, a convert to Rome, becoming the second Archbishop of Westminster in 1865 [James Pereiro, *Cardinal Manning*, Oxford 1998, p. 115].

married woman, and experiencing hostility from her husband. Manning, having experienced a similar difficulty, replied that a wife was not in surrender to her husband – only to God. Spiritual direction through correspondence was a favourite method of Manning, a practice he continued in the Roman Catholic Church.[149] It is possible, because of Butterfield's friendship with Butler, that he visited Manning for his own guidance on some matter.

In his letter to Anne, Butterfield continued to hope 'that all kinds of orderly rules are in full operation for the children, and that the Christian life must have no listlessness about it.' But he mellowed his strictness by urging her to tell the children that, for God's glory, the end to which the discipline was imposed upon them was 'a high and glorious future ... Let their life be cheerful and bright as if there were such a future.'

On the next day he felt 'very much obliged to Anne for thinking well of my remarks, and for giving me credit for having only one end earnestly in view – the making your children refined, well-bred, and above all, Christian-like.' He is moved in this letter to return to a former adjectival signature, as 'Your affectionate brother...'[150]

Later Anne wrote to ask what her brother thought of her intention to have an engraving in her schoolroom of three Grecian-type figures representing 'Faith, Hope, and Charity.' Butterfield objected that there was something pagan about such personification and abstract deification of an attribute ... It is more Christian to commemorate saints distinguished for those virtues. The Incarnation of our Blessed Lord has made it imperative on us to exhibit certain virtues in human flesh.[151]

Years after these letters were written, he was to summarise his thinking on the family, in a letter to *The Guardian*: 'Parents and Home lie at the root of Church and State. There must be piety

---

[149] Edmund Sheridan Purcell, *The Life of Cardinal Manning*, Vol. I, pp. 110, 233, and 496–498.
[150] Starey File, SY 78/8, 6 September.
[151] ibid, SY 78/9, undated.

and prayer, good government and affection in our households. Each family must be a small, well-administered kingdom in itself.'[152]

Butterfield's sister's son, William (1846–1912),[153] was curate of Wantage from 1869 to 1879, curate of Horton, also in the Diocese of Oxford, from 1879 to 1880, becoming vicar there from 1880 to 1883. He went to a curacy in Tottenham in 1883, where his vicar was a certain Mr Moreton. To his nephew, Butterfield wrote in 1890, 'I have been reading Mr Moreton carefully as to Confirmation. In order to establish an idea (which I thank him for) that it is a species of Lay Ordination he seems to me to make needless havoc of other views. If I read however with care there is much to be extracted from his thesis ... Most people are very vague in their views [of Confirmation] ... Where are the people, for instance, who have been Confirmed in Tottenham during these last fifteen years? What has become of them? What fruit are they bearing?' He was sad that 'how little Christian information of a theological kind our people have. They seem to perish for lack of knowledge ... Parents do nothing for them.' He continued that he was glad his nephew was reading the *Tracts for the Times*, but he guarded him against *Lux Mundi*. 'Leave modern books alone,' he adjures.[154] Which is odd, for *Lux Mundi* was a pastorally and socially orientated embodiment, a further exposition, of the theology of the Tracts and of the Incarnation.[155] Some months later there were further warnings to his nephew about the new generation: society without shade or belief will be seriously untrue and uninteresting, and quite unchristian, ready for the Antichrist.[156] Three weeks after that his nephew received

---

[152] 16 September 1885, signed *A Layman*.

[153] Trinity College, Cambridge, BA 1869, MA 1873; deacon, 1869, priest 1870.

[154] Starey File, Ref. SY 103/5, 11 March 1890.

[155] He might have been conscious of a charge of heresy against Gore for his apparent acceptance of a late-nineteenth-century Lutheran interpretation of the doctrine of Kenosis – the self-emptying of the Second Person of the Trinity at the Incarnation – an over-literal understanding of Colossians chapter 2 verse 9 which threatened the doctrine of the divinity of Jesus. Gore later expounded his view more precisely.

[156] ibid, SY 103/6, 17 January 1891.

a note urging him not to live as if the preaching of sermons was the great object of a clergymen's life. 'Anybody must get dull if that were the whole view. A clergyman has a relationship primarily to the Church, secondarily to his parish,' he wrote, gnomically.[157]

William's brother Augustin Starey (1849–1888) was trained by Butterfield to be an architect, but was later ordained. His opinion of his uncle was, 'He is made of goodness and unselfishness.' Another brother, John (1848–1928), although he felt his uncle's opinions more important than his father's and was glad of his very salient good advice, nevertheless found his uncle too conservative and unenterprising when he consulted him on his business endeavours. Lucy Storey, sister of the above (1844–1866), who died after a lingering illness, was looked upon by the family as 'saintly'. She was quoted in a privately printed memoir 'In Praise of Lucy Starey' as regarding Butterfield as one of those rare inspiring examples of men 'who have spent their lives with no other thought but working for Christ, and look upon this life as . . . a preparation for the heavenly.'[158]

The letters Butterfield wrote to *The Guardian*, *The Times*, *The Builder* and the *Building News* between 1874 and 1899, under various pseudonyms which 'reserved' his anonymity, but expressed his innermost feelings about his faith as it applied to the church and the society of his time, are remarkably revealing. In a letter to *The Guardian* dated 20 May 1874, signed 'A Layman', he fired a salvo in favour of the Book of Common Prayer: 'The Prayer Book is our terra firma, but how few, intellectually and faithfully stand upon it?' he asked. 'I have no sympathy with lawlessness of any kind, whether Episcopal, Evangelical, or Ritualistic. The Archbishop of York [asserted recently] that the Cope is the proper Altar Vestment. Has anyone seen the Archbishop of York so attired since the delivery of this judgement? I think not.' By 24 November 1880 he had evidently tempered his views of Ritualists as lawbreakers, having apparently seen in a different light the issues at stake: 'Can

---

[157] ibid, SY 103/7, 27 February 1891.
[158] Quoted, Paul Thompson, ibid., p. 20

nothing be done to stay the further prosecution of faithful clergy? These imprisonments make infidels say, with some of our Roman friends, that the English Church is but a creation of Henry VIII, and it must be ruled by the secular power. Surely our Bishops and clergy believe it is part of the Catholic Church, and don't intend playing into the hands of either Roman Catholics bent on presbytising ['proselitysing?'], or enemies who believe in no God. How much longer can we bear the sneer?'[159]

A year later he crosses swords with the Bishop of Bedford,[160] accusing him of assuming 'entire ignorance and childishness amongst his flock at large. The Church,' he writes, 'is a supernatural power. Her leavening properties are unlimited. A small beginning on a real Church foundation would produce a marvellous result and a lasting one.' The ignorant and childish are not to be dismissed, he believed, and he proceeded to give examples from his own experiences. 'I have seen the poorest and most ill-clad congregations saying the Church's evening service throughout (not "portions of it"),[161] kneeling on the floor of some gutted dwellings arranged reverently in a church order. I have knelt with them. I have heard them chant the musical parts of that service and generally respond with a vigour and thoroughness which I do not find in congregations which the Bishop of Bedford would consider as used to, and able to take part in, our beautiful church services, and to whom he is satisfied to permit the use of the entire Prayer Book. Such poor folk as I allude to certainly appeared to need no extraordinary condescension to their supposed mean capacities.' He summarises his point by asserting that 'Condescension of this sort is not needed … the Church of England will sadly defraud the East End of London if she goes to work in such a spirit as this. She has failed in that part of London for long enough, and [will go on] to a much greater

---

[159] 24 November 1880, over the name 'An English Churchman'.
[160] William Walsham How, from 1879 to 1888, Suffragan to the Bishop of London at the time; later Bishop of Wakefield.
[161] The bishop had suggested that a simplified form of the Prayer Book services might be more suitable for such people.

failure if she brings to the work this merely human wisdom, or unwisdom. The East End of London must be treated fairly and not thus niggardly; it must be recovered by men free of conceit and self-consciousness, with a full, simple faith in God, and therefore in the Church and her ways, rather than their own.'[162] The pastoral spirit of the Oxford Revival could not have been more clearly put.

In a letter to *The Guardian* dated 20 August 1884,[163] between some brief contributions of his to a continuing debate in the newspaper's correspondence columns regarding loyalty to the Prayer Book Rubrics, Butterfield related some revealing activities in his life, during the formative years 1827 to 1830, and it is worthwhile reproducing at length:

> The only education I ever received was at a National school. When about thirteen … I had to see about helping to earn my bread, and so was cast off into the world. But having been connected with the Church (my father always attended services and took me with him), and knowing her catechism and liturgy as I do now, the natural inference was that I should continue to attend her worship. But, although young, I was conscious of a deep need in my soul, for which I could find no satisfaction, which led me …to wander off into a life of godless indifference to drown this inward conviction. But being in a district where dissenters were numerous, I soon found that there were those around me that were far happier than myself, and in the end their companionship led me to one of their chapels, where I found 'peace in the work of Christ,' and, what is my great point, made me a 'Dissenter.'… The people with whom I was now associated at once found me work to do for Christ, and taught me how to do it.
>
> In course of time in the ways of Providence my path led

---

me over 300 miles away from home to [a place where there is] a large scattered parish, thinly inhabited, the land wholly belongs to a great nobleman [and] I am the only Dissenter in the parish, effectively debarred from worshipping his God according to his custom. The people who did attend church were the respectable and educated of the inhabitants, and not 5% of the labourers ever entered the church doors except to a marriage or a funeral. Seeing the ignorant and deprived, those who had been taught 'to do their duty in that state of life in which it has pleased God to call them,' the very ones that needed the Gospel were the least likely to get it, I took my Bible and went out in the front of the various scattered clumps of cottages and proclaimed what I knew of God's 'Good News' to lost men. The consequence was I got these poor wretched people … to 'hear me gladly,' but few, if any, of those habitually went to Church. I soon found myself making a stand at a regular time, under a certain oak on a small green, that they all came regularly to hear me … as many as 300 people, some from three miles away, for that purpose. Winter came, and I was offered the largest room in an old cottage, and with the room packed to suffocation, many had to be turned away. The place was not in my parish, but some from there came, and once one of the Rector's Sidesmen, remarked to me, after every one had left, 'Why can't our clergy get these people to hear them…the majority that were here never go to church at all.' All I can say is there is something wrong about a church that has lost her hold on her people.[164]

It would seem that, like other Tractarians – Gladstone, Manning, and Newman and others – Butterfield was well established on sound evangelical convictions when becoming a follower of the Oxford Renewal.

---

[164] The letter was signed 'A Layman'.

To *The Guardian* on 20 October 1897,[165] after several letters
in the 1880s and 1890s, Butterfield wrote on the subject, generally,
of episcopal deviation from the Book of Common Prayer
Confirmation service, or discussion of a revised translation of the
Bible (the last sentence of his letter dated 26 May 1897 reads,
'This is a day of talking and preaching, but not of praying. It
seems deficient in a high order of faith'), Butterfield returns to
detailed prescription, in the course of a series of letters, on the
subject of 'Teaching children the Bible'. He was inspired particularly
to respond to letters from one who signed himself 'Dragon', who
advocated, among other things, a selective Bible which omitted
all the 'difficult' parts. Butterfield responded that 'the only way
to teach the Bible is as a whole ... as a whole it is a wonderful
book – those who have tried it, know.' He continued, ' "Dragon"
does not seem to have the gifts which qualify him for teaching
children. His difficulties are within himself.' Butterfield admits
that Leviticus, a large part of Numbers and a large part of
Deuteronomy (chapters 18–27) pose difficulties but, 'as life goes
on, the Bible must be understood as one *whole* by any who believe
with St Peter that it "came not in old time by the will of man,
but holy men of God as they were moved by the Holy Ghost."'[166]
He quotes from his experience of teaching a family of poor
children, who were in a church school in which compulsory
attendance at church teaching was treated as cramming as a few
weeks before Confirmation. He asked them questions regarding
the Catechism, and whether they knew anything about the baptism
service. They did not. He then took the children through the
service, and read to them the first three chapters of Genesis, at
which they showed great interest; and thereafter as the Old
Testament was united with the New Testament at meetings on
Sunday afternoons. 'The difficulties experienced by "Dragon" and
his suggestion of an expurgated Bible never arose,' he said.[167] In

---

[165] p. 1681.
[166] A quotation from 2 Peter 1, vv 20 and 21.
[167] Signed, 'Another Layman'.

a further letter, in response to Dragon's replies on this subject, Butterfield observed that his reactions to his children 'seems to imply that they have been encouraged to understand that scepticism is interesting, and a mark of intelligence.' He quotes Dragon's answer to the question 'Did the ass of Balaam really speak?' as essentially ' "No – the animal looked at Balaam and his master understood him" ' – ignoring 2 Peter Chapter 2, verses 15 and 16.' This, said Butterfield, 'was an effort to reduce divine operation to vulgar common sense.' Other respondents wrote with similar observations. The effects of the German School of Biblical criticism – treating the Bible as any other literature, and attempting to refine it of all supernaturalism – were causing much consternation, along with evolutionism and hard-edged narrow rationalism among church people.[168]

Butterfield went on to tell an anecdote with a different moral, one of strong faith instead of doubt and mistrust, in the will and power of God. It was told to him by a valued friend who was the vicar of a parish: 'A poor journeyman, working for the great houses in the manufacture of shoes in Northampton, living in his own cottage in a village a few miles from that town, was lying on his deathbed . The Vicar called on him … and found him singularly depressed. He asked the reason and the man said, "I have had a visit from a fellow workman in Northampton, who heard that I was ill. But he was no comfort to me. He has no religion, and he talked against it in many ways." He said to me "You don't believe that the whale swallowed Jonah?" To the vicar's question "And what did you say?" he replied "I told him," sir, "that if God wished the whale to swallow Jonah, the whale could do it." He knew that the man was not attacking the whale, but God. And he knew that all things are possible to Him. It was a noble reply … the faith of that poor dying man was enviable.'

One of Butterfield's pseudonymous discussions of the state of the church as he saw it is found an expression in a letter to *The*

---

[168] *The Guardian*, 1 December 1897, p. 1930.

Guardian of 28 December 1898[169] over the name of 'Churchman'.
It was a contribution to an examination of 'obedience' and
'disobedience.'[170] Someone signing himself 'Antistes', a bishop of
the Anglican Communion, who had seen the Book of Common
Prayer as forbidding Reservation (of the sacred elements of
Communion) for the sick or terminally ill. 'He bases his remarks
on an entirely past period, never, we believe to return,' wrote
Butterfield. 'To do our work obediently with the materials which
Providence has supplied us is our present duty, I believe, and to
wait, in God's time, in faith, for change, commends itself to many
of us as the only way to ensure safe progress.' For Butterfield,
the only faithful way to make changes was not to acquiesce in
the scepticism of the age, no matter how well argued, but in
obedience to the leading of God. In a subsequent issue of *The
Churchman*[171] he refers again to the subject of obedience and
disobedience. 'Reading the correspondence in various newspapers
[on the current Bible/Prayer Book malaise], one is much struck
by the absence of any ecclesiastical or even religious principles.
Strong wills are engaged, there is a discreditable mutiny but little
more ... It is a lack of faith and spiritual-mindedness from which
we suffer; things essential, but not necessarily supplied quickly
... We have to start as penitents.'

In a very long letter to *The Guardian*[172] Butterfield makes a late
public expression of his anxieties for the church in its betrayal of
sound biblical and Prayer Book theology. 'It is well known,' he
wrote, 'that for the last two or three centuries the clergy have made
light of the Prayer Book, and have, with few exceptions, kept the
churches closed from Sunday to Sunday. To arouse them from their
slumber was the object of the Oxford Movement. But, for all those
ages of amazing neglect, there has never been any serious expression
of penitence and humiliation for disloyalty and disobedience. There

---

[169] ibid., pp. 2020 and 2021.
[170] 'Disobedience' he called 'the enemy of faith and the source of all ruin'.
[171] 13 September 1899, p. 1237.
[172] 30 August 1899, p. 1182.

is one Tract for the Times (No. 86) which is almost prophetical of our present trouble. Its title is "Indicators of a Superintending Providence in the Preservation of the Prayer Book, and in the changes it has undergone." It presses obedience and repentance … Would that our shortcomings had been met by this generation in a due spirit of humble penitence' ['A Churchman'].

In all these pseudonymous writings Butterfield was revealing both his opinions on coeval developments in the church, and his own theological standpoint in the Tractarian Revival and its true coherence with the theology of the Book of Common Prayer. The outworking, the application of his faith in practice, his professional principles, his dealing with his staff and co-workers, and his generous attitude to finance in the context of God's Kingdom, were all founded on these theological principles.

One of Butterfield's greatest admirers, and most percipient interpreters, was the poet Gerard Manley Hopkins (1844–1889). His observations on his approach to architecture and the Tractarian Revival are penetrating. In his younger days Hopkins did many drawings and watercolours, and this developed while he was at Oxford into a keen interest in architecture.[173] Hopkins went up to Balliol College in 1863, and wrote to his mother about Butterfield's rebuilding of the College Chapel (1856–57): 'Our graceful chapel, which cost only a fourth as much as Exeter,[174] and did *not*, as that did, run us into debt. We have no choir, organ, or music of any kind, but then the chapel is beautiful, and two of our windows contain some of the finest old glass in Oxford.'[175] By 1866 he was staunch in his admiration for Butterfield, and among the criteria of this selection were his 'Christian qualities.'[176] Stimulated principally by All Saints Margaret Street

---

[173] Catherine Phillips, *Gerard Manley Hopkins and the Victorian Visual World* [Oxford University Press, 2007], pp. 41 and 95.
[174] 1856–1860, Giles Gilbert Scott.
[175] Phillips, p. 92. Other Oxford College work by Butterfield was at Morton (new buildings, 1865).
[176] ibid., p. 101.

church, and its application of the theology of the Tractarian Movement: 'Almost a third of the church's length was given to the Chancel, emphasising the pre-eminence of the sacraments, establishing the ... Eucharist on Sundays, the regular recitation of Morning and Evening Prayer, providing spiritual counselling, the sacrament of penance and reconciliation, and appealing to the senses – lights, candles, vestments and the elevation of the sacrament.'[177] Hopkins admired the religious significance of each part of Butterfield's designs,[178] re-emphasising, as was said above, that Pugin wrote in 1836, 'In the temples of the pagan nations, every ornament, every detail, had a mystical import ... is it to be supposed that Christianity alone, with is sublime truths, with its stupendous mysteries, should be deficient in this respect and not possess a symbolic architecture for her temples which would embody her doctrines?'[179] Hopkins wrote in 1877 to thank Butterfield for sending him a list of his buildings, which he had asked for; he felt ashamed that he had not realised how long the catalogue would be. He added the hope that 'you will long continue to work out your beautiful and original style.'[180] Also in 1877 Hopkins wrote to Butterfield, I do not think this generation will ever ... understand how to look at a pointed building as a whole having a single form governing it throughout, which they *would* perhaps see in a Greek temple: they like it to be a sort of farmyard and medley of ricks and roofs and dovecots. And very few people seem to care for pure beauty of line.'[181]

Following Ruskin, Butterfield believed that, in the interests of Truthfulness and Reality, structure should be seen and truly understood. Pugin, in his *True Principles* wrote that a structure acknowledged and expressed could provide a greater sense of that

---

[177] ibid., p. 102.
[178] ibid., p. x.
[179] A.W.N. Rugin, *Contrasts*, Introduction by H.R. Hitchcock [Leicester University Press] 1969, p. 8. (Originally published by Charles Dolman, 1836; second edition 1841.)
[180] Phillips, ibid., p. 108. She adds that George Edmund Street had expressed this view twenty years earlier.
[181] ibid.

pure beauty of line ... than the obscuring involved in classical design.[182] Butterfield had made notes from Ruskin that 'The virtue of originality which men strain after is not newness, it is only genuineness: it all depends on this glorious faculty of getting to the spring of things, and working out from that ... There is reciprocal action between the intensity of moral feeling and the power of imagination.'[183] Hopkins appreciated the clear link between surface appearance and structure. He praised a church that revealed the mind of its architect:

> Who shaped these walls, though thick through stone,
> What beauty beat behind.[184]

It is that conviction of a link between surface appearance and structure, the unity of 'outer' and 'inner', admired in Butterfield's buildings, to which Hopkins alludes in the term he uses frequently: 'Inscape'. By this he means the unique inner quality, or essence, of a subject: a substantiation of the definition of a sacrament – 'An outward and visible sign of an inward and spiritual grace.'

Paul Thompson suggests that the vibrant sense of colour in Butterfield's designs offended Victorians morally as well as aesthetically.[185] But Ruskin could claim that 'None of us appreciates the nobleness and sacredness of colour ... All good colour is in some degree pensive; the loveliest is melancholy, and the purest and most thoughtful minds are those which love colour the most.'[186] Butterfield's contrasting brick courses – black, red, white, and so on – also appealed to Hopkins' observations of nature. In a letter he described a rainy day: 'The clouds westwards were a pied peace – sail-coloured, brown and milky blue ... far in the south spread a bluish damp, but all the nearer valley was showered

---

[182] ibid., pp. 5 and 6.
[183] Quoted, Paul Thompson, ibid., p. 375.
[184] Quoted, Phillips, ibid., p. 110.
[185] ibid., p. 229.
[186] *The Stones of Venice*, ii, pp. 144 and 145. Quoted in Phillips, ibid., p. 103.

with tapered diamond flakes of fields in purple and brown and green.'[187] His poem 'Pied Beauty' ('Glory be to God for dappled things') shows his appreciation of coloured themes in nature.

Lack of colour was characteristic of classical architecture, which came from Graeco-Roman admiration for cerebral inspiration and a disdain for raw nature. Charles Eastlake thought that the design for All Saints Margaret Street was 'a bold and magnificent endeavour to shake off the trammels of antiquarian precedent, which had long fettered the progress of the Revival ... to add the colour of natural material to pictorial decoration ... to adorn the walls with surface ornament of an enduring kind.'[188] 'Butterfield expressed through colour the triumphant Joy of Faith, and through line and pattern the insecurity of an age of doubt and change. He could express the spirit of the age at a deeper level than is usual with architecture.'[189]

William Butterfield was privileged to express in beautiful and functional buildings, and his ethical conduct of his art, the Incarnational emphasis of the Tractarian theological world-view in all its fullness and implication.

---

[187] Quoted in Phillips, ibid., p. 106.
[188] *A History of the Gothic Revival*, 1872, pp. 259, 253, and 254.
[189] Paul Thompson, ibid., p. 377.

3

Thomas Percival Heywood (1823–1897), Banker, 2nd Baronet Heywood of Claremont in the County of Lancaster

Thomas Percival Heywood was the eldest son of Sir Benjamin Heywood (1793–1865), MP for Lancashire, the head of 'The Manchester Bank', which was founded in 1788 in Exchange Street Manchester, moving to St Ann's Street in 1795.[1]

Benjamin became sole proprietor in 1828, and one of the acknowledged leaders of Manchester business.[2] The name of the business was changed to 'Benjamin Heywood and Company' when his four sons became partners as they reached the age of twenty-one. In April 1874 the entire business was sold to the Manchester and Salford Bank for the sum of £240,000.[3]

Benjamin's youngest brother was James, FRS (1810–1897), MP for Lancashire North from 1847 to 1857. James's parliamentary career was most notable for his promotion of reform at Oxford and Cambridge Universities, and as being one of the half-dozen who supported Owen's College (later the university), Manchester, to which he gave its first library of 1200 volumes.[4]

---

[1] The building he erected there in 1848, built of large ashlar rock, 'is a model of civil reserve and good manners combined with strength and character, a fitting tribute to the man and all that he did.' Royal Bank of Scotland, *3 Banks Review*, Vol. 3 (1949), p. 34.

[2] ibid, p. 30.

[3] It became later Williams Deacon's Bank, and then the National Westminster Bank. It is now part of the Royal Bank of Scotland.

[4] *Dictionary of National Biography*, OUP, pp. 967ff.

Benjamin Heywood was a part of another historical event: he was riding his horse at the opening of the world's first inter-city railway, the Liverpool and Manchester Company, in 1830 when William Huskisson (1770–1830)[5] was badly injured after stepping in front of the locomotive 'Rocket' (Huskisson later died). Heywood's horse was commandeered to send a messenger to Liverpool with the news.[6]

From early times the Heywoods were predominantly Unitarians in their Christian allegiance, which explains the 'ejection' in 1662 of ancestors who were ministers of religion: Oliver (died 1702), an incumbent in Halifax, and Nathaniel (1633–1677), Vicar of Ormskirk. In the nineteenth century many Nonconformists, and in particular Unitarians, made their transition into Anglicanism smoothly and almost imperceptibly, especially if they wished to enter Parliament.[7] From the age of 10 until he was 13 (1803–1806), Benjamin went to a boarding school at Fairfield, near Warrington, run by the Revd Edward Lloyd, and was under the influence and teaching of the Established Church.[8] At first he was attracted by the liturgy,[9] but he and his son Thomas Percival 'came to embrace wholeheartedly the theological position of the Tractarian Renewal.'[10]

Benjamin Heywood was a man who applied his faith to social concerns. He was prominent in the movement to establish amenities for the cotton mill operatives, especially in the provision of public parks. Through his membership of the Manchester Statistical Society

[5] MP for Morpeth, 1796–1801, and for Liskeard from 1804.
[6] Isabel Mary Heywood, Reminiscences of Thomas Percival Heywood, drawing on her father's *Memoranda* and Sir Benjamin's *Memoir*, 'All Saints Day, 1899' [printed for private circulation by Thomas Fargie, Church Booksellers, Manchester (the last page is inscribed as printed by Lloyd and Taylor, 77 Market Street)], p. 3. Hereinafter she is referred to as 'Isabel Mary', and Thomas Percival as 'Percival' Heywood, as he was always known, in distinction from several senior members of the family who were named 'Thomas'.
[7] D.W. Bebbington, *Unitarian Members of Parliament in the 19th Century*, article on the Internet, December 2009, p. 2.
[8] *A Memoir of Sir Benjamin Heywood, Bt*, by his brother Thomas Heywood, FSA [printed in Manchester for private circulation by Thomas Fargie, 20 Cross Street, 1885], pp. 7 and 12.
[9] Bebbington, p. 2.
[10] Isabel Mary, p. 65.

he conducted an enquiry into *The Condition of the Working Classes in Manchester*, which was published in 1834.[11] He was opposed to the Corn Laws, to monopolies in trade, and especially to slavery in the colonies ('A disgrace and a curse to my nation,' he said). He was elected to parliament in 1831, was instrumental in the Reform Bill of 1832, but retired from parliament with ill-health in that year.[12] One of Sir Benjamin's notable philanthropic achievements was his founding of The Mechanics Institute in Manchester in 1824. This was devoted to basic science, mathematics and chemistry, and the inaugural meeting brought together prominent members of the science and engineering communities. These included John Dalton, 'the father of atomic theory' (who became the Institute's vice-president for the years 1839 to 1841); Robert Hyde, cotton mill owner, later a Member of Parliament; Peter Ewell, millwright and engineer; Richard Roberts, machine-tool inventor; David Bellhurst, a builder; William Henry, a pioneer in the scientific chemical industry; William Fairbairn, Scottish engineer, associated with water-wheel technology and the Britannia Tubular Bridge – a man with a scientific approach to engineering, who became the first secretary of the Institute – and Sir Benjamin himself, president from 1824 to 1841. A committee was elected, which Heywood chaired when the Institute was opened in 1825. It was 'One of the first to be established in this country ... surpassed by none in the success with which it has accomplished its purpose.'[13] The Institute passed through several changes of name and refined expansions of syllabus in the following years, and in 1883, as the Manchester Technical School it offered London City and Guilds qualifications.[14]

---

[11] *Dictionary of National Biography*, OUP, p. 966 (it was the basis of Friedrich Engels' 'Condition of the Working Class in England' of 1845).

[12] *Three Banks Review*, Vol. 3 (1949), p. 31.

[13] *A Memoir of Sir Benjamin Heywood* by Thomas Heywood, p. 40.

[14] In 1917/18 it became Manchester Municipal College of Technology, which in 1956 changed its name to Manchester College of Science and Technology. By 1966 it was The University of Manchester Institute of Science and Technology, which achieved full degree autonomy in 1993. On 1 October 2004 The Victoria University of Manchester and UMIST ceased to exist when combined as the new single 'University of Manchester' [Internet].

Sir Benjamin's influence on his family was substantial. His son Oliver (1825–1892), became an honoured citizen in Manchester, taking over the chairmanship of the family bank, and presidency of the Mechanics' Institute, and was an ardent supporter of the anti-slavery movement. He has a commemorative statue opposite the Town Hall in Albert Square, together with one of Gladstone, John Bright (Liberal Statesman), Prince Albert, Bishop James Fraser, Second Bishop of Manchester and the Queen Victoria fountain. He was urged by his father to have sympathy for the aims of the Chartists, while eschewing the use of violence to attain them: 'The people must be treated with more consideration,' he said. 'It is likely enough we might be Chartists ourselves, in their circumstances of privation and disappointment and ignorance: we must sympathise with them.'[15] He urged Oliver to establish firm knowledge of the banking business, and to read Adam Smith's *Wealth of Nations.* The value of that knowledge, he wrote, was not only for the safety and success of the business, but for the position it would give Oliver on the great public questions of the time (1846).

Sir Benjamin exhorted his eldest son, Thomas Percival, to 'a cultivated mind and active and useful occupation; I cannot doubt you will desire for yourself, and probably it has already been in your thoughts, to lay down some plan ... in reference to it ... and to include some system of self-examination. Try yourself by your own rule ... I think you know my own little form of self-examination. Keep yourself in constant and familiar communion with your heavenly Master as an *ever-present friend.*'[16] In the following year he advised Percival, 'You should give both money and time to the improvement of the people in your neighbourhood ... It is desirable that you should lay by of your substance, using it in proper proportions in relief and service of others.'[17] A footnote to Thomas Heywood's *Memoir* of his brother lists his reading as

[15] Benjamin, writing to Oliver, 10 April 1848.
[16] 25 June 1846.
[17] 20 September 1847.

the writings of St Francis de Sales, Thomas a Kempis, Archbishops Sumner, Whately, and Trench; Bishops Andrewes, Jeremy Taylor and Wilson; Deans Stanley, Hook, Alford and Magee of Goulburn; Herbert, Hooker, Barrow and Baxter; Arnold, Vaughan, Pusey, Keble, Newman, Manning, Melville, Bradley, 'etc, etc.'[18] Benjamin Heywood was appointed Baronet in the Queen's Coronation List on 9 August 1838.

Sir Benjamin's eldest son, Thomas Percival the second baronet, was born on 15 March 1823 at Acresfield, a country house only three miles from Manchester. Like his father he was educated privately at various schools, latterly, having been baptised in the Name of the Holy Trinity, at Cuckfield School, Sussex, where the Head Teacher was a Mr Fearn, who later became Rector and Archdeacon of Loughborough. Percival had a great respect and regard for him. Percival went up to Trinity College, Cambridge in 1841,[19] but left before completing his degree because of a persistent fever, which weakened him for life; he was in constant pain from headaches,[20] an ill-health which seems to have precluded him from much involvement with the bank itself.

After his marriage on 19 May 1846, to Margaret, daughter of Thomas Heywood Esq, Thomas Percival settled at Doveleys, which had been his father's house, near Uttoxeter, on the Staffordshire side of the River Dove. This was in the parish of Rocester, where they were welcomed by the vicar, Mr Chippendall, who greatly appreciated their help in every way: Percival as churchwarden, his wife teaching evening classes, and by the financial relief they sent constantly to the vicar for those especially distressed in the parish. After a therapeutic visit to Kissengen, a town of salt springs in Bavaria, in 1851, Percival felt stronger and better than usual, and he received a letter inviting him to become High Sheriff of Lancashire.

His private journal records that in November 1854 he went to Cambridge to hear Bishop Selwyn advocating support for the

---

[18] p. 108.
[19] Isabel Mary, pp. 5, 8, and 10.
[20] ibid., p. 31.

Gospel Propagation Society (later USPG). He gave the bishop a promise to donate £100 a year for five years, desiring 'by God's grace that this may [affect] me with the sense of my responsibility, by all means in my power, to bring souls to Christ.' A further entry on 1 December of that year reads, 'I desire to put myself in contact with the sick and poor, and to administer both to their bodily and spiritual wants. I desire to give liberally, not as a gratification to myself and to ease my conscience, but as unto my loving Saviour who gave himself for me.'[21] These developments of the implications of his Tractarian faith caused him to see the nearby hamlet of Denstone as the 'most neglected of hamlets,' and he established a Dame School there. 'By degrees we worked on to have afternoon services which were taken at the school by Dr Fraser, the Vicar of Alton. This developed into one of the great interests of our lives, the consolidation of Denstone in Rocester with parts of Denstone in Alton – Quixhill and Prestwood – into an ecclesiastical parish, founding there a church, a vicarage, and a school.'[22] Heywood wrote to his father in 1861, 'I am very anxious to raise up a church that shall commend itself to those who worship in it as well as fitted to its object, perfect in all its parts and yet quite free from all fanciful decoration.' In his manuscript book of private prayers is a prayer in his wife's handwriting which they used in the preparation for the building of All Saints, Denstone: '... Grant that we may be permitted to build a house which shall bear thy Name, where the sacrifice of prayer and praise shall come up before thee – where the glad tidings of the Kingdom shall be proclaimed, and thy Holy Sacraments duly administered ...' He wrote to his brother Arthur in January 1859 about his plans: 'We think we can spare £1,000 a year for our object ... and hope by the end of next year to have the church and parsonage built, and ... the glass windows and the fittings of the church and churchyard will be £500.' He

---

[21] ibid., pp. 50 and 51.
[22] ibid., pp. 32 and 33.

clearly had some misgivings at the scale of his commitment, for he continued, 'The work is *very nearly* beyond our power, but we shall not accept any help from beyond my own family, if it were offered;' although later he wrote of receiving help from Arthur and his father.[23]

Quite apart from what Isabel Mary described as 'the customary opposition from "Principalities and powers of evil in heavenly places",'[24] there was less than willing co-operation from some of those who had existing territorial authority in the area. The Vicar of Ellastone was 'vehemently opposed to the taking of Prestwood into the proposed ecclesiastical district; the incumbent of Rocester (not by that time Chippendall) was still more vehement in his opposition to ceding the part of Denstone in his parish, and of Quixhill. A pamphlet was published, addressed to the Queen, praying her to put a stop to the 'naughty proceedings'.[25] However, Dr Fraser gladly gave up the Denstone part of his Alton parish, and helped in every way. The parishioners in Denstone and the bishop[26] agreed with the proposed work, and the Ecclesiastical Commissioners ratified the scheme, on the condition that Heywood endowed the church with £150 a year.[27] The total population of the new parish was to be about 1200 – similar to that of Rocester and of Alton. Prestwood and Quixhall were settlements of 70 and 30 people respectively. From 1871 the hamlet of Stubwood, in the former Alton part of the parish, had a chapel (St Luke's) in a farm building.[28]

The architect chosen for the new parish church building was George Edmund Street (1824–1881), who together with George Frederick Bodley (1827–1907) worked in the office of George Gilbert Scott, learning the English Decorated Gothic form which

---

[23] ibid., pp. 59 and 60.
[24] A reference to the Epistle to the Ephesians, chapter 6, verse 12.
[25] Isabel Mary, p. 61.
[26] John Lonsdale, Bishop of Lichfield, 1843–1868.
[27] Isabel Mary, p. 61.
[28] *Kelly's Directory for Staffordshire*, 1921, p. 168.

replaced the purist Gothic Revival of A.W.N. Pugin and the Cambridge Ecclesiological Society. Heywood does not record the reason for the choice of architect, simply stating in his *Reminiscences* of 1893 that 'we did not hesitate to choose Mr Street ... his work was there to prove the wisdom of the choice: that "a thing of beauty is a joy for ever" – the church is lovely in every detail.' It has been described as 'a country parish church of great power and charm ... a masterful composition of simple forms.'[29] Heywood had chosen the dedication of 'All Saints' that 'we may try to realize the fullness of meaning of a "Communion of Saints."'[30]

Bishop Lonsdale consecrated the church in the summer of 1862, and the offertory was devoted to the cathedral restoration fund. Heywood was a firm devotee of the movement, then in its infancy, for free and open churches, and the words 'Every Seat in this Church is Free' were set in stone near the door. At the meeting of the Church Congress held in Stoke on Trent in 1875 he delivered a long and well-constructed speech against the inherent bias of pew rents: that considerations of social and financial status were of prominent importance in the Church's attitude towards its parishioners. He listed the objections to free seats in church – First, overcrowding; second, having the different classes sitting near to each other; and third, that pew rents contribute to the stipend of the clergy. In response to the first he advocated giving thanks to God for such a blessing, and holding more services; to the second, he had never experienced such a problem – quite the contrary, it would be 'impossible to worship God aright if we felt uneasy at the near proximity of someone in a much humbler position of life.' He conceded that the case of the income from pew rents posed a grave difficulty, but that the laity, properly taught, would make the offertory a source of that revenue, given as a wholehearted gift to God and the work of his Church. In the same speech he argued that church buildings ought to be left unlocked; the closed church door during

---

[29] C.M. Smart Jnr, in *Muscular Churches* [London: University of Arkansas Press, 1989], p. 101.
[30] Isabel Mary, pp. 61 and 58.

the week intimated 'that the world is to be worshipped for six days and God only on the seventh.'[31] He would have warmed to the words of John Duke Lord Coleridge, in a letter in 1854: 'It seems to me ... a weak and effeminate fear of the world's ridicule ... which hinders us from going simply and openly to kneel before God's altars, or to sit and meditate in God's churches day by day on his ways and wonders.'[32]

The first vicar of the new parish was Joseph Cockerham, previously curate of Norbury and Snelstone, just across the River Dove (in the Diocese of Derby) from 1850 to 1860. He served from 1860 to 1881, although for the last six years he was an invalid, and *Crockford's Clerical Directory* showed him as still incumbent in 1890. This has the implication that Heywood, as Patron, was responsible for two stipends until that year, for Cockerham was succeeded in 1881 by Henry Meynell, who came from the parish of Faulds, near Whitchurch, Salop. Meynell later told Heywood's daughter Isabel that her father saw it as his duty as Patron to introduce their new priest to his parishioners: he took him round every one of them, house to house. Meynell had been impressed by the bright and kindly manner with which his patron greeted them all, and the intimate knowledge he seemed to have of their home life and surroundings. 'He put me at once at ease with them, and ... gave me much information about them of a practical kind which was most valuable to me afterwards as a parish priest. I noticed, however,' he added, 'that he said little or nothing of their faults or failings ... only their merits ... leaving the rest ... to find out for myself. Throughout my life at Denstone vicarage nothing escaped him or was too slight to interest him, if it referred in any way to the welfare of the people, or to the glory of God in the church of which he was Warden. His kindness to all was untold.' Meynell related how, one winter which occasioned unusual distress among the poor, Heywood

---

[31] Official Report of the Church Congress, 1875.
[32] *John D.L. Coleridge, Lord Chief Justice of England*, Ernest Hartley Coleridge, Vol. I [London: William Heinemann, 1904], p. 220.

asked him to go round the parish with him, to see what the people needed. 'He told me that what he wanted to see was that when Christmas came everyone within his reach should have a warm bed to lie on, decent clothes ... and something ... for their Christmas dinner.' He described how the expedition was bitterly cold, how they started early and worked on till late at night, on frozen roads as slippery as glass. 'They visited house after house ... up lanes and all sorts of awkward places until he was thoroughly tired. But Sir Percival never flagged, greeting everyone cheerfully, and making his enquiries as to their welfare with delicacy and courtesy. They trusted him as a real friend,' he said, 'and that was but one instance out of many. He was honoured and loved by everyone.'[33] Heywood's daughter Mary Monica (died 1951) recalled that on occasion, returning from riding with her, 'he would call at a cottage on the way back to visit some sick person, and remembered a poor woman in Rocester telling her how ... he tied up his horse at the village smithy and came to sit awhile with her dying husband.'[34]

Isabel Mary records that Denstone once had a bad name, being 'a sort of 'No-Man's Land', out of the way of good influences. There was drinking and fighting and all sorts of wickedness which went on unrebuked. The devoted, earnest and incessant work carried on in the church and school and the houses of the people has completely changed the character of the place.'[35] Exactly the application of the pastoral *Ethos* of the Tractarian Movement. Henry Meynell wrote to Heywood on 11 December 1875 to say, 'This church was, and is, an untold blessing, and every year I see this plainer.' Some who had gone to live elsewhere 'come back to cheer us by saying what good has come to them from their early days here ... there is much to make us thankful, and not least the warm love by the people towards you and yours at all time.'[36]

---

[33] Quoted, Isabel Mary, pp. 62 and 63.
[34] Isabel Mary, p. 234.
[35] ibid., pp. 62 and 63.
[36] ibid., pp. 64 and 65.

Heywood's daughter comments, 'The new life which thrilled through the Church in consequence of the Oxford Movement strongly influenced the Founders of Denstone.' Her parents 'had the most profound reverence for Dr Pusey especially: his name and that of Mr Keble were household words.' Many of the leading churchmen of that day came to stay at Doveleys and preached at All Saints. 'The services and the teaching were in accordance with the spirit of the originators of the Movement, and not with that of the more modern ritualistic development'.[37] This comment of Isabel's raises the question of how far the lay members of the Movement were in favour of the development of elaborate ritual.

Ritualism

The early Tractarians, Keble, Newman and Pusey, were not Ritualists in the pejorative sense of the term. Keble applied Tractarian principles to his parish at Hursley,[38] but 'To at least one family Keble's teaching seemed nothing new, only the consequence of what they had always learned.'[39] However, in the sacramental teaching of the Founders there was being promulgated a doctrine of the Eucharist and of the Real Presence which demanded a greater reverence in liturgical standards. The architectural societies of Oxford and Cambridge were urging a closer study of worship, and as early as 1840 at least one church, in the Diocese of London, introduced candles, a surpliced choir, and the intoning of services.[40] Ritualism was powerfully inspired to re-create the visual and material forms of medieval worship, in art, artefact, and architecture.[41] It was a valid development of the Incarnational theology of the 'Tracts' – of communicating its truth to the lay

---

[37] Ibid., p. 65.
[38] Kenneth Ingram, *John Keble*, [Philip Allen, 1933], pp. 174 and 175.
[39] Raymond Chapman, *Faith and Revolt* [London: Weidenfeld and Nicholson, 1970] p. 61.
[40] J.R.H. Moorman, *A History of the English Church* [A and C Black, 1953], p. 352.
[41] Dominic Janes, Victorian Revolution [OUP, 2009], p. 205.

followers, through the media of all the senses: not only hearing (Word), but sight – colour and movement, and smell, in terms of valid symbolism. But there is no doubt that a tendency grew which seemed to take a delight in such things as important in themselves, a distinction between those who were thoroughly inspired by the Oxford Renewal, and those who used the opportunity to develop liturgical practices which went far beyond the Prayer Book loyalties of the Founders. Such excesses were the Perpetual Reservation on the High Altar, Benediction, Shrines of the Sacred Heart, Corpus Christi processions through the streets, the disuse of the English language, and the regular use of the Latin missal.[42] Although John Keble admitted that he had no real sympathy for the 'ritualists', he had even less sympathy with those who were preparing to attack them by means of an Act of Parliament. He declared that 'they were opening the door to Parliamentary interference with spiritual matters. Once the power of the state had been involved, there would be no stopping the Parliamentary juggernaut – today at your request the state new-models your ritual, tomorrow it will be new-modelling your creeds and prayers.[43]

After her father's death, his daughter recalled warmly that 'one of the Denstone poor people' said to her 'how much he was missed,' and that 'he seemed to bring heaven with him when he came into the church,' adding, 'I could not have loved him more than if he had been my own father.'[44] Heywood always treated the servants with kindness and consideration, and many stayed with the household for years. His children saw them as faithful and trusted friends, sharing joys and sorrows and entering into their interests. One of those whom he took to (Uttoxeter) market remembered later in life that he would often give a lift to some market-woman who was toiling along the road with her heavy

---

[42] Moorman, p. 399.
[43] Georgina Battiscombe, *John Keble* [London: Constable Ltd, 1963], p. 350.
[44] Isabel Mary, pp. 82 and 83.

basket, chatting pleasantly to her to dispel her shyness at her novel position.[45]

From the early 1870s Heywood began to come forward more publically as a 'Defender of the Faith.' He made a speech on 31 January 1873 at a great meeting in St James's Hall, Piccadilly, in defence of the Athanasian Creed. Among the other speakers were A.J.B. Beresford Hope,[46] Henry Hucks Gibbs,[47] Lord Salisbury,[48] the Revd H. Temple and Dr Liddon. Heywood spoke first, and declared his view that nothing derogatory should be done to the Creed in the Prayer Book of the Church of England, for 'so surely [would] it make the Book no longer then a reflex of the Bible.'[49]

The Next Step: Denstone College and the Woodard Schools

Nathaniel Woodard (1811–1891), an Anglican priest, had a vision and the determination to see it realised: it was to set up a foundation of schools throughout England for the education of the middle classes. He saw the rapidly expanding society of the mid-century, with its social conflicts and its deprivation, and the need for the provision of an education, based on sound principle, true knowledge and the firm foundation of the Christian Faith. He wanted to achieve the 'union of the classes' by a common system of education especially aimed at the poorer middle classes, seeing that the aristocracy and the richest had Public Schools.[50]

---

[45] ibid., pp. 82 and 84.
[46] *Nobody's Friend*, No. 212.
[47] ibid., No. 156.
[48] ibid., No. 202.
[49] Isabel Mary, p. 73.
[50] Of which the Clarendon Commission of 1861 enumerated nine: Eton, Winchester, Westminster, Charterhouse, St Paul's, Merchant Taylors, Harrow, Rugby and Shrewsbury. (Two ancient schools, King's Canterbury and St Peter's York were both founded in the seventh century, but as descendents of cathedral choir schools were not seen in 1861 as being in the same category.)

The poorer classes were provided for, albeit inadequately, by 'voluntary schools' – church or individual enterprises – and by 1831 The National Society. But the middle classes were not provided for.[51] In 1863 the Social Science Association in Edinburgh proposed a Commission on Middle Class schools, as distinct from the Popular Education Commission or the one on Public Schools, and it met on 28 December 1864. Dr Frederick Temple was asked to be its head, and among the assistant commissioners were Bishop James Fraser of Manchester, Mr Matthew Arnold, and Mr (later Professor) Thomas Henry Green.[52] Its report was published in March 1868, declaring that 'Secondary education in England required to be organised. Hitherto schools for the middle classes had been left to themselves, as isolated units.[53]

Woodard started on a small scale in 1848 at New Shoreham in Sussex, St Nicholas' College (which later became Lancing College),[54] having discovered, as a curate there, that even the sea captains did not understand the art and science of navigation.[55] In 1850 he gave up his curacy and founded the first 'Woodard' school at Hurstpierpoint in 1851. This was followed by Lancing (1854), Bloxham (1860), and Ardingly (1870). In 1844 a girls' school had been founded at Hove (later at Bognor), but not until 1864 was the property conveyed to the Trustees of St Nicholas' College.[56] A central committee for the Woodard project was formed in London in 1855, with Lord Robert Cecil as chairman,[57] and the Revd Robert Gregory, future Canon, then Dean, of St Paul's, as honorary secretary.[58]

---

[51] K.E. Kirk, *The Story of the Woodard Schools* [Hodder, 1937], pp. 12 and 13.
[52] E.G. Sandford, Ed., *Memoirs of Archbishop Temple, 1821–1896* [London: Macmillan and Co. Ltd, 1906], pp. 132–135.
[53] ibid., p. 137.
[54] Kirk, ibid., p. 21.
[55] T.W. Bamford, *The Rise of the Public Schools* [London: Thomas Nelson and Sons Ltd, 1967], p. 30.
[56] Brian Heeney, *Mission to the Middle Classes* [London: SPCK], 1969, p. 35.
[57] Robert Arthur Talbot Gascoyne-Cecil (1830–1903), later (1868), the Marquis of Salisbury and Prime Minister from 1885 to 1902, was a strong supporter of the Tractarian cause.
[58] Heeny, ibid., p. 43.

The enterprise was brought to Percival Heywood's notice in 1866, and it appealed to him immediately. He saw it as providential that he had recently purchased Moss Moor, a nearby farm of 50 acres, and he offered it as a site for a college in the proposed second centre, the Midlands, to Woodard. As 'Head of St Nicholas's College, Lancing' Woodard replied on 15 November 1866 to thank him for 'the gift of land, and of £1,000 towards the cost of building' such a college. In 1870 Woodard was appointed as a residentiary canon of Manchester Cathedral, which gave him official standing and an income to enable him to pursue his vision. Woodard said, of the chapel at Lancing College,[59] 'No system of education would be perfect which did not provide for the cultivation of the taste of the pupil through the agency of the highest examples of architecture.'[60]

Meetings were organised to publicise the endeavour and to raise funds. At the one in St James's Hall, Piccadilly on 24 June 1861, a characteristically eloquent speech by Mr Gladstone was interrupted by the violent Protestant C.P. Golightly. In the same year the meeting in the Sheldon Theatre, Oxford, was attended by pamphleteers, protesting at what they saw as intentions which amounted to 'Semi-Romanisms'. These incidents set off a ferment of disputation between the followers of Woodard and those of Golightly.[61] By the end of the 1860s the Protestant controversialists had successfully branded Woodard and his schools as 'Tractarian Party Establishments'. Much damage was done to the project by such opposition, which became extended towards all middle-class education, although the project had also attracted a great deal of support and not all of it from High Church sources.[62]

However, Woodard was firmly committed to his educational aim for the middle classes, whose energies and creative imaginations were

[59] The architects were Richard Cromwell Carpenter (1812–1855) and his son Richard Herbert (1841–1893).The elder Carpenter was associated with the Cambridge Camden Society, and a friend of A.W.N. Pugin.
[60] Quoted in Roger Dixon and Stefan Muthesius, *Victorian Architecture* [London: Thames and Hudson Ltd, 1978], p. 249.
[61] Heeney, ibid, p. 42.
[62] ibid., pp. 82 and 83.

the engine of enterprise and prosperity in the world's first industrial nation and the application of Adam Smith's *Wealth of Nations*, but whose children had fallen between the public schools of the aristocracy and the minimal state provision for the working classes. Furthermore this conception had, as its sound foundation, a 'definite doctrinal Church teaching.' Heywood had found a cause for his heartiest support, rejoicing in a leader who enlisted fellow workers who displayed an absolutely selfless devotion of time and money to the service of God, and the good of their country. 'No grander work could be done than to bring up children as God-fearing men and women,' he said.[63]

The corner stone of Denstone College was laid on 22 October 1868; in his speech Heywood said he had spoken frequently in advocacy of the cause, 'And found no difficulty in doing so, and was thus brought into contact with many of the leading Churchmen of the day, and some of the leading statesmen. My hold on the doctrines of the Church has been thereby strengthened ... I always have had a love of architecture ... and have for these twenty-five years taken intimate counsel with our architect [Carpenter[64]] in every detail of our plans.'[65]

In a letter to Heywood dated 18 December 1866 Nathaniel Woodard expressed his pleasure at his earnest support, and his being overwhelmed by the degree of success which the work had generated: 'I am almost afraid to say anything, or do more than the leadership of Providence, and to wait and see in every case what the will of the Lord is. It will indeed be amazing,' he said, 'if, after losing so large a section of the middle classes for more than two hundred years, the Church should once again be a mother to these, her lost sons.' In a letter of 12 October 1869 he informed Heywood that he reckoned about two million pounds sterling would be necessary

---

[63] Isabel Mary, ibid., pp. 92 and 93.
[64] Richard Herbert Carpenter (1841–1893), Denstone College Chapel, 1879–1887. He also designed Ardingly College in 1864. His father, Richard Cromwell Carpenter (1812–1855) designed St John's College, Hurstpierpoint, 1831–1832, and began Lancing College in 1854, completed by his son in 1883.
[65] Isabel Mary, ibid., p. 94.

to complete their plan (sc. for the whole country). 'If we succeed, we shall be the only Church in Christendom that has completed a system of education in her own hands,' he observed.[66] He wrote again, on 9 August 1872 from Manchester Cathedral, expressing his gratitude 'to Thomas Percival and Lady Heywood for their being happily led by God in the Great and arduous struggle for the salvation of souls and the prosperity of our country. Difficulties we must have,' he wrote, 'but my motto is *Solvitur ambulando:* the greatest problems are solved by working in faith … Faith not only removes mountains, but it marches over them.' A curious piece of exegesis, but his point was well made.

Denstone College school building was finished in 1872, liberal financial contribution coming from Charles, 19th Earl of Shrewsbury and the 4th Earl Talbot. It was dedicated by the Bishop of Lichfield on 29 July 1873, and opened on 9 October that year. The foundation stone of St Chad's Chapel at the college was laid on 29 July 1879: 'Provost Lowe presented a silver trowel to Sir T. Percival Heywood and requested him in the name of the Fellows to add another to the many valuable services he had rendered to the College. Sir Percival laid the stone with these words: "In the Name of Jesus Christ we fix this stone on this foundation, in the Name of the Father, the Son, and the Holy Ghost; that within these walls here to be raised, bearing the name of St Chad, first Bishop of Lichfield, the true Faith of God may be taught, and the Sacraments duly administered; and that this place may be for ever devoted to faithful prayer and holy praise, to the honour of our Lord Jesus Christ, who with the Father, the Son and the Holy Ghost liveth and reigneth, ever one God, world without end. Amen".' In his speech Heywood made thankful reference to two Bishops of Lichfield who had been called away – Bishop Lonsdale,[67] who almost with his last breath had advocated the claims of this institution, and Bishop Selwyn[68] who had also gone

---

[66] ibid., pp. 95 and 97.
[67] John Lonsdale, Bishop of Lichfield, 1843–1867.
[68] George Augustus Selwyn, Bishop, 1868–1878.

to his rest. He hoped that in their present bishop[69] they might have the same faithful and loving friend they had had in them. He also paid tribute to the united efforts of 25 men who bound themselves together, despite opposition, to raise the buildings. He called to remembrance Charles John, Earl of Shrewsbury, Hugo Meynell Ingram, who said that if we were to give the people anything, we would give them something worth having; Mr Bagot of Leigh,[70] and Mr Sneyd.[71] He added that he, as one of the Trustees of the College, had placed beneath the corner stone a copy of the Book of Common Prayer. 'On that Book the Chapel will be raised, and by that Book I stand,' he declared.

It is clear that Heywood's Catholicism was definitely Anglican, according to the principles of the Oxford Movement. He continued with an affirmation: 'That we should keep faith with the public. We have told the public that we have founded this College on the teaching of the Church of England and from that we shall not deviate.' In the luncheon that followed the ceremony, in response to the Bishop of Lichfield's proposed health, Heywood enlarged on what he had said: 'There has been ill-will against the College, but for ten years I have not heard one single syllable spoken against it by anyone who knows what was going on within its walls.' He also said that if 'Before all things it is necessary to hold the Catholic Faith, and the Faith is to be held "whole and undefiled";'[72] he had no doubt about the project, 'and the measure of success as is good will be given.'

---

[69] William Dalrymple McLagan, 1878–1891; later (1891–1908), Archbishop of York. No. 33 in the list of members of *Nobody's Friends* in 1881, p. 236.

[70] The Revd Lewis Francis Bagot, MA, incumbent of Leigh, near Uttoxeter. A member of the family of the Bagots of Blithfield Hall, Staffordshire, who produced several clergy, including two bishops, one of whom was Richard Bagot (1782–1854), successively Bishop of Oxford and of Bath and Wells.

[71] The Revd John Sneyd of Ashcombe Hall, Cheddleton. One of a family of estate owners in the area.

[72] A quotation from the Athanasian Creed, appointed in the Prayer Book Rubric of 1662 to be read instead of the Apostle's Creed at Morning Prayer on Christmas Day, the Feast of the Epiphany, Easter Day, Ascension Day, Whit Sunday, Trinity Sunday, and on the Feast Day of certain saints.

The Chapel of St Chad was dedicated on 27 July 1887, by the Bishop of Lichfield, and the Archbishop of Canterbury[73] who preached the sermon. To complete the buildings, the dining hall was opened in 1891 by the new Archbishop of York, Dr McLagan.[74] The Revd David Edwards was appointed Headmaster in 1890, having been Vicar of North Nibley, Gloucestershire, from 1857 to 1889.

Heywood was to be well acquainted, like Job, with severe tests of his faith, quite apart from doctrinal opposition to that to which he was devoted. He lost an eye in a shooting accident on the Isle of Caldy, Wirral, in 1871;[75] his home, Doveleys, was burned to the ground, with all his possessions, in a fire in 1874;[76] he was thrown from his horse and broke his thigh in 1885;[77] and in 1894 the college at Denstone was severely damaged by fire – the headmaster's house being demolished, and part of the dormitory.[78] He bore all this care and anxiety with 'patient submission', although he confessed to his brother Oliver to feeling 'desolate and weak', acknowledging that 'Here we have no abiding city.'[79]

A survey of one of the Woodard Schools, Queen Elizabeth's Grammar School, Barnet, showed that over the years 1876–1885, out of the 450 boys, 393 (those who disclosed the occupation of their parents) the breakdown was as follows:

Shopkeepers, 89; Travellers, Warehousemen, Brokers, Agents, 70; Merchants and Wholesale Tradesmen, 50; Manufacturers, 26; Artisans and Labourers, 26; Architects, Artists and Engineers, 24; Civil Servants, 22; Mercantile Clerks, 18; Clergy, 12; Journalists and Schoolmasters, 11; Lawyers, 11; Bank Managers and Clerks, 10; Army Officers, 10; Farmers and Bailiffs, 9; Medical Men, 5.[80]

---

[73] Edward White Benson, Archbishop from 1883 to 1896.
[74] Isabel Mary, pp. 103–106.
[75] Heywood, *Reminiscenses*, quoted by Isabel Mary, pp. 118 and 119.
[76] ibid., pp. 120 ff.
[77] ibid., pp. 126 ff.
[78] ibid., pp. 107ff.
[79] ibid., p. 127.
[80] Heeney, ibid, Appendix F (p. 248).

A rather more comprehensive assessment of the term 'middle class' than might have been expected – just over 6 per cent were children of artisans and labourers, although these were partly funded by exhibitions from elementary schools.[81]

Woodard attracted some professional criticism at the time for his bold venture, particularly at the start from Thomas Arnold, who had clear ideas of his own in the same field. Woodard was both admired, and hated that he had not taken into account that the influence of the Church was in decline.[82] 'But by normal standards of starting schools he was enormously successful.'[83]

The Parish of Miles Platting, Diocese of Manchester

One of the responsibilities Thomas Percival Heywood inherited at the death of his father in 1865 was the Patronage of a newly developed parish in the rapidly growing high-density housing area of Miles Platting in Manchester.[84] Sir Benjamin had a large cottage property there, as a part-payment for a bad bank debt, and he had made continuous efforts to ameliorate the living conditions for the local people. He built a school, enlarging it later, and public swimming baths and hot water bath-and-wash houses, sparing no effort or money. The foundation stone for the parish church was laid in April 1855, the architect being John Edgar Gregan (1813–1855), born in Dumfries, practising in Manchester. He was responsible for Sir Benjamin's bank building in St Ann's Square, and also (his last design), the new building for the Mechanic's Institution in David Street.[85] The church was consecrated in December 1855. The first incumbent was William

---

[81] Although Woodard was fully aware of the possibility of social mobility; T.W. Bamford, *The Rise of the Public Schools* [London: Thomas Nelson and Sons Ltd, 1967], p. 31.
[82] Bamford, ibid, pp. 32–34.
[83] ibid., p. 33.
[84] The population of the parish in 1857 was 4000; by 1869 it was 5153 [*Crockford's Clerical Directory*].
[85] Dixon and Muthesius, p. 128.

Richardson,[86] and he served there until 1869 when Sydney Faithorn Green was appointed. He had been a curate of Thomas Percival's brother Henry at Swinton, near the Heywood's home at Claremont, Manchester, for four years. On 28 June 1865 Benjamin Heywood, less than six weeks before his death, had advised his son and heir to 'Ask of God to give you a collected and contented mind.'[87] It was a prayer he was going to need: life for Thomas Percival Heywood was about to become considerably more turbulent.

There had been ill-will against the College at Denstone – charges of 'Popery' by the enemies of the Oxford Revival – but the intensity of the subsequent attack on Sydney Green and the parish was to cause him much more anguish. Miles Platting was described in 1881 as one of the poorest districts in Manchester, 'densely inhabited, grimy, and altogether unlovely. The one group of buildings which break the depressing monotony are the church, the school and the clergy house.'[88] H.E. Sheen remembered the parish as 'an area of mean streets, dirty public houses, of which there were very many in the neighbourhood, chemical and dye works, engineering works, glassworks, cotton mills with tall chimneys, bottle-shaped furnaces, leather works, quilt manufactories, oilcloth and clay pipe works, as well as timber and builders' yards and railway carriage works. Most of the menfolk in the parish were employed locally. The Irish element was strong in the district. Two policemen always walked together because it was unsafe for one to go alone. Oldham Road and the contiguous districts are sacred to ruffians ... Reports of murder and manslaughter in the press [largely refer] if not to Salford, to Oldham Road or Ancoats Lane.'[89] Sydney Green's object was to make the church *the* beautiful

---

[86] Thomas Heywood, FSA, *A Memoir of Sir Benjamin Heywood, Bt (1793–1865)* [privately printed, 1885]. Richardson was later Vicar of Poulton-le-Fylde and Rural Dean of the Fylde.
[87] Isabel Mary, p. 82.
[88] Thomas Hughes, QC, *James Fraser, Second Bishop of Manchester* [London: Macmillan and Co., 1889], p. 279.
[89] H.E. Sheen, *The Oxford Movement in a Manchester Parish: The Miles Platting Case* [Unpublished Master of Arts Dissertation, Manchester University, March 1941], pp. 74 and 75.

spot in their lives as far as he could. When he went there, he was the only resident priest or any other sort of minister in the parish.'[90]

Sydney Green at once proved himself a zealous and able rector; the bishop, James Fraser, a man of wide and wise sympathies, fully recognised his good works, and despite the Catholic practices in the parish, they were on cordial terms. Thomas Percival found the chancel of the church 'lacking in dignity', and he had a great interest in trying to make it beautiful, although he found the design otherwise generally speaking to be admirable.[91] Heywood was not a Ritualist, and he did not contend for a ritual which he personally preferred, but when the uproar emerged against Tractarian practices, 'he could not, and would not, see a united congregation, with its devoted parish priest, insulted and molested by persons who had nothing to do with the church or parish, and who relentlessly persecuted for obeying, in perfect good faith, the Rubrics of the Book of Common Prayer.[92] 'Mr Green adopted a ritual alike dignified and devotional, and the great bulk of his people entirely approved. He was an excellent pastor. The ritual was far less advanced than that adopted in two other of the Manchester churches, but the Church Association[93] selected it for attack. It was my bounded duty,' wrote Heywood, 'not my selfish object, as patron of the living, as it was my great privilege, to defend Mr Green from the scandalous attack upon him ... He was a true and loyal churchman, and his people were devoted to him.'[94]

Sydney Faithorn Green, in his acceptance of the living,[95] had

---

[90] ibid., p. 91.
[91] 1873, Heywood's *Reminiscences*, quoted Isabel Mary, p. 139.
[92] Isabel Mary, ibid., pp. 138 and 139.
[93] The Church Association was founded by Evangelicals in 1865 with the specific aim of combating the Tractarian Movement, and preserving Protestant principles; it campaigned for the Public Worship Regulation Act of 1874, by which Tractarian priests were brought to Parliamentary justice [Peter Toon, *Evangelical Theology, 1833–1856*: London: Marshall, Morgan and Scott, 1979, p. 6].
[94] Isabel Mary, ibid., p. 140.
[95] Letter to Heywood, 12 June 1869.

said, 'In these days of bitter party feeling it would take very little to have the church desecrated by mobs of roughs, egged on by Orangemen and others. I need scarcely say that it will be my object to have all things done, some time or other ... in the Church's way.' 'He devoted himself entirely to his people; by day and by night also if necessary, he was at their service. He taught them with the utmost care, never introducing any ritual which they did not understand and appreciate ... The sick and sorrowful found in their new Rector a comforter and friend. The church became the centre of their love and devotion ... The parochial gatherings were marked by a wonderful unanimity and brotherly feeling. From time to time ... parties of parishioners went over for the day to the Patron's house at Doveleys and were warmly welcomed and hospitably entertained. But these happy days of quiet growth and development ... were not to last. A cloud was rising; it became darker and darker ... to leave a desolation which took years to overcome.'[96]

A Mr George McDonagh, a local Orangeman, was the first to mar the peace. At the Annual Easter Vestry Meeting on 3 April 1877 (the Easter Communicants had numbered over 200), there was a large attendance of strangers, owing to the more than usual interest – an organisation had been formed for the purpose of securing a stranger as Parishioners' Warden. George McDonagh was seconded by a Mr McGowan, who was also a stranger to the congregation. They had come to the meeting, although they had never been in the church in their lives, to protest against ritualism, even though, as one member of the church observed, as Orangemen they were the greater ritualists.[97] The next parish to the west, St Mark's, was well-known as an 'Orange' church.[98] On 17 May 1878 McDonagh raised a petition to the Bishop of Manchester against 'the propagation of false doctrine and error by the Rev.

---

[96] Isabel Mary, ibid., pp. 142 and 143.
[97] H.E. Sheen, ibid., pp. 95–97.
[98] Eric Saxon, in *The Church in Cottonopolis*, Chris Ford, Michael Powell, and Terry Wyke, Eds. [Manchester: Lancashire and Cheshire Antiquarian Society, 1997], p. 135.

S.F. Green of St John the Evangelist's Miles Platting. We do so in responsibility to our Lord Jesus Christ whose solemn charges to the Seven Churches of Asia are now speaking trumpet-tongued to our own. If error so contrary to our articles and homilies is taught in our Protestant and Reformed Church, we testify that a bloodless revolution will have taken place, as effective as if the Roman Catholic Church was established in her stead ... We therefore pray that your Lordship will use the great power committed unto you, and irradicate [sic] this abominable idolatry.'[99]

The bishop, having written to the rector and received a very courteous reply, though 'pleading guilty' to the charges and explaining them, replied to the petitioner on 20 May 1878 acknowledged the petition, 'signed (you inform me) by 320 parishioners, publicly testifying to the false doctrine and deadly error by the Revd S.F. Green ... I respectfully submit to the petitioners that as no particulars either of the "idolatry" or of the "false doctrine and deadly error" alleged, are given, I can take no steps, either by way of remonstrance or otherwise, against the inculpated clergyman. I have not counted,' the bishop continued, 'the signatures to the petition, but I observe, upon a cursory examination of it, that whole families of five, six, and in one instance, seven persons have signed it at once, and that whole groups of signatures are evidently in one handwriting, and are not, therefore, the signatures of the persons whose names they profess to give. This fact very much weakens the value of the petition in my eyes.'[100] McDonagh replied on 22 May 1878, challenging the bishop's enquiry regarding the names and residencies of the signatories, to which he received an answer to the effect that the charges were vague and without dates, and a little more precision of language would be desirable in matters of ecclesiastical discipline. The response was that McDonagh forwarded the case to the Church Association, and it was now in their hands.[101]

---

[99] Thomas Hughes, ibid., p. 281.
[100] ibid.
[101] Thomas Hughes, ibid., p. 284.

The parish magazine, *St John's Monthly Record*, for January said in the Editorial on page 3, 'We regret to announce that certain mistaken persons, for the most part entirely unknown to us, are endeavouring by means of the Public Worship Regulation Act, to interfere with our church and services.' The April edition recorded that 'During the night of 1 April 1879 some persons committed a work of spoliation, not apparently for the purpose of robbery, but for the gratification of simple spite and malice. The altar ornaments were stripped off the ledge and thrown behind the altar ... In the vestry, the cross made for the church by a member of the congregation seven years ago ... was broken, and [those] registers which were accessible were torn up and heaped on the floor, with the contents of drawers, where they were set fire to... There had been a deliberate attempt to set fire to the church, but providentially it had burnt itself out without spreading.' The bishop wrote to express sympathy and denounce the outrage.[102] On 2 December 1878 Bishop Fraser received a 'presentation' signed by three so-called 'parishioners'.[103] *The Monthly Record* for June of that year reported a letter sent to the *Manchester Guardian* setting out the facts and sequence of events for the benefit of a wider readership, that 'Some months ago the congregation worshipping at St John's church, Miles Platting were startled by the announcement that their pastor, the Revd S.F. Green, had been selected by the Church Association as a fit and proper person for persecution and annoyance ... Not a single communicant of the church (and there are about 240 on the Communicants Roll), nor any member of the congregation, has had anything to do with the matter [and] all, without exception, are entirely united in supporting the Rector ... who refuses (and we heartily agree with him) to recognise the right of three men of whom he knows nothing to regulate the services at St John's. ... Nearly all the church officers were in post before Mr Green's appointment [a

---

[102] Thomas Hughes, ibid., p. 286.
[103] Isabel Mary, p. 146.

rebuttal of a charge that it was an eclectic church, drawn from all over Manchester].'[104] The pleas of the communicants went unheeded. The objection of the three petitioners was heeded.

A meeting of Council of the Church of England Working Men's Society passed a Resolution 'deploring with the deepest indignation ... the late disgraceful and cowardly attempt to destroy the church of St John the Evangelist, Miles Platting, Manchester, by fire, and earnestly hope the perpetrators will speedily be brought to justice ... They have also heard with grief that the Bishop of the Diocese, on complaint of three persons living in the parish but not communicants of the church, has set the machinery in motion of the Public Worship Regulation Act, 1874, thus harassing the Rector, disturbing the quiet of the congregation, and threatening to destroy the spiritual work of the parish.' They prayed that the rector would be guided and strengthened by the Holy Spirit, remain faithful, and 'bear witness to the spiritual freedom of the Church of England against Erastianism and the usurpation [by] the secular courts. The Council was followed by similar expressions of sympathy from the Society at Southport, and pledge themselves to give "all legitimate and constitutional support".'[105]

The case for the prosecution went before the Privy Council, under the chairmanship of Lord Penzance. The matters charged against Green were (i) the mixed chalice [wine and water]; (ii) lighted candles; (iii) unlawful vestments; (iv) kneeling during the prayer of consecration; (v) elevation of paten and cup; (vi) placing the alms on the credence table instead of the Holy Table; (vii) using the sign of the Cross towards the congregation; (viii) consecrating so as to prevent the people from seeing him break the bread or take the cup; (ix) unlawfully and in a ceremonial manner, and as part of the service, raising the cup; (x) a large cross of brass on the Holy Table, or on a ledge immediately above the same and appearing to form part thereof; (xi) a baldachino. 'The accusations were partly true and partly untrue,'

---

[104] *The Monthly Record*, pp. 2 and 3.
[105] ibid., May 1879, p. 4.

comments Heywood's daughter, 'demonstrating that some of the points were false, and were merely the ordinary improvements in divine service adopted in hundreds of other churches, clearly showed the character of the complainants, and that they were probably never present at the Holy Communion at St John's.'[106] *The Monthly Record* answered 'two questions which are constantly being put to us – "Why do you not obey the law?" and "Why will you not obey the Bishop?" We reply (i) that our Rector has taken his present course because he believes that obedience to the law of the Church demands that he should do; and we think that he has acted rightly because in accordance with the Rubrics of the Prayer Book in its "plain, literal and grammatical sense," and we cannot discern that he has broken them. (ii) That the Privy Council judgements cannot all be obeyed – they contradict each other – and the Bishop of Manchester has allowed Mr Green to be persecuted for wearing the vestments because the Privy Council has declared them to be illegal, whilst the Bishop has declared publicly that he will not make a "guy" of himself by wearing a cope which the same Privy Council says he should.' The writer pointed out that the 'law of the church in the Rubrics of the Prayer Book are disobeyed in many churches, and the persons responsible ought to be asked the same two questions (but they are not).' Examples given include the omission of the Athanasian Creed on the appointed days; churches closed from Sunday to Sunday; Holy Days and even Ascension Day go unobserved.[107]

The findings of the Privy Council, seen as being inconsistent with the Rubrics of the Book of Common Prayer, were not acceptable to Sydney Green, nor was he able to accept the rulings of a secular court in matters concerning the faith and ritual of the Church.[108] Which was precisely the position of the anti-Erastianism of the Oxford Revival. The Dean of St Paul's Cathedral, London,[109] speaking in the discussion of Ecclesiastical Courts by

---

[106] Isabel Mary, ibid., pp. 147 and 148.
[107] July 1879, pp. 2, 3, and 4.
[108] Isabel Mary, ibid., p. 148.
[109] Robert Gregory, 1891–1911.

the Lower House of Convocation in February 1899, said, 'The Church of England has had its own courts very much longer than the Army and Navy have had courts for themselves, and yet the clergy were expected to yield at once to secular courts that intrude where they have no business, and the clergy are to be satisfied to be tried by people who have no right to try them ... I say these courts are unhappily and grievously discredited.' The Dean of Lichfield,[110] speaking after Dean Gregory, said, 'With regard to the court ... of which the Dean of St Paul's has spoken in withering terms – the court of Lord Penzance – that court is consigned to obscurity, and is absolutely no good to anyone.'[111]

'By this court Mr Green was condemned in 1879, and was imprisoned in Lancaster Castle on 19 March 1881, being arrested very unexpectedly at 11 am by the Sheriff's officer. The churchwardens of St John's sent a telegram to the Vicar of Lancaster, the Revd Dr Allen, and he made arrangements for Mr Green to be as comfortable as possible during his stay. The room in which the Rector was confined was originally part of the Banqueting Hall of the Castle before its conversion into a gaol, and was known as the Quakers' Room because it had been used more than 200 years before as the place of imprisonment of ...Quakers on account of their religious opinions.'[112]

Five 'Ritualist' priests were imprisoned for contempt of Lord Penzance's Court:

Arthur Tooth (Horsemonger Gaol),	1877,	for 27 days.
T. Pelham Dale (Holloway),	1880,	for 56 days.
R.W. Enraght (Warwick),	1880,	for 51 days.
S.F. Green (Lancaster),	1881,	for 595 days.
J. Bell-Cox (Walton, Liverpool),	1887,	for 16 days.

Life in the parish was maintained as near to normal as possible: the regular services were taken by the assistant priest, Harry

---

[110] Herbert Mortimer Lucock, 1892–1909.
[111] Isabel Mary, ibid., pp. 148 and 149.
[112] *St John's Monthly Record*, April 1881, p. 2.

Cowgill,[113] without any change.[114] The editor noted that The Junior Communicants Guild were invited to tea on 25 June at Tabley, Knutsford, by Lord de Tabley's chaplain.[115] The Hon. Charles Lindley Wood, President of the English Church Union, spoke to St John's Communicants after a visit to the Rector in Lancaster; he informed them the ECU was appealing to the House of Lords in the case.[116] Earl Beauchamp[117] moved the Second Reading of the Ecclesiastical Regulation Bill in the House of Lords on 9 August 1881, the object of which was the discharge of the Rector from Lancaster Castle at the expiry of six months from the date of imprisonment. The Bill passed the Second Reading without difficulty but several changes of name and intention in Committee thwarted it eventually.[118] Another staunch advocate of the opposition to the Church Association was Mr J.G. Talbot, MP.[119] He wrote to the Archbishop of Canterbury's Secretary asking that the attention of the authorities should be called to the rector's imprisonment. The Archbishop wrote to Mr Gladstone, but heard nothing further.[120] The truth seemed to be that nobody knew who 'the authorities' were – all agreed that he had been imprisoned, but no one was responsible.

Heywood addressed a meeting of the Church of England Working Men's Society during the Church Congress Meeting in Derby in 1882, and he gave expression to his dismay, receiving 'loud and prolonged cheering' when he said he did not accept the bishop's notice, in a letter of 27 September, that Mr Green was deprived, and the benefice had become void. He declared

---

[113] Master of Arts, Oriel College Oxford, assistant master at St Chad's College, Denstone, 1874–1877; later, Vicar of Shireoaks, Worksop (Patron, the Duke of Newcastle), 1892–1914.
[114] *The Monthly Record*, April 1881, p. 2.
[115] ibid., June 1881, p. 1
[116] ibid., p. 3.
[117] No. 239 in the membership of *Nobody's Friends*, p. 221.
[118] *The Monthly Record*, September, 1881, p. 2.
[119] No. 41 in the January 1875 list of members of *Nobody's Friends*, p. 208.
[120] *The Monthly Record*, October, 1882, pp. 2 and 3.

that 'Lord Penzance had no power to deprive a clergyman of the Church of England, a man whom the Archbishop of Canterbury had spoken as "of unblemished character", and his family turned out into the streets. It is a villainous cruelty,' he said, 'to tell me that if I, as patron, put a new man into the living of Miles Platting, Mr Green will be released, thereby insulting Mr Green and his loyal churchwardens and parishioners, who are praying for him to be restored to them. The very foundation of your Church will be shaken if we are beaten in this contest.'[121]

Foremost among 'those in fact responsible' was the Home Secretary, Sir William George Granville Venables Vernon Harcourt (1827–1904). In open disagreement with Gladstone, he supported the Public Worship Regulation Act of 1874, as a 'devoted Protestant.'[122] He wrote to Gladstone at Hawarden, pursuing his aim of not releasing Mr Green from prison. Gladstone replied on 13 December 1881: '... I am afraid we are not likely to make progress in the case of Mr Green (as to which I am told by somebody that in August next his benefice will be void). In my opinion it would be most objectionable to establish deprivation instead of imprisonment as the punishment for contempt, especially if a penalty of this kind, which would usually mean ruin, is to be applied to the clergy only. But quite apart from this objection [which] others may not share, I do not see that it is for the Government ... to charge itself with the settlement of an affair for which it has no responsibility. The Archbishops made the Act, and they should deal with the results. There is a great deal more to say as to the administration of the law, but I doubt not that I have said enough.'[123]

Sydney Green, for his 'contempt of court', was charged with the costs, about £450, and the sale of his 'goods and chattels' to pay that amount took place at the rectory on the 4th and 5th of August 1881, the bailiffs having taken possession of the rectory

---

[121] Isabel Mary, ibid., pp. 161–163.
[122] *Dictionary of National Biography* [OUP], Vol. 25, p. 140.
[123] *Letters on Church and Religion by William Ewart Gladstone*, Vol. I, p. 402, D.C. Lathbury Ed. [London: John Murray, 1910].

to make their catalogues.[124] The Lord Chancellor expressed his surprise that the bill should be so large in an undefended suit. He considered that £5 or £10 ought to cover all the expenses. At his suggestion the family returned to the rectory, after nearly three weeks banishment from their home on 6 April 1881. The counsel for the Church Association explained the expenses, saying that it was necessary under the Public Worship Act to have everything proved by *viva voce* evidence, which necessitated the bringing up of witnesses for every single thing. It was on the application of the Church Association that the rectory furnishings and contents should be sold.[125] All the furniture went on the first day of the sale, and the second day was given up to books, nearly all of which were secured by the English Church Union, although by some mismanagement several were allowed to go. In spite of the protests of church officers, some of the property of the church, although in regular use, a silver-plated flagon, a silver-plated censer, and a small vessel used for baptism were seized and catalogued as Mr Green's goods.[126] Heywood, as Patron, visited the parish often, and by his arrangement others gave the people their support, among them his son Arthur, his brother Oliver, the Revd Henry Meynell, H.R. Heywood, Vicar of Swinton, Manchester, C. Heath, the Vicar of Walkden, Fr Dulley SSJE of Cowley, Oxford, J. Outram Marshall (Organising Secretary of The English Church Union), T.A. Lacey, Assistant Priest of St Benedict's Ardwick, Manchester, and S.Y. Beechy, Rector of Newton Heath Manchester. On Sunday 27 March 1881 the Revd The Earl of Mulgrave, Vicar of Worsley, preached at Evensong on St Luke chapter 14, verse 33: 'Whoever he be that you who forsaketh not all that he hath, he cannot be my disciple.' He said that the people of Miles Platting now had in their midst 'One who was brave enough to forsake home and wife and children and friends for the truth's

---

[124] Isabel Mary, p. 149.
[125] *The Monthly Record*, June 1881, p. 1.
[126] ibid., September 1881, p. 1.

sake.' He made eloquent defence of the priesthood, and the futility and impotence of the enemies of the Church.[127]

Heywood wrote to *The Times* on 1 August 1881 to bring the injustice of the case to wider knowledge. He said that Mr Green had appealed to the Lord Chancellor for the protection of his wife and children, which he was no longer able to give them. 'It is difficult to believe,' he continued, 'that in this country such an outrage ... can be permitted. To imprison a husband first, and then turn the wife and children into the street is worse than cruel; it is brutal.'[128] '[These] proceedings ... are an intolerable aggravation of my friend's sufferings,' he said. Heywood tried every possible means to obtain Mr Green's release, appealing to those in high places, and spoke at meeting after meeting.[129] At one of these, of the Church of England Working Men's Society in Reading Town Hall, he read a letter from Dr Pusey, and also one from Mr Green, part of which described Miles Platting as 'a very poor district of Manchester, a neighbourhood of the most uninviting kind, where the commonest grass will not grow ... The congregation is entirely made up of the poorer classes – many of the very poorest – who love the church as their home.[130] An attempt to give those who dwell in such a place something of beauty in the house of God, even if unwise, may have been forgiven. The three nominally "aggrieved parishioners" never at any time attended the church. To assent to the Public Worship Act, and to submit to its judge, would be to give the British Parliament spiritual jurisdiction over the Church, and to submit the Kingdom of Jesus Christ to a body the members of which are not expected to be Christians.'[131]

On 7 November 1881 at a meeting of the same society in the great hall of the Cannon Street Hotel, not only was every seat

---

[127] ibid., April 1881, p. 3.
[128] Green had five children, the eldest of whom was six years old [H.E. Sheen, ibid., p. 8].
[129] Isabel Mary, ibid., pp. 149–151.
[130] The Revd William Radcliffe Dolling, another priest accused of 'ritualism', is quoted as saying, 'If there is one place which needs a magnificent church, it is a slum' [J. Lewis May, *The Oxford Movement*, John Lane, The Bodley Head, 1933], p. 253.
[131] Isabel Mary, ibid., pp. 151 and 152.

occupied, but also all the gangways and every foot of standing. There was an overflow meeting in another room, in addition to the thousands outside who were unable to get in. The latecomers were chiefly working men who were hindered by their work from coming earlier. Letters of sympathy were received from the Bishop of Ely;[132] Bishop Abraham; Archdeacon Denison; Lord Bath; Lord Salisbury, and others. At a meeting in February 1882 in Brighton, Sir Percival told the gathering that he had spent 'long that day' at the Home Office, pleading everything he could bring before the Home Secretary on behalf of Mr Green, but all he got as an answer to the delivering of the prisoner was an implacable 'Yield, and you shall be released; refuse to yield and you shall remain as you are.'[133]

Dr Pusey, in a letter to the English Church Union which appeared in the *Church Times* on the first anniversary of Mr Green's imprisonment (19 March 1882), began by saying, 'Mankind in the year 1892 will, I think, be much ashamed with us in 1882: ... all evil is growing, crimes are more atrocious than they were some years ago; atheism flaunts itself, all unbelief is more aggressive, and the exterminating party, as a remedy to all this, does what? It keeps in prison one who is the ... diligent pastor of a large congregation in a parish ... numbering nearly 5,000 souls, who is shown to live in the affections of his people. And for what? For wearing a garment which was worn in the English Church in the reign of Edward VI, a vestment enjoined by Cranmer, and the direction to wear which stands in our present Prayer Book ... It has been fashionable,' he continued, 'to call the "Ornaments Rubric", for which Mr Green is in gaol, "ambiguous"; but the sentence is as plain as any in our language.' He quoted a calm and dispassionate judge,[134] who said of it, 'The clause in question, by which I mean the Rubric in question, is perfectly unambiguous in language, free from all difficulty as to construction.' Another[135] said, 'After repeated attentive perusal

---

[132] James Russell Woodford, 1873–1886.
[133] Isabel Mary, ibid., p. 154.
[134] Sir J.T. Coleridge.
[135] Sir R. Philimore.

141

of the language, it [the Rubric] does *quite* appear to me as plain as any which is to be found in any statutory enactment …' Dr Pusey wrote to *The Times* on 24 August 1882 on behalf of Mr Green, and again on the 31st – his final battle, for he died on 16 September 1882: 'Three priests imprisoned have been released. The fourth, whom we cannot extricate from its grasp, will, I hope, preach to the hearts of the English people the tolerance which the intolerant will not exercise towards him. It was said by a Bishop in Convocation "There are hundreds of clergy who are disobeying rubrics … (the meaning of which there is not a shadow of a doubt) who are not only left unmolested but are taking part in the action which led to the imprisonment of Mr Green. The English have a great reverence for law, but also for honesty and fair play."' [136]

The problem between the two parties was the Ornaments Rubric of the 1552 Prayer book, which stated: 'Such Ornaments of the Church, and of the ministers thereof at all times in their Ministration, shall be retained, and be in use, as were in this Church of England, by the authority of Parliament, in the second year of the reign of King Edward the Sixth.' [137] It ordered the surplice and hood for Morning Prayer, Evening Prayer and Burials, and a rubric for the Holy Communion ordered the alb, vestment or cope and tunicle for that service. [138] The Puritans wanted the Prayer Book altered, and many avoided its use, and in 1562 they attacked bitterly the sign of the cross in Baptism, kneeling at Communion, the wedding ring, and every sort of vestment, including the cope and surplice and black gown, proposing that these, and organs in church, should be abolished. [139] At the Church Conference in 1660 the Presbyterians wanted the Prayer Book revision to be made like the liturgies of the Reformed churches. The nine

---

[136] Isabel Mary, ibid., pp. 154–158.
[137] Quoted, J.R.H. Moorman, *A History of the Church in England* [London: A. and C. Black, 1953], p. 201.
[138] Percy Dearmer, *Everyman's History of the Prayer Book* [London: A. and R. Mowbray and Co. Ltd, 1912], p. 71.
[139] ibid., pp. 90 and 91.

surviving bishops replied that the closer both their forms and ours come to the liturgy of the ancient Greek and Latin churches, the less they are liable to the objections of the common enemy. The Puritans demanded that the Ornaments Rubric be omitted (showing that it was still in legal force at that time), but the bishops replied, 'We think it fit that the Rubric continue as it is.'[140]

It has been argued that the object of the Reformers was not to revolutionise but to reform: to retrace the steps whereby the English Church had drifted from primitive practice. It was Reform in the sense of 'purify' and not revolution, in the sense of abolishing the old and substituting a new order. 'There is no new faith propagated in England; not a new religion set up but that which was commanded by our Saviour, practised by the Primitive Church, and approved by the Fathers of the best antiquity.'[141] Viscount Halifax, in a paper at the Church Congress of 1890, held in Hull quoted some words by Queen Elizabeth: 'In the Declaration ordered by Elizabeth in 1569 to be read in all churches it is expressly stated "We deny to claim any superiority to ourself to deyne, decyde, or determyn any article or Poynt of the Christian Fayth and Relligion, or to change any ancient ceremony of the Church from the Forme before received and observed by the Catholic and Apostolick Church".'[142]

A contributor to *Lux Mundi* argued strongly for symbolism and appealing to all the senses and not only to hearing: 'The unreal spiritualising which consists in a barren ... disparagement of ritual observance or of outward acts, of earthly relationships or of secular life, of natural feelings or of bodily health, clashed with Christian teaching as sharply as it does with human nature and with common sense.'[143] The choice of words here points

---

[140] Dearmer, ibid., p. 117.
[141] Evan Daniel, *The Prayer Book: Its History, Language and Contents* [London: Wells, Gardner, Darton and Co., 1894], p. 26.
[142] Official Conference Report, p. 419.
[143] Chapter on the Sacraments, by F. Paget, p. 310.

exactly to the theological issue between the Church Association and the English Church Union. The Calvinistic doctrine of total depravity and the Puritan rejection of the natural man as being completely opposed to the spiritual man would reject the Incarnational doctrine espoused by the Oxford Movement. True 'ritualism' was not a superficial development: it was the inevitable outworking of that theology. From the Incarnation comes the concept of an outward and visible expression of God's inward and spiritual love. On these arguments the 'Ritualists' based their behaviour.

The radical 'revolutionary' position of the Evangelicals was expressed in October 1850, when *The Christian Guardian*, 'following the debacle of the Gorham case, urged the re-writing of the Prayer Book so that it could not be interpreted in anything but a Protestant sense ... the avoidance of ambiguous terms ... not positively supported by the plain statements of Holy Writ. There was a need to complete the work of the Reformers of the sixteenth century because the liturgy of 1662 did not speak with the clarity of the 39 Articles on doctrinal points.'[144]

A long, pastorally minded letter, dated 12 August 1881, went to Sydney Green from the Archbishop of York, William Thompson, who was also in correspondence with the Archbishop of Canterbury about a possible resolution of the impasse. York deplored the fact that a clergyman should be in prison for a refusal to obey a judgement of a [secular] court.[145] They had written to the Bishop of Manchester with various suggestions of how to proceed, but the latter declared, 'I do not think that his fate excites much sympathy or commiseration amongst the laity, in Lancashire or elsewhere.'[146] Sheen comments on this, 'In view of the comprehensive support that the Rector had received from his congregation ... and his patron, it seems impossible to believe that the Bishop

---

[144] Peter Toon, *Evangelical Theology, 1833–1856* [London: Marshall, Morgan and Scott, 1979], pp. 93 and 94.
[145] H.E. Sheen, ibid., p. 148.
[146] Thomas Hughes, p. 290.

was unaware of the sympathy of such laity as Lord Bath, Lord Salisbury, Lord Clinton, Lord Nelson, Lord Edward Churchill, and Dr Philimore.'[147] The bishop did write to Gladstone on 22 September 1881, asking if he might appeal to the Queen to exercise her prerogative of pardon and Green be released from gaol,[148] but the Prime Minister, while sympathising, and promising all within his power, explained that this jurisdiction fell to the Secretary of State for the Home Department [Harcourt] in consultation with the Lord Chancellor, the Lord Selborne.[149] The Prime Minister's son, the Revd Stephen Gladstone, Rector of Hawarden, wrote to Green on 26 April 1881. He said he 'wished indeed that he could help him, [but] it seems to me your bishop ... has taken a worldly line (I fear) and at least a narrow unworthy one. But your calm and positive resistance *must* tell in the end ... blessed are they to whom God gives the opportunity, and for love of him and the Church to go through such [suffering].'[150] Bishop Fraser apparently vacillated between the extremes of wanting the whole business to be resolved amicably, and expressing a testy impatience with Sydney Green. During a meeting of the York Convocation in February 1882, after some intemperate words from Dean Lake[151] about his handling of the Miles Platting case, Fraser said of Green, 'I do not like this posing as a martyr when you are only playing role of an anarchist and bad citizen.'[152]

In July or August[153] 1882 an official 'deprivation' of Green of his living was declared and the benefice became vacant, but no action was taken and he remained in Lancaster Gaol. Responsibility for the next step was referred by the Lord Selborne, the Lord Chancellor, to the Bishop of Manchester. The bishop replied that he had been distinctly told that Green would be guided by the English Church

---

[147] Sheen, ibid., p. 145.
[148] Hughes, ibid., p. 294.
[149] Sheen, ibid., p. 161.
[150] Sheen, ibid., p. 164.
[151] William Lake, Dean of Durham from 1869 to 1894.
[152] Thomas Hughes, p. 321.
[153] 'There seems to have been a question as to the exact date' [Hughes, p. 299].

Union, and as the Union had proclaimed by the mouth of its president that it would treat the 'deprivation' with the same contempt that it had treated the 'monition', and as Sir Percival Heywood, the patron, had declared that he would not recognise the deprivation but would assist Mr Green with all his power to maintain his rights as rector of the parish, he (the bishop) was not prepared to take on himself the responsibility of applying for Mr Green's release. However, this resolution was modified by further correspondence with the Chancellor, who suggested that as the Bishop's right to fill the vacancy, which would not arise until 16 February 1883, notice would be given to the Ecclesiastical Commissioners not to pay a stipend to Mr Green, and that a curate-in-charge should be appointed. The bishop in the end consented to make this application. On 30 October Fraser gave notice that he would apply on 4 November to Lord Penzance for the discharge of Sydney Green from custody. At the same time he appointed Walter Ruthven Pym, Curate of Lytham, a priest of two years' standing, on whose courage and temper he could rely, to take charge of the living. He had already given Sir Thomas Percival Heywood, as Patron, notice that the living was vacant, and that unless he made a new appointment within six months from 27 September 1882, it would lapse, and remain in the bishop's gift.[154]

So ended one issue of the controversy; but the bishop's presentiment of 'A crop of new difficulties'[155] was at once fulfilled. Sydney Green, in a loyal wish to free his patron from the pledge he had given, chose to recognise his deprivation and resigned the living. John Diggle pointed out[156] that 'It is impossible to understand the Miles Platting story without distinctly remembering that it is a narrative of a struggle, not between two individual persons, but between two rival ecclesiastical associations, representing two antagonistic ecclesiastical contentions.' By the latter phrase he

[154] Hughes, ibid., pp. 300 and 301.
[155] Hughes, ibid., p. 302.
[156] In *The Lancashire Life of Bishop Fraser* [London: Sampson Low, Marsden, Searle and Rivington Ltd, 1890], p. 416.

referred to the two perceptions of the very nature of the Church of England, both strongly represented in its ranks since the sixteenth century: was it established as a new body at the time of the break with Rome as a Protestant Church (as the Lutheran and the Reformed Churches were)[157] or was it the same Church, 'Catholic and Reformed', consisting of the same people in the same churches as before the break? The two views were essentially irreconcilable, though maintaining a unity by means of attempting to compromise both theological positions.

'Standing in the annals of St John's Church as perhaps the most sad day in all its history was All Saints Day, Wednesday, 1 November 1882, was the announcement of Sydney Green's resignation as Rector. He had written to his patron from Lancaster on 27 October, feeling that it was "the wisest course, in view of the fact that the Bishop was proceeding to sequestrate the benefice, and that however much he loved the people of St John's, things could never be the same, and it was time for them to start afresh".'[158] Green's letter, which was the greatest blow of all to Heywood, gave three reasons for his resignation: First, he had learned from the newspapers that the bishop was going to apply to Lord Penzance for his release, and did not wish the degradation of a bishop going in the manner of a supplicant on his behalf (the bishop had informed Mr Cowgill, the curate, who had been acting for eighteen months as priest in charge of the parish, that the benefice income was to be sequestrated and another priest sent to St John's in his place – a further insult to the patron); second, he could not allow his benefactor to suffer any longer in circumstances which could end only one way; and third, that he felt that even if he did return to the parish, the relationship with the faithful at St John's could never be as before.

The first point engaged with the issue raised at the beginning of the Tractarian Movement – the manipulation of the Church's

---

[157] See Peter Toon, p. 210.
[158] *The Monthly Record*, November 1882, p. 3.

finances and pastoral administration by a parliament consisting of nonconformists (including Roman Catholics), Jews, and agnostics. The time when the 39 Articles of Religion could be completely binding upon the Church of England 'in their plain and full meaning' had passed. Articles XVII and XXI are clearly a product of Geneva, and of unacceptable authority – 'Princes' now being the secular legal power; Article XI – Justification by Faith Only, is not of the authority of the Bible: the phrase 'faith only' appears only once, and there it says we are not.[159] The phrase *Sola Scriptura* (Luther) does not appear in the Bible, and in any case our understanding of the Scriptures depends upon a tradition of interpretation, which is a product of our pre-suppositions.[160] Article XXXV had lapsed entirely, not least because of Newman's exposition of the contents of the *Homilies*, which, although only those of the Second Book are detailed, it declares unequivocally that the Homilies in the First Book contain 'godly and wholesome doctrines.' The First Book affirms the authority and the teaching of the Primitive Church, and the ancient bishops and doctrine of the final eight centuries, and that the godly Fathers were endued without doubt with the Holy Spirit. They also declare the Real Presence in the elements of the Holy Communion, and that Ordination and Matrimony are sacraments, and that the so-called 'Apochryphal' Books of Tobit and Wisdom are Scripture.[161] Article II: Was Christ crucified to reconcile his father to us, or to reconcile us to him? Article VI seems to be unaware of the doubts surrounding the authority of certain of the canonical books of the Bible; for instance of James and Jude, 2 Peter, 1 and 2 John, and the Book of Revelation. The doubts were resolved by AD 382, but it was not true to say they 'never existed'.[162]

With such attacks as these on the heartland of the Protestant Establishment, it is hardly surprising that the Oxford Revival came

---

[159] The Epistle of James chapter 2, verse 14–26.
[160] *Vide* F.F. Bruce, *Tradition Old and New* [London: Paternoster Press, 1970].
[161] J.H. Newman, *Apologia Pro Vita Sua*, pp. 50 and 51.
[162] *Encyclopaedia Britannica*, 1955, Vol. 3, p. 514.

to be seen as a Papal Trojan Horse in their midst. The utterances of certain leaders of the Oxford Movement were indeed totally inflammatory. For example, William George Ward (1812–1882) declared that 'he and others remained in the Church of England while holding and promulgating Roman doctrine.'[163] Frederick Oakeley, in 1841, following Hurrell Froude, had spoken of the Reformation as 'more of a curse than a blessing.'[164] This was certainly an 'unscriptural' view: the tradition of the Old Testament spoke clearly of a balance between priest and prophet – for the necessity of a balance between stability and continuity on the one hand, and the need for attention to the spirit of Godly correction to human imperfections on the other, in the divine/human body of witness to the Kingdom of God. When William Goode the Younger (1801–1868) the leading theologian of the Evangelicals, sent an Address to the Queen expressing disgust over recent developments (the Catholic Emancipation Act of 1829, the 'Papal Aggression' of 1850, and the rise of Romanising party in the Church of England), and requesting her to preserve unimpaired the Protestant character of the Church of England, it is easy to understand how others could be led to violence and riotous behaviour.[165]

The rector's letter 'caused untold grief to the people of St John's.'[166] Their grief was hardly allayed by the announcement on All Saints' Day that the bishop had informed Harry Cowgill, the *de facto* (though not *de jure* curate – Cowgill had never been licensed to the parish) that another priest was to be sent to take charge of St John's, and to reduce the ritual to the Cathedral Standard.[167] On 31 October 1882 a meeting was held after church in the school, at which a letter of farewell from Sydney Green was read,

[163] Raymond Chapman, Ed., in *Firmly I Believe* [Norwich: Canterbury Press, 2006], p. 12.
[164] Peter Toon, ibid., p. 73.
[165] ibid., p. 207.
[166] *The Monthly Record*, November 1882, p. 3.
[167] The Bishop's nominee, Walter Ruthven Pym, was Curate of Lytham (1880–1882). He left in 1883 for the Diocese of York, becoming Rural Dean of Rotherham (1895–1898), and Bishop of Mauritius from 1898.

to great distress, and a resolution, representing how close and real a thing was the spiritual relationship which bound this flock to their pastor, and assuring him of the continuance of their most tender regard and affection. On the following day, Sunday, 5 November – noted as 'Guy Fawkes' Day' – 'The Protestants of Manchester' also celebrated their victory at Miles Platting. At the Communion Service at the usual time of 7.30 am there was, despite a vast congregation, not one communicant. But the Archdeacon of Manchester came to the service of Matins at 10.30 am, with Pym and the bishop's secretary present, where the reporter in the parish magazine noted wryly that the subject of the first lesson was Daniel's disregard for the Public Worship Regulation Act of King Darius.[168] Also in the December 1882 issue of the parish magazine (pages 2 and 3), it was reported that a letter, drawn up by the church, was sent to Mr Pym expressing the view that, although deploring his appointment, they would be attending church as usual to glorify God, not as an indication of loyalty to him.

Sydney Green was released from Lancaster Gaol on the evening of 4 November, the bells of St John's ringing in celebration. Heywood, being in the parish that day, gave to Cowgill, the churchwardens and the East Grinstead Sisters, working in the parish with the children and the poor, to whom they had ministered 'with the greatest love and tenderness,' a cheque to be used for the benefit of the poor.

Green's case was heard on 10 and 11 December. Judgement was reserved until 22 January 1884 when the verdict and summary were given for the defendant, with costs. Sir Percival, after some demur, had accepted Green's resignation and at once notified the bishop that he appointed Harry Cowgill, Green's curate, to succeed him, the gentleman the bishop had already refused to licence as he had continued all the disputed practices. On 18 December the bishop refused the right of nomination. On 4 February the

---

[168] The Book of Daniel, Chapter 6, verses 6–15.

bishop, having declared as lapsed Sir Percival's right of presentation, because Heywood had indicated his intention to nominate 'another rebellious cleric', instituted the Revd Tom Taylor Evans, a young man he had ordained in 1878 and who had done good work in Burnley and at St Matthew's, Campfield, Manchester.[169]

During this period the Archbishop of Canterbury [Tait] lay on his deathbed, and in one of his last acts appealed to the Revd Alexander Heriot Mackonochie, Vicar of St Alban's, Holborn, London, one of the most 'infamous' pursuers of ritual practices, to resign his living, 'so that the scandal of a second contumacious clerk might be averted.' After some hesitation, and the Bishop of London's agreement to appoint him to the parish of St Peter's London Docks (equally a parish of the same disputation), Mackonochie agreed. Much pressure was applied on the Bishop of Manchester to acquiesce in the archbishop's appeal for a peaceful solution to the Miles Platting case, mainly from the Dean of Manchester and four rural deans, the most common argument being, 'Will you be the only Bishop to refuse the dying Archbishop's legacy of peace?' Bishop Fraser's reply, courteous and closely argued, centred on two things – one, that he had only insisted on obedience to the law of the land; and two that, in the blurring of the lines of the Prayer Book as previously understood, he could discern nothing for the Church but continued disquiet for the present, and disaster, possibly destruction in a future only too threatening and imminent.[170] The second of his reasons was a significantly unperceptive assessment. Archbishop Tait, in one of his never-concealed personal opinions, said, of the refusal of the complainants in the Miles Platting case to accept Bishop Fraser's invitation of an interview, that he would have been justified, to say the least, in refusing the suit to proceed.[171] Fraser himself, some years later,

---

[169] The name of the parish derived from the site of the Roman Fort of Mancunium. Evans left Miles Platting in 1890 to become Vicar of Holy Trinity, Bolton, where he served for over 20 years.
[170] Hughes, ibid., p. 302.
[171] Quoted, H.E. Sheen, ibid., p. 197.

came to much the same opinion: 'If ever such another case should arise within my jurisdiction, and the complainants refuse to submit the case to my direction, and I further know that some extraneous association, like the Church Association, is at the bottom of the business, I will put my *veto* on the proceedings. The interference of such associations between parishioners, clergy and their bishop is a great injury to the peace of the Church.'[172]

Heywood had done all he possibly could to gain support for the cause. He continued to visit the parish regularly, and to invite parties of parishioners to his home, Doveleys, reached by train from Manchester London Road station to Denstone;[173] but eventually the diverse authorities to whom he had appealed presented an unassailable opposition. His last effort as patron consisted in serving a writ of *quere impedit* on 23 January 1883, but it produced little effect.[174] On 10 May 1883 Sydney Faithorn Green proceeded to the degree of Master of Arts in the University of Cambridge, the cost of which was paid by a number of undergraduates who wanted to show their appreciation of his stand for the liberty of the Church.[175]

All hope having been given up, there was a congregational meeting in the schoolroom on 12 February 1884, where about 400 sat down to tea, a figure which increased considerably during the course of the evening. The Revd Harry Cowgill presided, and was supported by, among others, the Revd Sydney Green; the Patron, and his brother the Revd Henry Robinson Heywood (1833–1895), the Vicar of Swinton; the Vicar of All Saints, Margaret Street, London (Beardmore Compton); the Revd Dr Marshall, Vicar of St John the Baptist, Hulme; Mr Oliver Heywood; and the Revd W. Climpson, Curate of St Alban's, Cheetwood, Manchester. Sir Percival praised the 'grand work' of the faithful men and women, carried on for years and years, and the 'gracious

---

[172] John W. Diggle, p. 403.
[173] Reported in *The Monthly Record* for August 1883, p. 1, and September 1883, p. 1.
[174] ibid., March 1883, p. 3.
[175] Isabel Mary, ibid., p. 177.

work of love that the Sisters have done in the parish.' 'By the Providence of God,' he said, 'the dark clouds still hang over you ... but once, when a great storm was raging, the good Lord drew near and said, "It is I – be not afraid." Remember these words.'[176] His brother Henry, in his speech, quoted a god-fearing man of business, and a large employer of labour, words which shed important light on apparent defeat which may be success [of] the most real, and true and lasting: 'Success! What is success but bending reverently, submissively, thankfully, to the will of God?' Beardmore Compton spoke with great warmth: 'The world in general has not yet learned what the principle is [that] is being contended for. It is not a principle that has anything to do with ritual. [It] is "Shall the Church govern itself, or be governed from without by a body which is not the Church at all?" In asserting that principle the people of St John's have met with great disaster ... [but] the man who can bear witness when trodden underfoot can bear witness in the courts of heaven.' He thought it was a burning shame, after he had visited Sydney Green in prison, that Miles Platting had been selected for attack, whilst others – his own for example – had been left alone.[177] The reason was, in all probability, that unfortunately for the Bishop of Manchester, the Orange Movement was much stronger and more aggressive in Manchester than in the south of England. His latent hostility to Roman Catholicism was provoked by the existence of the newly founded R.C. Diocese of Salford, taking in the area of the Diocese of Manchester. It sheltered 196,000 Irish immigrants, which also stimulated Orange hostility.[178]

St John's *Monthly Record* ceased publication with the edition of March 1884. The editorial attempted to summarise the new situation: 'Under the new Rector most of the old congregation found themselves unable to worship at St John's, and the "intruders"

---

[176] ibid.
[177] ibid., p. 179.
[178] James Bentley, *Ritualism and Politics in Britain* [Oxford University Press], 1978, p. 106.

are mainly non-parishioners, thus degrading it to the level of a sect.' The new incumbent had told some of the 'remnant' that no conditions were imposed upon him by the bishop at his institution, and if only the congregation had remained he would have made the services agreeable to them. The bishop's inconsistency, in the writer's mind, was revealed in a sermon which he preached in June 1871 at St John the Baptist, Hulme, a notoriously 'High' place of worship, where he had been taken to task for preaching there, but had asserted his right and duty to preach everywhere: 'The only thing he cared for,' he said, 'was to encourage every man, be he High or Low Church, who is striving to win souls for Christ ... A Church which at the same time had two such men as John Keble and Charles Simeon ought not to be ... narrowed down to the dimension of a sect ... through this service ... a decorated, rich, and gorgeous service, I have seen and heard nothing which is in any sense disloyal to the Church of England. These are not the days when we can wreck a Church for the sake of a posture or a vestment.' These eirenic words clash with the bishop's opinion in a speech to the Convocation of York in February 1882, on the subject of Miles Platting and after the Dean of York had criticised the bishop's handling of the case.[179]

In the parish magazine for March 1884 (pages 2, 3 and 11), it was recorded by the Sunday School teachers, in a letter to the parents of the scholars, that 'because of the vindictive prosecution by the Church Association, supported by the Bishop of Manchester and the consequent changes in our church (the rejection of the Revd Harry Cowgill and the interference with the rights of the patron), we are compelled to discontinue the work of the Sunday Schools.' On the final Sunday, 17 February, the Sunday Schools, founded by Sir Benjamin Heywood before the erection of the church, were closed. The scholars gathered that day numbered 450, and the teachers between 50 and 60. Soon afterwards came the farewell to the East Grinstead Sisters, who had lived in the

---

[179] Quoted earlier, p. 145.

parish for over two years, and to their work with the St Agnes Guild for Married Women (30 in number), the St Agnes Guild for Young Women, the Mothers' Meeting, with over 60 members, all of which had to be disbanded. The Sisters went across the City to another parish (St Alban, Cheetwood).[180]

Mr Hayward, a prominent member of the congregation, writing to a local paper, declared, 'we can help good churchmen, whether "High" or "Low" in building up the Church. But God helping us we will not, neither at Miles Platting or anywhere else, assist in pulling it down.' The editor adds the principles of Building Up and Pulling Down, based on what they had learned under Mr Green. They were:

Building Up
A Free and Open church (a large number of seats being previously appropriated [pew rents]).
Daily Morning and Evening Prayer.
Observance of Holy Days.
Greater regard for the Sacraments of the Church.
Increased reverence for holy things.
Due respect to the adornment of God's House; and speaking generally an investiture of the dead body of modern respectable churchmanship with the living spirit of the Church's order, and an opening out of the practical application of the truths enshrined in her Creeds.

Pulling Down
Repudiation of the following Article of the Creed "I believe in the Holy Catholic Church" and the substitution of "A Protestant Sect".
Attendance at church generally once a week, usually on Sunday evenings.
Irreverence during services, expressed by sitting or lounging

---

[180] Isabel Mary, ibid., p. 183.

during prayers and other similar indications of careless indifference.

Non-observation of Holy Days.

Utter neglect of the Sacraments, even by those who lead the service.

Disregard of the sanctity of God's House and all holy things, and generally a persistent stifling of the Christian life, and the blessed truths which breathe in the order of her services.[181]

The people of St John's continued their corporate worship elsewhere at neighbouring parishes in the changed circumstances. For instance, on Easter Day 1884 about 230 made their Communion at the cathedral: 170 of them before breakfast at the 6.30 am service – causing the subsequent celebrations at 7.30 and 8.30 to be delayed by half an hour. The old and even the sick and infirm were present at the earliest service, having faced a cutting east wind.[182]

The weary years of exile, however, were at last to be rewarded: in May 1890 the new Bishop of Manchester, Dr James Moorhouse (1826–1915) lost no time in exercising his episcopal authority by resolving at a stroke the antagonisms. He brought peace by appointing Tom Taylor Evans to another living, and restoring Sir Percival Heywood to exercise his rights as Patron. Bishop Moorhouse, when he was made Bishop of Melbourne, Australia, in January 1877 wrote in the late 1870s that 'The hatred of Rome here is incredible ... I could have gained my object here long ago but for that ... Nothing will induce me to join in the bigoted howl against Rome.'

With his previous experience of urban ministry in Sheffield (his birthplace), and London, and his intellectual engagement with the problems of the day and interpreting them for working lay people, he was an admirable appointment for Manchester. The

---

[181] *The Monthly Record*, March 1884, pp. 2 and 3.
[182] Isabel Mary, ibid., pp. 184 and 185.

Revd Arthur Anderton, curate for many years with Canon Hornby, Rector of Bury (from 1850 to 1884), who had been a supportive friend to Miles Platting parish, accepted Heywood's offer of the living, and was inducted on 11 July 1890. Anderton worked on quietly, little by little restoring the former services to their former beauty and dignity, and welding together with great care and tact both elements of the congregation, the old and the newcomers.[183] The community of East Grinstead Sisters returned and took up their work again on 24 September 1891, the Guilds were revived, and the Sunday School re-opened. 'The Church is once more the pride and joy of the people, many bringing gifts to make the House of God more beautiful.'[184]

After the death of Sir Percival Heywood in 1897, it was proposed that a memorial window should be placed in the church. There was no difficulty whatever in raising the required sum: the money came in quickly, entirely from past and present members of the church. Not one rich person contributed. Among those who did were the Revd Sydney Faithorn Green, Vicar of Charlton, Dover, and the Revd Henry Cowgill, Vicar of Shireoaks. More than enough had been received in three weeks, and so portraits of the Patron and of the Founder were placed in the vestry, and also a portrait of the school, beneath which is a brass tablet with the inscription 'To the dearly treasured memory of Sir T. Percival Heywood, for over thirty years patron of this benefice, and a warm friend to the poor of this parish.' There still remained a considerable balance, which was forwarded to the Denstone Memorial Fund.[185] A letter from the Marquess of Salisbury added his name to the project of a commemorative portrait at Denstone College, for his 'conspicuous service to the cause of religious education, adding that few persons have established a better claim

---

[183] Anderton stayed there until his death in 1929; '39 years of faithful service' [H.E. Sheen, ibid., pp. 214 and 215].
[184] Isabel Mary, ibid., p. 188.
[185] ibid., pp. 187, 188, and 189.

to the gratitude of all who are interested in this important subject.'[186]

A close friend of nearly 30 years standing, George Body, DD, Canon Missioner of Durham, wrote a summary of Heywood's life in an Introduction to Isabel Mary Heywood's *Reminiscences* of her father. He said:

I treasure the thought of him as that of a man, of all whom I have known, who realised most fully the ideal of a true Christian layman, and of a true son of the Church of England ... Two words describe his life: it was Faithful and True. The ruling principle of his life at Doveleys ... was one of the most beautiful things I have ever seen, and, under God, it was his creation. [At] The family prayers in the morning, in which he ministered, and the evenings in which the family life found its climax, God was a felt presence. There is no aspect of the Christian character more admirable than that of the Catholic layman formed according to the model of our Church. *This type has its ideal in consecrated duty in daily life. He walked with God**. He was, as everyone who realises what a Catholic life is, a true Evangelical: he lived in personal relations with the only true God and Jesus Christ. The Blessed Sacrament was his most cherished privilege. The Communion of Saints was to him a fact. I may seem to be drawing a picture too ideal to be true; I am but with strictest fidelity saying what he appeared to me to be, in a long acquaintance. *The most ordinary and secular occupations were carried on in the consciousness of the presence of God, and of his over-ruling Providence.**

He made notes on his daily Bible readings, interpreting and applying the texts to his own life. His generosity was unfailing. On himself he spent nothing ... but for others he was constantly doing kind things. Behind the curtain of

---

[186] ibid., p. 245.

his courteous manner [was] the abiding holiness of character and singleness of purpose that gave the sterling ring to all he was and did.
[*emphases added.]

Postscript

Percy Dearmer was so disturbed by the 'Lamentable confusion, lawlessness and vulgarity' which were conspicuous in the Church by the end of the nineteenth century, that he founded the Alcuin Club. Formed in 1897, it sought to offset the influence of those heirs of the Tractarian Movement who were intent on 'Romanising' their Church. He introduced *The Parson's Handbook* in 1899 to set out the principles of liturgy and ceremonial as adhered to by the early Tractarians – that is, according to the ethos of the Book of Common Prayer and the convictions of their orthodox High Church contemporaries.[187] 'To John Keble,' wrote Kenneth Ingram, 'the Movement was simply and always a restoration of the religious principles for which the Church of England and the Prayer Book stood ... The Erastianism of government and nation was the result of the neglect of the Prayer Book standard. His pattern was the doctrine of Hooker and of Laud. He conceived no startling innovation, no development of a standard whose loyalty to the Anglican heritage could be questioned.'[188]

---

[187] Donald Gray, *Percy Dearmer* [Norwich: Canterbury Press, 2000], pp. 37, 38, and 131.
[188] Kenneth Ingram, *John Keble* [Philip Allen, 1933], p. 47. One historian lamented the appropriation of the term 'Anglo-Catholic' by later adherents of the Tractarian Movement, asserting that it originally denoted, like that of 'Anglican', simply membership of the Church of England (Peter B. Nockles, *The Oxford Movement in Context* [Cambridge University Press, 1994], pp. 40–41).

4

Lilian Mary Baylis (1874–1937): Theatre Entrepreneur

Lilian Mary Baylis, CH, was nationally and internationally known as a pioneer female theatre manager, having revolutionised the approach to such establishments in accordance with a clear vision and the resolution to achieve it. She took over management of the 'Old Vic' theatre in south London in 1912 with the determination to continue and develop the principles of the previous manager, her aunt Emma Cons, to bring the highest and best in drama to the poor of the district of Waterloo. Through the difficult years of a great war, the changing moral and cultural standards of the 1920s, and the Great Depression, and in a male-orientated society, she pursued what she believed to be her God-given vocation with a highly personal management style – autocratic and domineering, but laced with humanity and generosity.

To the grindingly poor local community Baylis brought performances of Shakespeare and opera – sung in English – employing some of the best artists of the day, usually at miniscule salaries. Later, in 1928, when she took over the derelict Sadler's Wells Theatre, she did the same for ballet. Her life was lived openly in close fellowship with God – it was to him that she gave credit when things went well, and to whom she appealed for help when they did not. She made a lasting impression on all three artistic disciplines in London, and created the companies that would become The Royal Ballet, The Royal National Theatre, and the English National Opera.

Lilian Baylis was born on 9 May 1874 at 19 Nottingham Street, Marylebone. She was the eldest child of Elizabeth Baylis, née Cons, a professional singer and pianist, and Newton Baylis, also a singer. He was a member of several church choirs, notably that of All Saints, Margaret Street, London, where he and Elizabeth were married, and where the first eight of their ten children were baptised.[1]

Music was one of the earliest influences on Lilian: her mother, Liebe Cons, was a professional musician as well as a devout Christian.[2] The other was a concern for the poor and the provision of adequate housing. This second influence was that of her mother's sister, Emma Cons (1838–1912), a close friend of Octavia Hill (1838–1912) who championed the amelioration of the lives of the poor, and managed houses in the slum areas of south London. Octavia Hill had been moved by the poverty she saw there, and in her teens worked for The Ladies' Co-operative Guild, a Christian Socialist initiative. She was a member of the congregation of Lincoln's Inn Chapel where she met F.D. Maurice, who proved to have a strong effect upon her and especially in the strengthening of her faith. She was brought up a Unitarian, but became baptised and confirmed in the Church of England, with Maurice as her sponsor for baptism.[3] John Ruskin was impressed by her abilities, and in 1864 began to support her work.

It was at a meeting of the Council of Promoters of Working Men's Associations in 1854 that Hill met Emma Cons,[4] who was to become a close and most supportive friend.[5] 'I find in her a

---

[1] Elizabeth Schafer, *Lilian Baylis: A Biography* [University of Hertfordshire, 2006], p. 28.
[2] Susie Gilbert, Opera for Everybody [London: Faber and Faber, 2009], p. 13.
[3] Gillian Darley, *Octavia Hill, A Life* [London: Constable, 1990], pp. 35, 44, and 48.
[4] The unusual surname was an adaptation of her family's 'Konss'. They were Germans who came to England in 1772.
[5] Darley, ibid, pp. 48 and 49.

strength and energy which is quite refreshing,' Hill wrote to a friend in 1857; 'she has amazing perseverance, a power, and a glorious humility.'[6] Emma Cons was in the forefront of housing provision and open spaces for the poorer residents of the area, and was the prime mover, for example, of The South London Dwellings Company in 1879, as well as a great proponent of women's suffrage. She was one of the three women members of the first London County Council, eventually becoming an alderman.[7] Beatrice Webb rated her as 'one of the most saintly as well as one of the most far-sighted of Victorian women philanthropists.'[8]

One of the few things on which Hill and Cons disagreed was teetotalism; Cons was firmly committed to it as part of the work.[9] The Waterloo area south of the Thames was indeed a very socially deprived community. A study of the Metropolitan Borough of Southwark, covering roughly the parishes of St George the Martyr, St Saviour, and Holy Trinity, Newington, showed that in 1902 St Saviour's parish was the poorest in the whole of south London, and that of the 33,000 inhabitants living between Blackfriars Bridge and London Bridge, 68 per cent were classified as 'poor'. In 1905 St George's parish had a population density of 212 people per acre, a death rate of 30 per thousand, and an infant mortality rate of over 200 per thousand. The average annual death rate in 1931 was 13.8 per cent, the third highest figure of all the boroughs examined in an essay of that year.[10] The population was described as the 'despair of those who work amongst it,' and Cons herself often felt overwhelmed by 'all the misery and sin' she saw there, and said that only her faith saved her from utter hopelessness.[11]

[6] ibid., p. 49.
[7] Cicely Hamilton and Lilian Baylis, *The Old Vic* [London: Jonathan Cape Ltd, 1926], pp. 249 and 281.
[8] Richard Findlater, *Lilian Baylis: The Lady of the Old Vic* [London: Allen Lane, 1975], p. 23.
[9] Darley, ibid., pp. 142 and 148.
[10] S.C. Williams, *Religious Belief and Popular Culture in Southwark, 1880–1939* [Oxford University Press, 1999], p. 29.
[11] Darley, ibid., p. 214.

The lack of public open space, 20 acres per 1000 inhabitants (1931 figure), elevated the importance of church gardens and graveyards as well as the public houses as recreational focuses in the area.

During the nineteenth century the music-hall began to emerge alongside the public house as another major institution of communal life.[12] By the end of the century, the music-hall was second only to the pub as a popular institution, and south London was the geographical focus of music-hall culture. In some cases their functions became combined, and the Grapes Tavern, later known as the Surrey Music-Hall, in Southwark Bridge Road, was the first pub-based concert hall to use the explicit title of Music-Hall. The various 'star' appearances were supplemented by a distinct form of drama – plays which were melodramatic but considered to be 'true to life', humorous but realistic portraits of working-class life. This was the background to Emma Cons' last development in her care for the working man and woman. She re-opened The Royal Victoria Theatre (originally the Royal Coburg Theatre), known locally as The Old Vic, as a teetotal Coffee Music-Hall in 1880. Emma Cons maintained that the venture was intended to combat 'Not poverty, but pauperism in its attendant vices – drunkenness, improvidence, mendacity, bad language, filthy habits, gambling, low amusements, and ignorance.'[13]

Emma bought the theatre freehold, raising £17,800 in three months by public subscription, sacrificing the drink licence, which had brought in a profit of £200 a year, and selling only coffee and tea. She handed the Title Deeds to the Charity Commissioners, to avoid the theatre's falling back into private hands.'[14] As an alternative to the gin palaces and bad public houses of that time, the Vic gave fresh impetus to the growing thirst for knowledge among the working classes which led to the establishment of The Workers' Education

---

[12] S.C. Williams, ibid., pp. 42 and 43.
[13] Findlater, ibid., p. 23.
[14] Baylis, in a talk, 'Shakespeare for the People', 1931 [Bristol University Theatre Archive, OVLB 000149, p. 1]

eoff ة

Association.[15] Cons instituted Tuesday evening lectures (admission one penny) given by a range of eminent scientists and travellers, and this gave rise to the establishment of Morley College – evening classes for men and women, at first on the same premises, but later in a separate building[16] – funded with financial support from Samuel Morley (1809–1886), a Bristol textile millionaire.[17] Such an institution 'was one of those late-Victorian products of philanthropic idealism, which, like the gas lamps of the period, spread little pools of light in the dismal materialistic darkness of that philistine age ... Future historians will probably reach the conclusion that the establishment of coffee halls and teashops was a major social innovation, contributing far more to the life and habits of Londoners than any other single event.'[18] In his obituary notice for Baylis, A.E. Johnson described Cons as 'slight and frail, with the face of a saint and the heart of a lion. Not without shrewd judgement did the older woman cast her mantle on the younger, and ... the double portion of her predecessor's spirit, for which the latter most surely prayed, was not withheld.'[19]

At the age of 25 in 1889, Lilian Baylis became part of her parents' concert group, 'The Gypsy Revellers', and they played in churches, hospitals, aristocratic socials, tennis parties, and workhouses all over England. By the age of 12 she was a competent violinist and able to supervise her mother's piano pupils.[20] The group set off in 1891 for South Africa, to tour in covered wagons, giving musical performances to audiences that had never been entertained before.[21] But after six years there she was summoned to England by her Aunt Emma to help her in her scheme for

[15] W.J. Turner, in *The New Statesman*, 4 December 1937, p. 918.
[16] Baylis, ibid. The director of music at the college was Gustav Holst. Baylis claimed that the first working man to graduate from Cambridge University was from the classroom of the Old Vic [article in *The Era*, 26 August 1936].
[17] Ian Campbell Bradley, *Enlightened Entrepreneurs* [Weidenfeld and Nicholson, 1987], pp. 48ff.
[18] W.J. Turner, in *The New Statesman and Nation*, 4 December 1937, p. 918.
[19] In *The Times*, 30 November 1937.
[20] Schafer, p.13.
[21] Sybil Thorndike, in *Lilian Baylis as I Knew Her*, Sybil and Russell Thorndike [London: Chapman and Hall Ltd, 1938], p. 11.

the running of the Old Vic Theatre. Charles Kingsley wrote of the theatre in *Alton Lock*: 'They say the Queen is a good woman and I don't doubt it, but I wonder if she knows what a den of iniquity her namesake is.'[22] The scheme was explained by Cons as providing, for the working and lower middle classes, recreation such as the music hall affords, without the existing attendant moral and social disadvantages.[23] The district was characterised by a leading journalist of the day as 'The site of one of London's ... biggest criminal "rookeries", and one of the most unpleasant examples of London that one could offer to a foreigner ... The Vic held more than a thousand people on a Saturday night ... sweating ... and quarrelling and fighting ... but all went quiet when the curtain rose ... The Vic was a safety valve, which saved the area from being a mere Devil's Acre.'[24]

On the death of her aunt in 1912, Baylis took over the management of the Old Vic. Thus began her extraordinary career, developing the avowed clean and healthy and uplifting policy of bringing the highest standards of drama and opera for the benefit of the poor, at a price they could afford, with seats from one penny to a shilling. She developed her aunt's ballad concerts to operatic recitals, given by great singers and recitalists at greatly reduced fees.[25] This innovation alternated with the Workers' Lectures, and it developed into full-blown opera performances on Saturday evenings. Her aunt's death affected her deeply, and in the same year she went on retreat, where she met the priest who was become her spiritual adviser and supporter for the rest of her life – Father Andrew, SDC.[26] She had been

---

[22] Quoted by Baylis in a talk 'The History of the Old Vic'; Mandel and Mitchenson Theatre Collection, Old Royal Naval College, London. [Collection removed to Bristol University in 2010.]

[23] Sybil Thorndike, p. 15

[24] Findlater, p. 4.

[25] Baylis, 'Shakespeare for the People,' 1931.

[26] Henry Ernest Hardy (1869–1946), Anglican priest and friar. Keble College Oxford, 1892, Ely Theological College, 1892–94. Curate of Plaistow, Superior of the Society of the Divine Compassion. Name in Religion: Andrew. He was a direct descendant of Nicholas Ferrar of Little Gidding (1543–1620) [Kathleen Burns, family tree in *Life and Letters of Father Andrew, SDC*, Mowbray, 1948, p. 87].

brought up in a robustly Church-centred family, regularly engaged in Bible studies, and she attended St Augustine's school, Kilburn.[27] This encounter with a devout holy man sharpened and deepened her relationship with God.[28] She also had a great admiration for Edward Stuart Talbot, the first Warden of Keble College and later, successively, Vicar of Leeds and Bishop of Rochester, Southwark and Winchester.[29] It must have given her great pleasure to receive from him a letter after a concert in which he wrote, 'When you came into the Box you must have seen how much we were enjoying ourselves ... thank you. To enjoy is one thing; to give enjoyment is another ... Miss Davies (my wife's maid) in particular enjoyed herself... and the rest (two Bishops in one Box) were well delighted.'[30]

The Motto of the Old Vic was a quotation from Shakespeare's *Cymbeline*:

> The Benediction of the covering heavens
> Fall on their hearers like dew; for they are worthy
> To inlay heaven with stars.[31]

Building on her aunt's inspirational achievement, Baylis went on to revolutionise the Old Vic theatre and, incidentally, the recognition of the competent management capabilities of women. The concerts, magic lantern shows and temperance lectures for the deprived communities south of the river developed into full-scale productions of 'Shakespeare for the Masses' and opera and ballet. From a strong committee, recruited by the actress Estelle Stead (daughter

---

[27] Schafer, p. 13.

[28] He was a constant support, encouraging her to continue meditation and retreats, writing to reassure her that her 'mission' was soundly based. 'Keep a good heart and go on with your fight. I really think that you are doing one of the finest things I know. Your provision of good fare and your brave assertion that theatre is a noble art brings a clear stream of noble suggestion into London' was a typical example [Bristol University Theatre Archive, OVLB 000003/18].

[29] Findlater, p. 51.

[30] 29 January 1934 [Bristol University Theatre Archive, OVLB 000116].

[31] Act V, Scene V [Lilian Baylis, *Reminiscences*, Ms. at Mander and Mitchenson Theatre Collection, Royal Naval College].

of the crusading journalist W.T. Stead),[32] formed in June 1914 of leading actors, chaired by Matheson Lang[33] and his wife Estelle Britton, came a scheme for running Shakespeare plays, starting in the autumn. Despite the almost insuperable difficulties of the beginning of the war, Lang and his wife produced three plays. However, having warned Baylis that he had promised only to start her off well, the time came when Lang gave her notice that he would soon have to leave London. He said, 'God knows how you will carry on.' Baylis's reply was to characterise the whole of the quarter-century of her time as manager: 'God alone knows, as you say, but he does know and he will show me the way.'[34]

In fact he had already provided a competent successor. On the last night of the second of the three plays 'a charming white-haired old man stopped me in the theatre and said "I am Ben Greet;[35] is there any way I can serve you? I love my Shakespeare and think this work you are doing is splendid".'[36] Greet viewed Shakespeare as a moral oracle who helps us all to achieve serenity of mind, and the way of gentleness and mercy, whose works should be brought to the widest possible audience. As if this were not sufficient qualification for the Old Vic, even more impressive were Greet's spiritual qualifications: 'He was a devoted Anglican, very High Church – it was his whole life,' said Sybil Thorndike. He was a pillar of the Church Union, and of the Church and Stage Guild.[37]

---

[32] Who had died in the *Titanic* disaster of 15 April 1912.
[33] Matheson Alexander Lang (1879–1948), born in Canada, educated in Scotland; actor, and playwright. Left in 1916 to act in films.
[34] Baylis, Bristol University Theatre Archive, OVLB 000149, p. 2.
[35] Sir Philip Ben Greet (1857–1936), actor-Manager. Born on a recruiting ship on the Thames commanded by his father, Captain William Greet, RN. Educated at the Royal Naval School, New Cross. For 49 years he presented Shakespeare in the open air and in theatres in London and the provinces. Took the morality play *Everyman* to the USA, where he became known as an actor and a producer of Shakespeare plays, 1902–1914. He worked at the Old Vic from 1914–1918. Gave up the work there at the request of the Shakespeare for Schools Committee of the LCC Board of Education to present the plays throughout London and the suburbs, resulting in over one million attendances. Gained Diploma and Gold Medal for English productions at the Paris Exposition in 1926. Knighted 1929.
[36] Baylis, ibid.
[37] Findlater, pp. 119 and 120.

In the one week during Baylis's second season, 4000 schoolchildren saw *As You Like It*.[38] The miracle was achieved partly by the Revd Stewart Headlam (1847–1924), a disciple of F.D. Maurice, founder in 1879 of The Church and Stage Guild, and member of the London County Council Education Board.[39] 'The programmes of opera and Shakespeare proved very successful, and were a source of refreshment and recreation to our men from the Front on their brief respites at home, as many letters of gratitude testified,' wrote Baylis in a record of her work requested later by the Vic-Wells Association.[40] In 1924 *Everyman* was performed on the Chancel steps of the Chapel of King's College, Cambridge – the first play given there since the visit of Queen Elizabeth in 1564.[41] E.G. Harcourt Williams[42] wrote of those times that despite the hardships of the early days, the parochial methods, the makeshift quality of the pioneer work which were entailed by sheer poverty, and by which Baylis was too often judged, she consistently improved her work. For one who proclaimed herself an ignoramus, and knowing little or nothing about art, this was a strange quality to possess. She knew that satisfaction with achievement would mean stagnation and disaster.[43]

Baylis's 'credo' she set out in a speech for broadcasting, 'The Art of Living – The Need for the Theatre': 'I so believe theatre is our greatest power for good or evil, that I pray my earnestness may give me words in which to express this faith and to hold your attention … I am cast tonight to speak on the Art of Living and the place of the Theatre in that life. The theatre isn't an excuse for wonderful evening gowns and jewels; it isn't a fad of people with long hair and sandals or the performance of 'varsity men and women; good drama

---

[38] Sybil Thorndike, p. 17. The Old Vic staged eventually every play that Shakespeare wrote [Susie Gilbert, p. 25].
[39] Findlater, p. 127.
[40] Baylis, ibid., OVLB 000144/2.
[41] ibid.
[42] Williams (1880–1957) was appointed by Baylis in 1929 as the new director of the Old Vic.
[43] *The Listener*, 1 December 1937, p. 1184.

isn't only for the students of training colleges and boys and girls swotting for the Oxford and Cambridge locals; it is a crying need of working men and women who need to see beyond the four walls of their offices, workshops and homes into a world of awe and wonder. Furthermore, art is a bond between rich and poor; it allows of no class distinctions; more than that, it is a bond between nation and nations, and may do much to help widely different peoples to understand the problems of life in each country.' She quoted Dr Dearmer[44] who said 'Art is a spiritual necessity. Civilisation cannot exist in its absence, for without it civilisation is but organised savagery.' 'The theatre is perhaps the most easily understood branch of art for the man and woman in the street.'[45] Baylis understood Dearmer's view that 'Art is the expression of spiritual values in terms of beauty,'[46] and also his belief that 'Goodness, Truth and Beauty were a Trinity of ultimate values (Love being a supernatural activity which embraced all three) – Art and Religion both being an attempt to express the things which are unseen and eternal.'[47] She believed that 'the adventures of heart and mind should ... be available and accessible to [all]'. She wanted everyone to have their slice of the 'elitist cake,'[48] and saw art as something more than pleasure, but as expressing spiritual values, to set within reach of the poorest.[49]

It must have been encouraging to Baylis when someone said in the interval of a performance, 'Them 'amlicks 'ad a lot trouble in their

---

[44] The Revd Dr Percy Dearmer (1867–1936), Canon of Westminster and Professor of Art at King's College, London. A quotation from his Preface to *The Necessity of Art*, Ed. P. Dearmer [London: SCM Press, 1924], page v.

[45] Bristol University Theatre Archive: Mander and Mitchenson Theatre Collection [BBC No. 21].

[46] Dearmer, *Art and Religion* [London: SCM Press, 1924 (Revised 1936)], p. 12.

[47] ibid., pp. 16, 53, 54, and 79.

[48] Gilbert, p. 461.

[49] An example of the authenticity of her vision was the 'barrow lady' who sold apples in the yard near where Sybil Thorndike lived: 'Me and my pals went to see you performing at the Old Vic about those Trojan Women [21 October 1919]. We 'ad a good cry, then a nice walk 'ome. As I see it that play is just us – 'aven't we been through the x war? 'Aven't we lost our x sons and 'usbands? It done us good to see them all crying and moaning and 'aving to get on with it, like us' (Thorndike, p. 43).

family.'[50] She quoted how she had been told by soldiers home from the Front of the heartening effect of recalling tunes from *Faust* and *Il Trovatore*, and how, in their whistling of them 'knocked against others who had become familiar with them in the same old theatre in London.'[51] She recalled that an Oxford professor sent her a donation of a guinea because his railway guard constantly sang the Flower song from *Carmen* or some other aria. When asked about this, the guard said he had learned them at the Old Vic.[52] After a performance of *Tannhauser*, a rough woman coming down the gallery stairs said to her, 'Gel, but that Pilgrim's Chorus makes me feel like I'd like to pray till I'm bust, and I ain't one of your churchgoers.' Baylis related how she knew of more than one luke-warm Christian made 'red-hot' for his faith again by the Master-Hymn in Mascagni's *Cavalleria Rusticana*, and good resolutions made by people, rich and poor, after hearing Gounod's *Faust*. How she saw a party of factory boys and girls sky-larking on the gallery staircase: one boy was mauling a girl when her pal called out, 'Now, Liza, what did Meph say to Marguerite? No messing about until the ring's round your finger.'

She had seen 'three of the leading intellectual figures of the time weeping like children for the lost simplicity of their faith during a performance of the wonderful Chester Nativity Play'. 'The world of medicine fully realises the help it receives from the recreation of the people, and the Church now realises what a handmaid it has in the stage,' but she felt that the passing of the Revd Stewart Headlam reminded her that the relationship of Church and stage 30 years before was anything but friendly. In 1885 the Bishop of London (Frederick Temple, later Archbishop of Canterbury) had taken issue with Stewart Headlam, who was secretary of the Church and Stage Guild, over 'the evil influence of the stage'.[53] Baylis was impressed by

---

[50] Quoted, Fr Andrew, November 1937 (Bristol University Theatre Archives, OVLB 000354).
[51] Baylis, ibid.
[52] Interview with J.L. Hodson in the *Westminster Gazette*, 28 April 1930.
[53] *Memoirs of Archbishop Temple*, Volume 2, E.G. Sandford Ed. [London: Macmillan and Co, Ltd, 1906], pp. 129–131.

the experience of appreciation of her theatre when the Builders' Strike Committee put their work at the Old Vic in the same class as their work for hospitals – the alterations taking only one week instead of seven. She was convinced that 'Opera is the door to the so-called finer arts of poetry and painting.' She quoted St John Ervine, who wrote that the tired businessman would get a great deal more rest out of a performance of Hamlet than from a performance of the latest musical comedy. 'Some people may think that a pretty wild statement,' she said, but she had often received letters from over-tired men and women thanking her for the refreshment and tonic, even to being 'saved from insanity' by the healing power of the plays.

She remembered from early days that Ben Greet had been a little jealous of the large audiences which crowded the theatre for opera, as at that time they tended to exceed those for Shakespeare, and he loved to tease her about her 'immoral operas'. But she knew in her heart that they helped the lives 'of our workers, rich and poor alike'.[54] Because of that conviction, she had faith to the strength of a vocation from God in what she was doing, which was able to move mountains of indifference, to defy adverse balance sheets, and have the ability to convey that faith to her staff. Even the most sceptical admitted that she could so inspire others because her 'mission' was patently disinterested – when she supported her theatre so committedly it was very obviously not for herself. She was 'not one of those who confound their own advancement with advancement of the cause they advocate'.[55]

Baylis was convinced that art, however local in its inspiration, was a gift to the world at large; that the highest art brought the highest benefit to mankind, and that truth is truth and beauty is beauty and worthy of homage wherever it is found.[56] 'During

---

[54] Baylis, ibid.
[55] Cicely Hamilton, p. 190. Hamilton was instrumental in Baylis becoming a member of the Soroptimists, an international federation of women's clubs, established in California in 1921. Its aims include the maintenance of 'High Ethical standards in business and professional life'.
[56] ibid., p. 204.

the War,' she said in the course of this talk, 'many [theatre] managers thought it good to put on a whole string of frothy and sometimes unpleasant plays, giving the men home on leave and the public generally a taste for poison and drugs. Some people are only just getting over this bad habit, but it is being overcome.'

The Old Vic venture was carried through in an atmosphere not of personal ambition, or of cheap popularity or self-promotion.[57] 'The Royal Victoria Hall,' said a review in the *Daily Telegraph*, 'was accomplishing what no other repertory theatre is able to do more than dream about. It has created a real taste for the comprehension of good drama among the class which forms the real backbone of the playgoing public.'[58]

Baylis spelled out the function of a theatre in a radio talk entitled 'Aims and Ideals of the Theatre'. Although declaring that she was better at getting on with her job than talking about it, she was quite bold, beginning with a favourite analogy: 'People rest and refresh their bodies by using different muscles – they want to recreate their minds and feelings by becoming other people sometimes. The instinct to "pretend", to day-dream, is fundamental, and gives us most that is worth having from religion to the greatest art, and to many the art of the theatre, where the ear and eye combine to the same end, speaks most easily and directly. People have the right to this re-creation – to this expansion of their own personality by the inclusion, however temporarily, of that of others.' 'Some of her listeners,' she said, 'may say that her aims and ideals sound well, but they are quite impracticable.' But she felt that the Old Vic had proved that a people's theatre had been accomplished, and it paid its way.[59] She pressed her case further by saying that many people cling to the old idea that Shakespeare is all murders and quotations, and not recreation. But often, as the audience dispersed after a comedy, there were many comments of surprise at how funny it

---

[57] ibid., p. 205.
[58] Quoted, Findlater, p. 162.
[59] Mander and Mitchenson Theatre Collection. Quotation is a conflation of Baylis's draft and final script.

had been. Ben Greet once had a bet with Baylis that there were more laughs in *The Comedy of Errors* than there were in *Charley's Aunt* which was running locally at the same time. 'He won, hands down,' she said.

Baylis did not forget the valuable experience she had had in South Africa, and when the English Association at the University of Witwatersrand, Johannesburg, invited her to speak on her work at the Old Vic, on 3 September 1924 in advance of a proposed tour of South Africa by a Shakespearean company, she readily accepted. Her lecture was entitled 'What the Old Vic Stands For', and she explained that 'the Old Vic is like no other theatre: it does not work for profit. It is the only repertory theatre in the United Kingdom which produces Shakespeare and Grand Opera for nine months every year ... and its mission is to give the humblest the chance of seeing the best.' Since 1914, she revealed, 'every play in Shakespeare's First Folio had been produced, and *Pericles* – a feat no other management in the history of the stage has equalled or even attempted.' Whole families come – father, mother, and all the children: they book the same seats each Friday and Saturday, and 'phone if they can't come. Patrons include the King and Queen of England and the King of Siam; the greatest people in the land [are] there, with a crowd of humbler folk.'[60]

Once, when she was being driven almost to despair at the large numbers of opera-lovers being turned away from the Old Vic on Saturday nights for lack of accommodation,[61] she seized upon the purchase of the derelict Sadler's Wells Theatre as a possible solution. All the departments of the Old Vic were against it at heart, because the huge problems of renovating and rebuilding and raising the purchase price seemed insuperable. 'When one considers the years of depression and discouragement,' wrote W.J. Turner in the *New Statesman*, 'the constant struggle to make both ends meet under

---

[60] Draft of her address for the visit, pp. 1, 7, and 8: Bristol University Theatre Archive.
[61] In a talk on 'Shakespeare for the People', she revealed that although her theatre was licensed to hold 1800, there were often 2000, with people standing [Bristol University OVLB 000149].

which she laboured all of her life at the "Old Vic," one can form some notion of the audacity and courage which enabled her to add another theatre to her burden.'[62] The problems were eventually overcome by her 'bulldog tenacity', and the complete conviction that, as it was God's work she was doing, it was up to him to sort them out. In a brochure celebrating the opening of the new 'Wells' in 1931, she placed it at the centre of her great mission – that of providing top-quality lively entertainment for no more than the price of a cinema ticket. She wrote:

Great music and great drama at cheap prices are very real necessities in the life of the people. I have said often before, and I repeat, that nowadays we cultivate physical fitness in every possible way; and everybody knows that the full enjoyment of one's bodily faculties is only possible after exercise and effort. But what about the mental fitness of our younger generation? This, too, can only be acquired by exercise and effort; and it is toward this full realisation of the great kingdom in our minds that we shall labour at Sadler's Wells.[63]

In an interview for *Time and Tide* (15 July 1921), she elaborated on her vision: 'If I am right, the Almighty is with me, and no one will/can [sic] beat me.' Her practical piety is referred to again when she says, *a propos* of the nervousness of some members of her 'Old Vic' family on first nights: 'I believe in the force of prayer, and they know I do. I have seen them sick with nerves – I kiss them, thump them, and I pray.' The interviewer concluded, prophetically, that 'if the family is the nucleus of the State, it may be that this "family" at the Old Vic is the nucleus "What women are Doing",' (14 June 1934, pp. 561 and 562). Reminiscing on the terrifying air raids during the war, and how audiences were affected by the dangers,

---

[62] *The New Statesman and Nation*, 4 December 1937, p. 918 [Bristol University OVLB 000364].
[63] Schafer, p. 170.

she remembered that one night the theatre took only £5 (300 people all told, at 4d or 6d), and that although it was a terrible experience, she never knew when she was beaten, and always said, 'When things are as bad as they can be, they must get better.'[64]

In a radio talk ('the BBC honouring the Old Vic by asking her to speak on their 'Aims and Ideals in the Theatre'), Baylis declared:

> It is to Recreate. People rest and refresh their bodies by using different muscles, and they want to recreate their minds and feelings by exercising their imagination – becoming other people sometimes. The ear must be refreshed by the beauty of sound, whether of music or poetry, the eye refreshed by the beauty of painting – scenery, lighting and costumes. To day-dream is strong in most of us, and the desire to escape from one's lower self has produced practically all that is most worth having in the world, from religion to the greatest art; and to many the art of the theatre, where the ear and eye combine to the same end, speaks most easily and directly. People have the right to this re-creation – to this expansion of their own personality by the inclusion, however temporarily, of that of others.[65]

In 1924 Baylis was honoured by the University of Oxford for her work, with the award of an honorary Master of Arts degree. In his presentation speech the Public Orator, Alfred Godley, said,[66] 'We are bound always to honour and admire those who by cultivating the scenic arts and give pleasure not only to our eyes, but to our intellects; but most of all are those persons to be praised which are so ordered as not only to delight us but to educate and shape our minds for getting knowledge of the best

---

[64] ibid.
[65] Mander and Mitchenson Theatre Collection – quotation conflated from Baylis's Draft and her Final Script.
[66] English translation from the Latin.

literature. You see now before you that lady whose name, as we believe, will be forever associated with the studies which are practised in this University ... William Shakespeare [himself] could not fail to regard her as his minister and high-priestess. She had learned how to draw the unlearned and ignorant to the seats of her theatre ... they come, people of the humblest classes; they crowd to the theatre, they applaud, they laugh, they weep. "Thus has the so-called Old Vic made a conquest of the crowd".' [The translator explains in a footnote that 'this line of poetry is actually of the Orator's own composition. In the Latin he has contrived a very neat alliteration. In English it would be something like "Thus has the veteran Vic verily vanquished the vulgar".][67] Cicely Hamilton commented on this event that it was the first time one of the older universities had recognised the work of the stage. 'In Shakespeare's day there was an absolute ban on theatres and plays – in the university precincts and on attendance, by any Master, Bachelor, or scholar.'[68]

Baylis received many letters of congratulation on being accorded this honour. One was from the Rt Revd Charles Gore, former Bishop of Worcester, of Birmingham, and of Oxford, one of the foremost Tractarian theologians and founder of the Community of the Resurrection, Mirfield. Writing from 6 Margaret Street, W1, he said, 'May I say with what *great* pleasure I saw that Oxford had sought to honour you?'[69] Another letter she would have found particularly warming was from Sybil Thorndike, who said, '... you are the only woman who carries on a concern [for] the people by prayer and sure and certain faith. Bless you.'[70] A letter from a secular source showed the breadth of appreciation of her work. The London District Secretary of the Workers' Educational Association conveyed 'Hearty congratulations on the degree which Oxford has bestowed upon you ... We esteem very

---

[67] Mandel and Mitchenson Theatre Collection.
[68] Hamilton, pp. 228 and 229.
[69] 7 May 1924. OVLB 000205.
[70] 19 March 1924. OVLB 000307.

highly the wonderful work which you have been, and still are doing at the Old Vic.'[71]

In 1929 she was granted admission to the Order of the Companions of Honour, one of very few women to join the Order.[72] In the *Theatre Arts Monthly* magazine in February 1938, Ivor Brown contrasted all her honours (she also received an honorary LLD from the University of Birmingham) with the fact that she who knew 'the exact profit on a hundred cups of tea and forty-two ham rolls ... inherited a coffee-concert house and left it a great playhouse.'[73]

In 1933, writing in the *Toc H Journal*,[74] Baylis returned to her central analogy – her sense of 'mission' in all her labour, through drama, music, and ballet. We could achieve our aim of acquiring a cheerful outlook on life despite its distresses and depressions by:

> Keeping our minds fit as we keep our bodies fit, by exercise, by escaping, now and again from this painfully real world by escaping into the great countries of the imagination with the thinkers of the ages as our guides. We may find this ... escape in books, in music; but the easiest, most accessible way, is still by means of the ... theatre and all it comprehends. As a vehicle for broadening people's minds, as a means of teaching, the theatre is still what the medieval church recognised it to be – the greatest weapon they possessed.[75]

Baylis returned to the subject of escape from a 'painfully real world' three years later, when she was asked to contribute to a

---

[71] 9 May 1924. OVLB 000314.
[72] *Oxford Dictionary of National Biography* [OUP], 2004–9
[73] pp. 108, 109, and 116. Mander and Mitchenson Collection.
[74] 'Toc H' – signaller's name, in a now-obsolete code, for Talbot House – an organisation formed in World War I for the rest and refreshment for servicemen at the Front, but later with branches throughout the Empire, devoted to social service and spiritual development. It was named after Gilbert Talbot, son of Edward Stuart Talbot, killed in action in 1915.
[75] British Library, System Number 002247518.

symposium published in *The Era* of 1 January 1936. It was a debate with the title 'Should Dramatists Show Life as Better or Worse?: Illusion versus Reality'. The contributors were all distinguished men and women in the world of stage and cinema – managers, producers and critics, some taking one side and some the other, although most had subtle arguments for both, varying at different times for different people. The editor, introducing the results of the symposium, suggested however that 'those who argue that there is no necessary conflict between Reality and Illusion in the field of drama, must be very poor students of the [then] current political scene [in Germany and Russia]. Most people want to be convinced that life is not just a dirty game, and for that reason the illusionists are always likely to be in the majority until everyone is so prosperous and contented that unhappiness itself takes on the character of illusion. Life, for dramatic purpose is either worse than it seems, or better than it seems. But … for the public the theatre is … a place from which they can draw the illusion that enables them to face reality.'

A film director and producer[76] thought that 'films should strive after presenting life as it is, rather than attempt to present an escape from Life … Holding up a mirror to life we can present the world in all its fascinating and infinite variety,' although he thought it wrong to be 'almost fantastic in [an] over-stress on reality'. The secretary of the Theatrical Managers' Association[77] thought that dramatic art should reflect life as it might be under certain and various circumstances imagined by the playwright.

More than one contributor mentioned John Galsworthy, who 'selected from life as it is, and hoped to convince us that it is not what it ought to be,' contrasting this with James Barrie, who 'reflected life neither as it is nor as it might be'. The BBC Director of Drama[78] was of the view that a play should make good entertainment, and that there have been dramatic masterpieces

---

[76] Michael Balcon (1896–1977), Gaumont British Studios, Ealing.
[77] Horace Collins.
[78] Val Gielgud, brother of John Gielgud.

which have reflected life as it might be, with the object of cultivating and preserving agreeable illusions in a vale of tears.

The Dramatic Critic of the *Daily Sketch*[79] was in philosophical mode when she gave her view that 'Dramatic Art should reflect and preserve the illusions. In other words it is not necessary to escape from the illusions. Life is real – and it's full of illusions. It is those who keep their illusions who get the best out of life.'

Lilian Baylis's contribution began in a characteristically forthright manner:

> If by 'Illusion' you mean unreality, I am all in favour of realism. If by the latter you mean dwelling on the uglier side of life, then your question becomes impossible to answer at all. Briefly, I believe that the function of the stage is to help the audience by translating them into a more intense emotional atmosphere, thereby extending their sympathy, and helping them to lose themselves for the time being. It seems to me that this can most easily be done whether by the actual life of today or yesterday, or by the ideal life of wished-for tomorrow, [but it] does not seem to me to matter. The main thing is that the emotional appeal of the play should be to something real, and should be founded on something which can awaken a response in the hearts of the various members of the audience. This, 'Illusion', if synonymous with unreality, can never do, I think.[80]

The editorial summing-up of the debate was that a portrayal of the real world must appeal to the reality of the audience in such a way as to give them a creative response ('illusion') to the circumstances of their individual lives, thus enriching them.[81] The Thomist philosopher Jacques Maritain (1882–1973), although speaking primarily of the painter but in application to all the

---

[79] Jesse Collings.
[80] *The Era*, 1 January 1936, pp. 12 and 13.
[81] ibid., p. 46.

arts, expressed the question in sacramental terms: 'The part played by an artist can be one of revealing a world more real than the reality of the senses ... he should be attuned to the deeper truths which inhabit the material world ... [his creation] may, to an extent, be a "resemblance", in the traditional sense, but a "spiritual resemblance" should also be inherent: "realism", if you like, but a transcendental realism.'[82]

In 1936, Baylis was a delegate to the Paris Congress of the International Federation of Business and Professional Women.[83] The theme was 'Women's Contribution to the Modern World.' The principal speaker was Miss Frances Perkins, USA Secretary for Labour, and the English speakers were 'Miss Lilian Baylis; Miss Caroline Haslett OBE, Electrical Engineer (Director of the Electrical Association for Women); Miss Irene Ward MP; and Miss Helena Normanton, Barrister.'[84] In her address Baylis said, 'Women have done great things for the theatre, not only in our times but in an almost unbroken line for over a century.' She listed the names of many outstanding theatre managers 'in London and in other great cities of England,'[85] including her own aunt Emma Cons. She went on to outline her own progress with the Old Vic and later the Sadler's Wells theatre. 'The Vic-Wells were the first theatres to have their amusement tax removed because the Government agreed that the Vic-Wells is an educational asset to the country, not only a place of entertainment ... We are the National Theatre in all but financial support from the State'.[86] Miss Caroline Haslett wrote to Baylis after the Congress thanking her for a contribution, saying also, 'It was sweet of you to leave me the ten francs for the taxi fare, but it was quite unnecessary,' (OVLB 000150/4).

---

[82] Maritain, Essay, 'The Frontiers of Poetry', in *Art and Scholasticism with other Essays* [London: Sheed and Ward], 1933, p. 96.

[83] 26 July to 1 August.

[84] Bristol University Theatre Archive, OVLB 000152.

[85] And also including Mrs Henderson at the Windmill Theatre, Lady Gregory at the Abbey Theatre, Dublin, Miss Horniman's Repertory in Manchester.

[86] *The Era*, 26 August 1936, p. 20.

One characteristic runs through all the accounts of Lilian Baylis's work in pursuit of her aims – that of 'an extraordinary sense of what one can only call family affection and family pride' within the theatre.[87] In the *Churchman's Handbook* for 1936, Baylis wrote an article on 'Church and Stage'. In it she told of the time when one of her staff was trying to make up her mind to go and hear sermons at church in Lent, or to attend the Old Vic performances of Shakespeare. Baylis recorded that she had replied, 'At church you will hear only the old, old story; you are given the *Winter's Tale* and *The Taming of the Shrew* at the Vic. Leontes had years of unhappiness through giving way to jealousy, and Katherine was never happy either till she had conquered her temper.' So she compromised by giving her member of staff two nights off a week – one for church and one for Shakespeare.[88] Baylis might have been a devout Christian, but she was able to distinguish between what is derogatively known as 'churchianity' on the one hand, and true Christian devotion and spirituality on the other: she could expound theological themes and instruction from Art as well as from conventional religion.[89]

Even Sir Ben Greet, as early as 1917, recognised that the Old Vic had a social function.[90] This feeling of corporateness extended to the audience. The *Old Vic* magazine, launched in 1919, saw itself as 'some tangible expression of the interest and affection felt by those before the curtain and vice versa.' Joan Cross recalled later that the audience responded, equally in drama and opera, with understanding, devotion, and loyalty ... It was their theatre as well as Miss Baylis's. The close relationship between audience and artists was a vital ingredient of Baylis's legacy.[91] The theatre was unique, both in policy and in clientele. Hugh Walpole described a long queue outside Sadler's Wells for a revival of *Die Meistersinger*

---

[87] Edward J. Dent, quoted Gilbert, p. 27.
[88] *The Era*, 3 January 1936, p. 2.
[89] On another occasion she rebuked an actor for 'droning like an old clergyman', rather than acting in character [BBC Memorial Programme, 29 July 1952, p. 32 of script, M & M Theatre Collection].
[90] Gilbert, p. 25.
[91] ibid., pp. 27, 28, and 29.

von Nürnberg on 5 January 1938: 'Inside there was so much enjoyment radiating from the stage out to the audience and back to the stage again. The spirit of Lilian Baylis lived on long after her death, and remained a constant and lasting inspiration for the company she had created. Baylis had made it very easy and simple for an onlooker to feel he is sharing in a creative art.'[92]

The Assessment of Others

Lilian Baylis was very unprepossessing in appearance, and she was not of a mind to make any radical changes in it. She was described, variously as looking like 'a seaside landlady', 'a charwoman', 'a schoolmarm', or, most frequently, like 'a parish visitor' or 'social worker'.[93] Dame Sybil Thorndike, who later became a very good friend, wrote to her brother, Russell, that 'she looks like a church worker, and is one'.[94]

Baylis always operated on the tightest of financial budgets. Her artists were never in any doubt that they were to be paid only meagrely, but they gave of their best nevertheless. They knew well that she was even harder on herself than on them. 'She was paid only a pittance to run the Royal Victoria Hall.'[95] They were also quite clear on her motivation – her work was a commission from God, and as he was very much with her in it, he would always provide what was needed. She had a great capacity for inspiring devotion in those who worked for her, who were convinced of her personal integrity and the worthiness of her high artistic ideals, Some people described her as headstrong, autocratic, fiery-tempered, over-forthright, especially when her inspirations and principles were questioned, but the sufferers were aware that it was all without malice. She attracted affection and loyalty from all sorts

---

[92] ibid., p. 63.
[93] Findlater, p. 19.
[94] ibid., p. 123.
[95] ibid., p. 19.

183

and conditions of men and women, an affection which survived even strong disagreements.

Sir Hugh Walpole distinguished three opinions which she generated in those who worked with her, or observed her methods:

1. Dislike: too careful about money; a prude about morals; ill-educated; a brute, selfish, conceited, a fanatical egoist. One or two hated her, simply detested her with that vehemence of hatred which only remarkable people can arouse.

2. Some regarded her as humorous, affectionate, a faithful friend; great, courageous and inspired...

3. Others saw her as a saint, completely unique as all geniuses are, a divine fanatic, a St Francis, a Florence Nightingale, a Madame Curie.[96] Walpole thought that 'In Lilian Baylis there were at least two personalities, apparently irreconcilable ... I have never known anyone at all like her ... [Her] supreme gift was getting other people to perform miracles for her ... her belief in God, as a practical ally, was astonishing in its intensity.'[97]

She was described by one biographer as 'maverick and eccentric', but the same writer spoke of her as 'A high-powered professional woman who enjoyed networking with other successful career women; the international traveller; the strategist who could (mostly) get what she wanted even when arguing about finances with [the] economist John Maynard Keynes.'[98] Her religious faith was manifested not only in her unselfconscious recourse to consultation with God before replying to a request for a decision on an urgent subject, but also in her honesty, for her respect and honour for

---

[96] E.G. Harcourt Williams, in *Vic-Wells: The Work of Lilian Baylis* [London: Ed. Cobden Sanderson, 1938], p. 2.
[97] Sir Hugh Walpole, quoted from the review by R.P.P. Rowe in *The Listener* Supplement VIII, 18 May 1938.
[98] Schafer, p. 5.

all with whom she had to do, her simplicity and lack of guile or affectation. Beatrice Wilson, one of her actresses, recalled being interviewed by her. She was told of the pay and conditions, and in the same breath was asked, 'Do you believe in God?' It was not a condition of employment, but the manager liked to know how much support she had from her staff. Later, Wilson was asked to stand in for an actress who was too ill to play. Baylis said, as she helped Wilson to dress, 'Good girl to come. Thank you. I asked God to send you, and he never lets down the Old Vic,' – an illustration of her unfussy way of expressing her appreciation, and concern for the people she employed, together with an acknowledgement of who was really in charge of the whole enterprise.

Among the many anecdotes quoted to exemplify her alleged meanness was her prayer during the early days of the Old Vic, during the Great War: 'O God, send me good actors, but send them cheap.' Beatrice Wilson commented on this, saying it was practical and natural, when men were at a premium and there was little with which to pay. Wilson was convinced that Baylis made her famous gaffes in a spirit of mischief, to amuse people. 'She could always laugh at herself. She was sincere and exuberant, seeming to be the only real person present.'[99] 'Jokes at her expense were all right. Laughing at the Old Vic, never.'[100]

Tyrone Guthrie, who had succeeded Harcourt Williams as Director of Plays in 1933, recounted an occasion when she swarmed up a ladder to the proscenium during the garden scene in Gounod's *Faust* to eject a drunken fireman who was blaspheming against God in the middle of a quiet passage. She fought him in the fly gallery and forced him down the ladder in front of her, praying to God to give her strength to hold him in case he slipped.[101]

John Gielgud, one of the many actors and dancers who worked

---

[99] Harcourt Williams, pp. 9–14.
[100] Findlater, p. 135.
[101] Harcourt Williams, pp. 15–16.

with her and laid the foundation of a glowing career,[102] wrote of her after her death as 'A great Christian, great personality, and a strong sense of humour. She had a clear trust in all who worked for her, and her own selfless example of perseverance. She inspired me with awe, with admiration, and with affection.'[103] At the age of 25 Gielgud had been at a turning-point in his career when, dissatisfied with the West End, he was looking for a place in which to develop his ideas and exercise his talents under guidance. An invitation from Harcourt Williams to join the Old Vic Company seemed a right opportunity, but he approached his interview with Baylis with caution, trying to look 'rather arrogant, as I always do when money is discussed'. She put him in his place at once, greeting him with, 'How nice to see you, dear. Of course, we'd love to have you here, but of course we can't afford stars.' By the end of the interview, Gielgud recounted, 'I was *begging* her to let me join the company.'[104]

Dame Sybil Thorndike remembered a comment made to her by Sir Oliver Lodge after a performance of George Bernard Shaw's *St Joan*. He said, 'You are a fortunate person – no one can touch *St Joan* without being bettered.' She replied, 'I feel that about Lilian.'[105] During the run of the play, she said later, she had realised how like the peasant saint Baylis was, and observed that Shaw had grasped what was meant by a saint – 'one who has a vision of God and the work she is called to do: no thought of self, just a shouldering of a burden with never-ceasing courage – never sitting down and saying "I've done enough …".'. Joan must have been as insistent – as impossible in her demands – as Lilian

---

[102] Among others were Edith Evans, Charles Laughton, Alicia Markova, Margot Fonteyn, Robert Helpmann, Alec Guinness, Lawrence Olivier, James Mason, Michael Redgrave, Alastair Sim, and Peggy Ashcroft.

[103] Harcourt Williams, p. 18.

[104] Findlater, p. 201. Val Gielgud, when adjudicating at the Buxton Play Festival in 1937, mentioned that his brother 'Probably owed the success of his career to having played for Miss Baylis at the Old Vic.' [Newspaper cutting, untitled and undated, in the Sadler's Wells Archive, the Local Library Section, Finchley Library, Reference 201A Moxley.]

[105] Harcourt Williams, p. 17.

was.' [As] Shaw said of St Joan, "She was miraculous, and she was unbearable".'[106] Thorndike unintentionally inspired something of a backlash against Baylis during her preparation for playing *St Joan* by being explicit about the fact that she was basing her characterisation on Baylis. 'She's so like you,' she said in a letter to her. Thorndike repeated this comparison many times during her long life, to the fury of some of Baylis's detractors.[107]

Baylis was unfailingly encouraging with the artists. An actor, Ernest Milton, recalled that after he had played in the *Merchant of Venice* in 1918, she said, 'Beautiful, my dear, beautiful. But you will do better.' 'I was her slave for ever,' said Milton. He was offered a new job elsewhere in 1922: 'Lilian wasn't at all anxious to release me. She was in two minds about it. As was her habit when faced with a difficult decision, she resorted to prayer in her office, and emerged from this retirement to announce "I'll let you go, dear; but they must pay you well".'[108]

Milton also witnessed to her private generosity: 'Her love for [humankind] was spontaneous. It needed no whipping-up by a desire to be good. Many an actor, fallen on hard times, had a helping hand from her; her private charities were efficacious, unobtrusive, unpublished.'[109] Milton continued, 'an innate taste made her repudiate the meretricious and the shoddy, even if it filled the house. I have heard her say "I can't bear this, Ernest. It isn't Shakespeare, it isn't anything." But she could go into transports of grateful pleasure if the success were also truly beautiful; and when a commercial failure was truly beautiful she prayed for the regeneration of the benighted who has not seen that beauty.'[110]

The conductor of her orchestra, Charles Corri, was suddenly taken ill at the launching of *Tosca* and *The Marriage of Figaro* at the Old Vic, and she asked his assistant, Lawrance Collingwood,

---

[106] Thorndike, p. 99.
[107] Schafer, p. 94.
[108] Quoted, Harcourt Williams, pp. 54 and 55.
[109] ibid., p. 57.
[110] ibid., p. 56.

if he would conduct the orchestra, which he did, and without a hitch. But Baylis told him that she felt Corri's illness was a punishment from God because she had lately been praying for an opportunity to introduce another conductor into the company, as Corri would, after 16 years of service, soon be wanting to retire. Her prayer was granted, but she was horrified to think that she might have been the cause of Corri's illness. This was an illustration of her compassion for her staff, but further theological reflection, or guidance from her spiritual adviser (which she may well have sought at her next Confession with Fr Andrew), would have made clear that her feeling of guilt was inappropriate: God answers prayers in a wide variety of ways, some very unexpected, and his answers, however shocking, included, integrally, a vast and comprehensive love and compassion for long-term welfare of all those involved, including the one who seemed to suffer the most.

An interesting comparison was referred to by Harcourt Williams, her Director of Plays: 'Lilian Baylis has been compared sometimes to St Teresa of Avila. Well, saints are [not] always easy people to get on with, but she certainly had something of that saint's driving power and humility. Humility before God, not before her antagonists! Her driving power was tempered with a ready wit, and her humility did not exclude the unshakeable belief that heaven and all the angels were on the side of the Old Vic and Sadler's Wells.[111] When founding a convent against strong opposition, St Teresa went to the only friend she could rely on: "My Lord," she said on her knees, "This house is not mine, it is yours; all that I could do is done. You must see to it now." The same may be said of Lilian Baylis and her theatres.'[112] A similar example of Baylis's continuous 'companionship' with God was when, during the war, an actress was taken ill, and she began to telephone for a substitute. As she stood with the speaker to her mouth she said,

---

[111] BBC Memorial Programme, 29 July 1952, Script p. 6.
[112] Harcourt Williams (Ed.), *Vic-Wells: The Work of Lilian Baylis*, p. 47.

'God, you've got me into this mess; you have got to get me out of it. You must help me.' A mystified operator said, 'I beg your pardon,' and Lilian explained, 'I'm so sorry. I quite forgot there was someone else on the line.'[113]

Few people had more opportunity to study her closely than her secretary, Evelyn M. Williams, who remembered 'Her courage in making decisions, which usually seemed lunacy but were always right. Some have suggested she was a superwoman [but] she was too near and too human – and in that lay her great strength.' Williams recalled two things in particular that were said to her: 'I'll have no free love in my theatre.' Then, having asked about her religious beliefs, 'I'm asking you this now, because if you came and worked with me we'll never have time to discuss them again.' Williams remarked, 'She was kind and cheerful, but she could also be maddening; there were days and weeks when she would just not make up her mind. ... It was a long time before one could accept this hiatus with optimism – actually, nine times out of ten ... she had been right in postponing action. By some miracle, she would make us all anxious to overwork, and unwilling to go home ... it was her humanity, not her brilliance, that would make us feel that the theatre was ours, and that we must give it everything we had, of intelligence, of energy and of thought. I think it was important that the standard she set was always attainable, but never the final one.' Evelyn Williams also remembered that 'When an artist had secured a well-paid engagement with another company at a moment when some were inclined to talk of "Sweated Labour" at the Vic, she could say triumphantly, "I knew the Lord would prove that we were helping our people".'[114]

Harcourt Williams commented that 'her whole life was a triumph of faith and intuition over cold facts. She was very much like the Wife of Bath in her warm humanity [and] her blend of religion and earthiness: she had amazing vitality and creative

---

[113] Findlater, pp. 141 and 142.
[114] BBC Memorial Programme Script, pp. 32–35. Mander and Mitchenson Theatre Collection.

powers.'[115] Evelyn Williams gave a talk on *Woman's Hour* in 1948, in which she testified to the impact that Baylis's faith had had on all around her: 'Her faith in God was that of the saints of old, who wrestled with him. He was so real that when things went wrong she tackled him as one would a friend; he had given her this job, surely he owed her the miracle which alone would enable her to get on with it. The Old Vic and Sadler's Wells exist today because a plump little woman without much education but with a wide humanity, ruthless drive, and a great faith, heard voices, and obeyed them.'[116]

Kathleen Clark, who worked in the box office, recalled, 'She knew each and every member of the companies, and the waits between scenes were enlivened by ... little intimate kindly enquiries about the wives, husbands, children ... of the actors and actresses. She always insisted, when honours were conferred on her, that it was *not* on herself but on the work – which, she said, included us all.' Regarding her 'blend of religion and earthiness', numerous are the anecdotal examples. Clark recounts that Baylis disliked the habit of girls wearing their trousers at their work, but when the actress Esmé Church argued that it was sensible garb for their acrobatics, fencing, eurhythmics and so on, Lilian said, 'Yes, I suppose you are right, dear, but if a girl has pretty ankles, it seems a pity to hide them.' She once referred to a distinguished opera producer as 'That man with the nice legs,' which was not the expected answer. 'You never did get the answer you expected, and that made it such fun,' said her secretary, Evelyn Williams. 'When we remember her it is not with tears but with affectionate laughter. She would have liked that.'[117]

After a dress rehearsal for *Measure for Measure* in which the Isabella was so chillingly chaste that the scenes with Angelo were becoming passionless, Baylis commented, 'Well, dear, all we can

---

[115] Harcourt Williams, pp. 29–33.
[116] Published in *The Listener*, 25 December 1948. Mander and Mitchenson Theatre Collection.
[117] ibid., p. 64.

do now is get on our knees and pray for lust.'[118] One of the clerks, Irene Beeston, recalled her pugnacity in another direction. In the early penurious days, when artists and stage and front of house staff were giving their services free, she did not see why they should have to pay for lighting during the presentations. 'Write to the electricity people,' she said, 'and tell them that if they will deduct the cost of this performance from their bill, I shall be very glad to print it on the programme. Tell them that if they don't feel they can let me have the light free, I'll print that too.' The 'electricity people' were happy to oblige.[119]

Sir Hugh Walpole said, 'People have talked and written about her conceit, but ... in all those years I never saw any sign of it. She was rather comic, but extraordinarily inspiring.' Harcourt Williams remembered one occasion when she was very tired, and said, 'I am going to pray for a bit more physique. I've got a rotten body.' She was asked, 'Do you think you will get it if you pray for it?' 'Of course,' she replied, 'if it is right for me to have it ... and it *is* right for me, just now.' 'That's rather like dictating to God.' 'Oh well, he understands me, my dear ... that's the great thing, to be quite natural yourself with God,' she replied.[120]

Towards the end of the war, despite the financial anxieties, she gave 'a dramatised version of Mendelssohn's *Elijah* on Sundays, and from the proceeds of these performances was able to send several hundred pounds to the Church Army and YMCA huts at the front.'[121]

Shortly after the war, with the mounting popularity of the theatre and its diversified use for drama and opera, the state of the building began to give the County Council cause for alarm. It was clear that a public appeal would have to be launched, and in 1921 the target was set at £30,000. It was launched in the November with distinguished signatories – Lady Frederick Cavendish, Dame Ethel

---

[118] Schafer, p. 246.
[119] Harcourt Williams, pp. 49 and 50.
[120] ibid., pp. 3, 4 and 5.
[121] Bristol University Theatre Archive, OVLB 000149/2.

Smyth, the Bishops of Southwark,[122] and Manchester,[123] and three political leaders – Asquith, Bonar Law, and J.H. Thomas.[124] It went well to start with, but by the first six months only £5000 had been raised. It was a bad time for Baylis; she was obliged to take a convalescent holiday after a bicycle accident, but while she was away her prayers were answered suddenly: the whole of the £30,000 had been offered by an anonymous donor, who was later revealed to be the theatrical manager, George Dance.[125]

Bruce Worsley[126] recalled that 'One day, when discussing possible retrenchment, the Lady said "No, no – we must have faith: Nature is tireless in her efforts to re-capture the ground she has lost".'[127] An Incarnational theology will see analogies with God's working in the natural world. Alan Pryce Jones[128] had some perceptive observations on Baylis's ability to 'create an audience'. 'She has given, or revived,' he said, 'an unacademic spontaneous atmosphere of delight in her theatre, which hangs about the entire building from the moment the doors are opened.' He also observed that 'In the theatre there is no division of plays into high-brow or low-brow. There is only good and bad. The one valid intellectual division is of audiences, which are perceptive or not, and it takes a Miss Baylis to train an audience in perception, by constantly presenting them with excellent things, but above all (since ordinary people are easily lost among masterpieces) by allowing her own personality to be felt at all times as something constant and human in a world of abstract values.'[129]

Professor Edward Joseph Dent (1856–1957), one of the theatre

---

[122] Cyril Foster Garbett.
[123] William Temple.
[124] Liberal, Conservative, and Labour, respectively.
[125] Findlater, pp. 168 and 169. George Dance (1857–1932), librettist, and theatre manager. He was knighted in 1923 for services to the theatre, including his gift to the 'Old Vic'.
[126] Ernest Bruce Digby-Worsley (1899–1980), highly successful fighter pilot in World War I, 1918. On retirement became manager of Sadler's Wells theatre.
[127] Harcourt Williams, p. 37.
[128] 1908–2000. Editor of *The Times Literary Supplement*, and Trustee of the Old Vic Theatre.
[129] Harcourt Williams, pp. 69 and 68.

governors, was at first very sceptical of the whole set-up at the Old Vic. He 'found Lilian Baylis difficult of approach on a first meeting; I was certainly not the only one. Ben Greet, in a letter to Sybil Thorndike, wrote, "There's a strange woman running a theatre in the Waterloo Road".' He quotes Granville[130] as saying, 'Queer woman, Lilian Baylis ... I don't think she knows anything about these plays, but I think she's got something.' Dent expressed doubts about the opinions of those who professed admiration for her: people who 'wrote about her as "a great lady"; anything less like a grande dame one could not imagine, though she had an ungainly dignity of her own. Her voice was about the most disagreeable that I have ever heard issue from female lips. The ugly aspects of her, her close-fistedness and her harsh and almost offensive manner of speaking were the results of her environment ... an unending struggle against poverty and despair, the repellent crust of hardness was a protective armour that she had either secreted subconsciously or deliberately assumed as a defence against all sorts of spiritual enemies.'

It is clear that Dent had serious doubts about her professional suitability, and was unappreciative of her religious motivation. He was highly suspicious of Father Andrew, whom he characterised as 'haunting' the theatre, 'his tall and sinister-looking figure gliding silently in the shadows of the theatre, suggesting a Grand Inquisitor from the score of some forgotten opera by Mercadentes or Donizetti'. He did, however, come to see Baylis differently, acknowledging that finding her difficult to get on with was his own fault, not hers. 'I had all sorts of prejudices to live down,' he admitted.[131] He had at first formed the opinion that the only hope of opera at the Old Vic lay with the removal of Miss Baylis,

---

[130] Harley Granville-Barker (1877–1946), actor, producer, playwright, Shakespeare scholar, and innovatory theatre manager.
[131] His own 'environment' was that of a son of the landed gentry class, born at Ribston Hall, North Yorkshire, seat of the Goodrich family for 300 years, and bought by Joseph Dent in 1836. He was educated at Eton and King's College, Cambridge, and was Professor of Music at Cambridge University from 1926 to 1941.

but came gradually to the view that 'she was the one person whose presence was indispensable'. 'A woman,' he said, 'of deep fundamental goodness and kindness of heart, and this made a peculiarly loveable woman who could hold that entire theatre – those two entire theatres – firmly together, united, if for no other cause than in personal loyalty to herself.' He was happy eventually to count himself 'as a humble member of the family'.[132]

Sumner Austin, one of Baylis's singers and producers, thought that two of her most salient characteristics were her perception of people, and her integrity. She never minced her words, but never went back on her word. She was not mean with money, but paid what she could afford. She took nothing for herself, and never spared herself, and she expected others to be altruistic. In the 1919–1920 season, at a time of more than usual privation, she paid the salary of the pianist (Lawrance Collingwood) herself.[133] One drama student, offered a 'walk-on' part in *The Merchant of Venice*, was paid 25 shillings a week for the first season, and received from Miss Baylis's own purse at the end a bonus of seven shillings and sixpence, 'For shoe leather, dear.'[134] 'For some fourteen hours a day [she] worked, talked, ate, and drank – but never slept – in her tiny office,' said Austin. 'For her, the words "tact" and "diplomacy" had no meaning … though once really cornered she could admit defeat with disarming frankness.' She insisted that Austin, the producer of the opera *Hansel and Gretel*, should go down to the leper colony at Moorhouse and give a performance. Sunday was the one day of rest for the principals, but the suggestion that the understudies should go instead met with intransigence: 'They may be only a small colony, but they shall have the best.' She took it for granted that the half-dozen principals should support her pet charity. 'The faithful support that we tried to give her,' Austin said, 'was but an echo of the genuine affection

---

[132] Dent, *A Theatre for Everybody* [London: T.V. Boardman and Company Limited, 1945], pp. 39–41.
[133] Findlater, p. 158.
[134] ibid., p. 132.

and staunch loyalty she had increasingly shown to us. The utter selflessness of her nature swept like a storm wind among the nooks and crannies of petty jealousies and personal ambitions ... There were few that did not sometimes feel poor and mean before her simple, generous, unflagging and undaunted soul.'[135] St John Ervine remembered that 'She once told me that she had been worried about Mr Ernest Milton when he was performing in a production of Hamlet in its entirety. I think he was giving two performances that day. "I thought he might be tired," she said, "so I gave him an egg for his tea." She was that sort of woman, always telling you to wrap up well, and giving you an egg for your tea. But she did not give herself many eggs.'

Clive Carey,[136] a singer and producer with the company, said that at first the opera productions were seen as a poor relation of the Shakespeare Company, but 'there was in these performances (*The Magic Flute, The Marriage of Figaro, Don Giovanni*) more than a spark of real fire, and that we were part of something that was going to grow into much greater completeness. It was without doubt the fire of Baylis's spirit that kindled us. She was out to give Shakespeare and opera to all the world, and it was up to us to help her to do it! She had faith that her work would grow, and with it her audiences and the money for the enterprise increase. And she was right.[137]

Laurence Olivier was born in 1907, the son of a Tractarian priest. In 1917 he became one of the 14 boarders of the school attached to All Saints Margaret Street, the church where Lilian Baylis had been baptised. It was not surprising, then, that he and she should be kindred spirits. After juvenile acting had shown his great promise, a major turning-point came when Tyrone Guthrie

---

[135] Harcourt Williams, pp. 84, 85, and 86.
[136] Francis Clive Savill Carey (1883–1968). Sherborne School, Clare College Cambridge; singer, opera producer, and composer. He served as a major in World War I, then on the staff of the Royal College of Music. CBE, 1955. [*Dictionary of National Biography*, OUP]. Volume 10, pp. 69 and 70.
[137] Harcourt Williams, pp. 91 and 92.

invited him to lead the Old Vic Company in the 1937/38 season, which firmly established him as an actor.[138] One critic's acute comment on Olivier's performance in the film *Henry V* (1945) was that 'Laurence Olivier's "Henry V" shone with a spiritual splendour, a quality as rare in actors as it is in other human beings.'[139] Olivier and Baylis had 'a mutual respect and affection'. With Ralph Richardson and John Gielgud he praised her shrewdness, loyalty, dedication, motherliness and all her other virtues.[140]

Several members of Baylis's 'family' were deeply influenced by her faith. Winifred Oughton[141] recalled, 'If she hadn't got the money, she went down on her knees in that poky little office of hers with anyone handy who would do the same thing, and bully until God sent her the money; and he did. There's no denying it. The money came.' Tyrone Guthrie also observed that 'There was a great deal of praying in her office.'[142] Elizabeth H.C. Corathiel, Press Agent for the Old Vic, remembered that the office 'Had an enormous crucifix on the wall, and a "crib" at Christmas, some holy pictures which changed from time to time, except one which remained constant – a picture of Durer's "Praying Hands".'[143] J.B. Marriott, in a memorial article on Baylis in 1968, recalled that 'She prayed to God for cash, and usually he sent her some quickly, by return on occasion … God certainly was in her head and [in her] understanding.'[144]

Spiritual Life

The Baylis children had been brought up in a family whose life was centred on religion. The children took part in study groups, and

---

[138] Robert Tannich, *Olivier* [Thomas Hudson, 1985], pp. 8 and 9.
[139] John Mason Brown, *Saturday Review of Literature*, quoted by Robert Tannich.
[140] Findlater, ibid., pp. 271 and 289.
[141] 1890–1964. Actress and writer.
[142] In an article in *The Stage*, 19 November 1950. Mander and Mitchenson Collection.
[143] *The Stage*, 19 November 1950; article, 'Old Vic Memories'.
[144] Press cutting, newspaper name not recorded. Mander and Mitchenson Collection.

Lilian began her education with a governess employed by a local vicar and later went on to a convent school – St Augustine's, Kilburn – and maintained a life-long connection with the nuns there. She grew up with an unswerving sense of the reality of the spiritual world, and the continuous presence of God in her normal life.[145] She recorded in private documents several occasions when she had direct experience of that presence: during the time that she was working as an assistant to her aunt Emma her parents returned from South Africa for a special operation, and because they were beset by financial troubles, she arranged for them to come and live with her. The strain of re-adjusting her household and the pressure of work caused her to have eye problems, and the report of the ophthalmologist was so alarming that she feared for her sight. She took her prescription to a chemist near the Queen's Hall, and because it was to take half an hour to make up, she went, ill and weary, to All Saints' church for 20 minutes. It was the only time, she related later, that she remembered entering a church and not kneeling. She 'sat and groused' about the burden of caring for her parents, and since her aunt had died only recently, the full weight of her theatre work. 'I told God that even the *Daily Telegraph*, which had seldom failed to note my musical programmes, had taken no notice of our last Wagner performance. I had no praise or thanks in my heart – just one hateful grumble.'

While she was there, the editor of the *Daily Telegraph* rang up one of his staff, who was keen on Baylis's work, telling him to go to the Carlton and interview (Dame Nellie) Melba, who had just arrived in England. Lilian's friend thought it would be a good idea if Melba were to go to the Vic for the performance of *Rigoletto*. 'It was like a royal visit,' said Baylis later. 'She promised to help my work, and the next day sent me a big cheque. I had longed for a word or two in the *Daily Telegraph*: the following morning I had several columns on Melba's visit. My friend told me he was back in his office by one-thirty, everything having been arranged while I

---

[145] Schafer, ibid., p. 13.

was in our beloved church.' 'For Miss Baylis, God was on the staff; she saw herself only as the instrument of God ... and that is why she saw other people, too, as agents of his will.'[146]

The first time she 'heard a voice out of the elements' was at the age of about 18 one lovely moonlit night in South Africa. She had walked up to the brow of a hill with a young man who had paid her much attention during the week that she and her family had given concerts in the district. He expressed his sadness at her leaving and asked for a farewell kiss, which was granted. Unfortunately his passion conquered him, and he held her to him, kissing her repeatedly. She distinctly heard the voice of her old schoolmistress (a nun), saying, 'Lilian, Lilian,' in surprised tones, and managing to release herself from his strong embrace, waved a friendly farewell and ran back to her parents. A few weeks later she had a letter saying the owner of the voice that had spoken to her had died on that day.[147]

About ten years later, while Baylis was working one Friday night – paynight – a ne'er-do-well brother of a dear friend came to the office to try to borrow money, which was refused.He then began to make violent advances to her. Immediately outside the door was a large box, in which after an opera many of the costumes were packed by the dresser, a woman who had worked at the theatre for many years. She was folding away the dresses on this particular evening. A young singer, who had been to borrow an opera score shortly before, was standing a few feet away from the door, and there was also a messenger, Bob, waiting to have his petty cash bill passed. All three were anxiously waiting for Baylis to dismiss her visitor and get on with the night's work. The man became more and more amorous; Baylis knew that if she called out, one of her staff would come to her aid, but she felt ashamed they would know she was being insulted ... She sent up a silent prayer to be helped to conquer the man without

---

[146] Findlater, ibid., pp. 109 and 110.
[147] Bristol University Theatre Archive, OVLB 000155/3; written in the third person.

calling for assistance. Suddenly, there was a violent knock at the door and the handle turned imperatively as if someone was at once entering the door. The man dropped her and she rushed to the door, opened it, and found the three people with their eyes on the door but all three answered that they had not knocked, and not one had heard a knock. The knock was so loud and determined and the handle turning so sharp just behind the man's back, that he heard it distinctly and pulled himself together.[148]

Some 15 years later Baylis asked Rosina Filippi[149] to run Shakespeare for her at the Old Vic. The season started with a full house, but the show being second rate – nearly all Filippi's pupils instead of a professional company – the audience dwindled to a few dozen, really empty houses. Baylis couldn't sleep and in her despair after soaking her pillow with her tears cried out to God to help her in the work she had not chosen but had been thrust into. A strong manly voice came out of the darkness. 'Why have you allowed my beautiful words to be so murdered?' She replied, 'I know something about music and can run operas, but I'm not an actress and I had to ask a good player to help me.' 'You must run them yourself as you do the operas,' said this strong calm male voice. 'I don't know enough about Shakespeare. I don't feel able to cast plays,' she argued. 'You are to choose your company of players and run the plays yourself,' continued this calm good voice. She fell asleep and next day started to get together her first company of Shakespeare players.[150] In an interview with J.L. Hodson for the *Westminster Gazette*[151] she defended this account, saying, 'I am a religious woman, but I am not a Spiritualist and I believe the voice was Divine.'[152]

About eight years later (aet 51) Baylis had a bad cycling accident, in which she hurt her knee and which shocked her nerves. She

---

[148] Baylis, ibid.
[149] Actress and drama school proprietor.
[150] Baylis, ibid.
[151] 28 April 1930.
[152] Mander and Mitchenson Collection.

ought to have had a good nurse with her but just let the maid help, and tried to keep the seriousness of the accident from her aged parents. The pain of the knee was beyond words ... and a sort of rigour set in, the whole body shaking, making the very bed vibrate. She felt cold and dreadfully ill; the pain was beyond her control and she could hardly refrain from crying out. After one of these bad attacks of pain, she lay for several hours shaking with cold and misery; she tried to say the *Veni Creator* but could not remember anything beyond the first few lines. She called on God for comfort and suddenly felt as if she were being lifted up on most lovely downy pillows, a soft beautiful bed of ease. All pain left her, all cold shivers disappeared and perfect comfort of body came to her. She was first conscious of a quiet peace, and then the ceiling of her room vanished and one unending sea of silver took its place; a glorious silver dove was directly over her and radiating from this dove (the Holy Ghost) was this wonderful sea of ... (the manuscript breaks off here).[153]

In the spring of 1931 Baylis motored to Shellness, Isle of Sheppey, to stay the weekend with a friend. One large garage housed all the cars for the visitors on a Saturday and Sunday, but she left her car outside, in case hers should be blocked in on the Sunday morning. But someone arrived late at night and it was well wedged in.

It took 20 minutes to shift the other cars before she and her chauffeur could start out for the nearest church, three miles away, at ten to eight. Although they had enquired the day before about the times of the Sunday services, they found on arrival that no service was being held. She decided to go another eight miles to the beautiful old church at Eastchurch, if only for the end of the service. The priest had just turned to communicate those at the altar rail, and she felt it was too late to go up, but she suddenly saw our Lord kneeling in the Lady Chapel. A year later she visited Sheppey again and stopped to pray at Eastchurch. She knelt in

---

[153] Bristol University Theatre Archive, OVLB 000153/3.

the Lady Chapel and looked at the place where our Lord had knelt. She wondered if the window had a large figure of Christ. With the strong morning sun she thought that if there was a large figure it might have been photographed in her eyes or reflected in some way, but the window, though beautiful, had no figure of Christ. She felt it so keenly that on leaving the church she called at the vicarage next door to tell the good priest her vision and how it had helped her when difficulties of work had to be faced. She found the priest had been dead some months and had been sick for a year before; he was greatly loved and respected by his people as he was very saintly. Baylis believed he was so near Christ and so longed for prayer by the Blessed Sacrament, that our Lord came to that little chapel at the good priest's desire – and that she saw Him also.

When very overtired before going to South Africa for a rest, she had two cables asking her to speak, and this so frightened her she almost longed to cancel her passage. Praying about her fears during the Children's Service on Corpus Christi Day, she heard a strong voice speaking from the Reserved Sacrament: 'My Grace is sufficient for thee,' and she felt calm and fearless once more.[154]

Baylis had other experiences of divine support and encouragement, which she recorded in her notebook. It was obvious why she wanted to keep them private, apart from brief mentions to close friends. Mid-twentieth-century views on religious phenomena, seen in the interpretive light of psychology and scientific positivism, were such that anything suggesting the 'paranormal', and lack of objective repeatable verification, was likely to evoke ridicule or outright rejection.

In private Baylis acted as a spiritual adviser to those who asked her for guidance. In a letter of 2 March 1918 to Ivy Smithson, a young friend, she apologised for not answering sooner a letter from her friend, but in these difficult times (air raids) expressed

---

[154] Baylis, ibid.

her confidence that 'if one can only hold on, all will be well'. The friend reported on a recent Retreat, and Baylis was glad that 'your church is really alive, and you must have great joy from it'. She said she was 'not a member of the English Church Union, though my father was one of the first members over fifty years ago. It is a splendid society.' But as she belonged to the Confraternity of the Blessed Sacrament and an associate of two religious communities, 'that is as much as I can manage.' She wrote of attending a Quiet Day at St Mathew's Westminster before Lent, and how Father Andrew, in his first address, on Art and Music, spoke of his joy at having such a theatre (as The Old Vic) made her feel really ill: 'Such praise from the pulpit by a saintly priest.' She felt unworthy of belonging to the Society of the Divine Compassion – Andrew's Order – 'with its motto "Put on the Divine Compassion", so great and loving are those men [sc. the Community].' She gives her friend, who finds 'great succour' in catholic devotions – saying that she herself 'doesn't believe much in books as in meditation – a lengthy commentary on the Stations of the Cross and the Mysteries of the Rosary,' indicating clearly how she conducted her own meditations.[155]

Father Andrew was her main support and interpreter for more than 30 years. E.G. Harcourt Williams, at the end of his collection of memories – first-hand witness accounts of Baylis from 28 of her staff and friends, *Vic-Wells: The Work of Lilian Baylis* – gave the last six pages over to Father Andrew, who headed his contribution 'A Friend of God'. 'Nobody would have dreamed,' he wrote, 'of suggesting to Lilian Baylis that she was a holy woman, for fear of what her answer would be. But without any doubt at all the marks of a vital sanctity were to be found in her character.'[156] In a tribute after her death he wrote, 'She was first of all a Christian: quite unconventional, she was never unorthodox. Her worship on Sundays and Holy Days, her observance of Lent, her spiritual reading, her

---

[155] Mander and Mitchenson Collection.
[156] Harcourt Williams, ibid., p. 101.

communions, confessions, prayers, these things not only had their part in her life, but were the foundation of her life.' As an Associate of Fr Andrew's Order, she kept her Rule with devotion. 'I have heard Lilian say "I have been pretty near swearing at God for the job he has given me to do, but," she has added, with a kind of petulant penitence, "he has never let me down ... I just ask myself, does God want my companies to keep in work and my theatres to go on and am I doing a beautiful work for him? To all this I can say yes quite certainly. Then there is nothing to do but to go on. It is terribly hard to keep my head and my temper, but I just know I have got to do it." She was a woman with a fighting faith, a faith that fought to be true to itself, but not a faith that had to fight for its foundations. Those were always there.[157] She would often say to God with simplicity, "You have got me into this difficulty, and you must get me out of it." She was indeed a woman of faith,' Andrew said, 'that really and truly takes God for granted, and depends upon him as a child depends upon his parents. Hers was a life of hope. Times of retreat were a necessity to her; she never missed a week's retreat in her year, and besides that week there were many days of quiet and hours of retirement that were the secret source of the buoyant hope which was always hers ... She really did pray without ceasing. If there ever was a loving servant of the public,' he wrote, 'it was Lilian Baylis, and there was never one who gave herself more selflessly for the poor and afflicted than she. It was to a colony of afflicted people that she constantly slipped away, taking with her members of her own company to sing and act and cheer those who were shut off by the nature of their malady from the joys that the theatre can give. To these dear people she [brought] brightness and beauty and unforgettable days of wonderful entertainment.'

In the last year of her life Baylis said to Father Andrew, 'I know that if I go on as I am going, my work will kill me; but I don't see why it should be otherwise.'

' "Now abideth Faith, Hope, Love," says the Apostle,' Andrew

---

[157] Bristol University Theatre Archive, OVLB 000354, p. 1.

quoted. 'Whatever National Theatre comes into being will really be born of her creative sacrifice, and she will be its patron saint.'[158]

Towards the end her health began to fail, but she would not give in, although diabetes was a fearful strain. To the last she was chatting gaily, encouraging all around her and listening to strangers with that quiet and eager courtesy which never deserted her.[159] On 23 November 1937 Lilian Baylis had a slight heart attack, and telephoned Fr Andrew to cancel the arrangement she had made with him for her confession the following day. When he offered to go and visit her, she replied that she was not fit to see. 'There was nothing to say to that,' he said later, 'except "God bless you, my dear".' 'I was waiting for you to say that,' were her last words to him. A further heart attack, which she did not survive, occurred on 25 November. 'Thus died a woman whose sympathies were feminine, but whose mind was cast in iron ... She had an amazing power of delegation. She trusted those under her implicitly. Had she lacked this power of delegation ... she would have failed altogether.'[160]

Among her papers, together with a list of people for whom she prayed every day, was found, transcribed in her own handwriting, this prayer by Bishop Carey:

O Holy Spirit of God, come again [in]to my heart and fill
    me:
I open the windows of my soul to let thee in
[I surrender my whole life to thee].
Come and possess me; fill me with light and truth.
[I offer to thee the one thing I really possess,
my capacity for being filled with thee].
Of myself I am an unprofitable servant, an empty vessel:
Fill me that I may live the life of thy Spirit,
the life of truth and goodness

---

[158] Ibid., p. 2.
[159] Magazine, *Great Britain and the East*, 2 December 1937.
[160] Fr Andrew, in Harcourt Williams, ibid., p. 101.

the life of wisdom and strength,
the life of beauty and love.
And guide me today in all things:
guide me to the people I should meet and help...
whether by my actions or by my suffering...
above all make Christ to be formed in me,
that I may dethrone myself in my heart and make him King.
Bind [and cement] me to Christ [by] all ways, known and
    unknown,
by holy thoughts, unseen graces, and sacramental ties,
that he may be in me, and I in him, this day and for ever.[161]

Lilian Baylis's Requiem Mass was celebrated on 30 November at St Agnes Church, Kennington by Father Hutchinson, Vicar of St John's Waterloo Road, and a much-loved friend and chaplain of the two theatres. The church was full, with people standing ten deep at the back. In his address the Bishop of Southwark[162] said, 'She has shown that it was possible, even in these days when such things are much more difficult than ever before, how to maintain a great life, true to the highest ideals and in such a way that the very poorest of the people, as well as all the rest, could enjoy it, enter into it, and have their lives lifted up by it.'[163] The opera staff formed the choir, singing the *Dies Irae*, the hymns, and the Russian Orthodox *Kontakion*, and the coffin was draped with a silver and gold pall of the Actor's Church Union. After the ceremony in St Agnes's, the body was borne through crowded streets to the Old Vic and then to Sadler's Wells and on to Golders Green crematorium, for Father Andrew to take the last

---

[161] Walter J. Carey, DD, MA (1875–1955), who served successively as curate of Lavender Hill, London; Librarian of Pusey House, Oxford; a naval chaplain in the First World War, the Warden of Lincoln Theological College, before his consecration as Bishop of Bloemfontain. Before ordination he received distinction as a Rugby Union Blue. [I am indebted to the Editor of the *Church Times* for this information.] The brackets and elision marks in the prayer indicate slight differences from the original.

[162] Richard Godfrey Parsons, Bishop from 1932 to 1942.

[163] *The London Evening Standard*, 30 November 1937.

rites. Both St John's church and the crematorium chapel were filled to overflowing, and a great congregation assembled on the following day for the Memorial Service at St Martin-in-the-Fields, at which the lesson was read by John Gielgud. The Lord Mayor's Elizabethan Choir augmented the singing, which included music from *Die Meistersinger*. Her ashes were carried to St Philip's church, Plaistow, to be laid in the Guild Ground of the cemetery there, according to her wishes, among the poor. In a letter to a friend, dated 9 December 1937, Andrew wrote, 'Lilian's Requiem and Memorial Service were quite beautiful ... She had the selfless, direct sympathy of a very high quality of sanctity.'[164]

The Revd C.W. Hutchinson wrote in the obituary for the *Church Times*,[165] 'Much has been written of her conception of her work as a divine vocation. That this is so there is no doubt at all, but as it has been popularly represented it almost gives the impression that she used self-conscious phrases about it. As far as my experience goes, that was never the case. Her work was definitely the work God gave her to do. It was a mission and a responsibility, but she was quite devoid of cant about it. The intimations of truth, beauty and goodness that belong to good drama, ballet, and opera, were intimations of God who was the source of all absolute values ... it was these values she was determined to communicate to those who could less afford to apprehend them by the usual means, those whose lives were impoverished of beauty and meagre in rhythm and colour ... Her work and her religion were all bound up together.' In a post-mortem appreciation, Harcourt Williams wrote, 'The beauty of her soul ... burnt its way like a steady flame of blue fire to the things she loved, because they belonged to her idea of God.'[166]

A sound test of whether the work and influence of a person of outstanding leadership achievements, in any walk of life, is of

---

[164] Kathleen M. Bourne, *The Life and Letters of Father Andrew*, SDC [London: A.R. Mowbray and Co. Ltd, 1948], p. 153.
[165] 3 December 1937, p. 649.
[166] *The Listener*, 1 December 1937.

God, or simply from force of personality, is the endurance of what he or she achieved or declared to be their aim. Edward Dent wrote in 1945: 'People said that the Vic and Wells [on Baylis's death] were bound to come to an end, since no one else could ever replace that singular combination of artistic insight and ignorance, personal goodness and hard-headed business capacity, and shrewdness of judgement and human character. None the less the two theatres have continued their work and prospered.'[167] Writing 64 years later, on the work of the English National Opera Company in 2009, Susie Gilbert stated, 'Over the company's existence of 138 years it has overcome countless difficulties – including two world wars. It has adapted to many social and political circumstances since its socialist and humanist idealism of the late nineteenth century and the Christian mission days of Lilian Baylis, to the bombed-out victims of the Blitz, to the young prisoners at Feltham Young Offenders institute in 1991.'[168]

Charles Kraus, chorus manager in 2008 and one of the longest-serving members of the company, confirmed that there was still a sense of loyalty to the company and an undiminished belief in performing opera in the language of the audience. 'I don't know why,' he said. 'Maybe it's the ghost of Lilian Baylis.'[169]

There can be little room for doubt that Lilian Baylis's life demonstrated a fundamental commitment to the spirituality of the Oxford Movement, and that she lived the ethical implications of its doctrines. It is also clear that the theology implicit in the pursuit of Beauty, Truth, and Goodness was exemplified in her work. The Catholic acceptance of the sacramental principle – that God can communicate through the arts, music, drama, painting, poetry and sculpture, was inherent in her commitment to the highest standards of artistic presentation, and that it was for all people, rich and poor, and not simply for a few.

Not only is this clarity referred to in the testimony of her

[167] Dent, ibid., p. 7.
[168] Gilbert, ibid., pp. 583 and 519.
[169] Quoted, Gilbert, ibid., p. 585.

contemporaries, but the endurance of her vision has been secure and lasting: this gives a godly witness to the spiritual strength of her life's work.

Conclusion

Although The Oxford Renewal was initially concerned with the setting out of the Church of England as having an independent identity from the state, it agreed with its establishment so long as the theological principles were preserved, and not subject to the secular arm. It set out the Church as continuing in the Catholic tradition – renewed but not severed by the Reformation, and one of the most significant of its influences has been that, since the Second Vatican Council (1962–1965), the Roman Catholic Church has referred, in its Ecumenical documents, to 'The Catholic Church, the Orthodox Church, the Anglican Church, and Ecclesiastical Communities which arose in the sixteenth century.' The Renewal proceeded to seek the re-emphasis of the eternal truths as set out by the Early Church, especially the doctrine of the Incarnation, and this led to an emphasis on holiness and personal commitment in both clergy and laity. An important element in the Renewal, for both clergy and laity, was the revival of religious orders – monks and nuns in the Church of England – beginning in 1841.

The high point of its influence on Anglicanism came in the middle of the twentieth century, with the promotion of the main Sunday service as 'Parish Communion', with the involvement of all ages and the whole community. Though not entirely Anglo-Catholic, the spirit of the 'Parish and People Movement' was to influence the Church on a widespread scale. With its emphasis on a more 'collegial' form of the parish priest's leadership, the laity were authorised to participate in the liturgy, and in pastoral schemes, such as the appointment of 'street wardens' (or, as preferred in some parishes, 'church visitors'). On the burgeoning housing estates, certain people were trained to keep a watch on their locality for the needs of their neighbours. They could visit on behalf of the parish church, and inform the incumbent of the more 'serious' cases. In these ways, the love of God, personalised in action, had a more profound effect on the populace than set-piece missions, valuable though these could be. The development in some parishes (though much more rare) of a 'Junior Parochial Church Council' encouraged involvement and debate among young members of the church, and the acceptance of their Resolutions by the adult committees.

The influence of the Tractarians remains prominent in the twenty-first century in the legal introduction to the services of Enthronement, Installation and Authorising of Bishops, Priests and Deacons. This declares that 'The Church of England is part of the One, Holy, Catholic and Apostolic Church. It professes the faith uniquely revealed in the Holy Scriptures and set forth in the Catholic Creeds ... Led by the Holy Spirit, it has borne witness to Christian Truth in its historic formularies.' In our time we are seeing an emphasis on the part played by the laity, and their own increasing participation in this ministry.

One of the most prominent of all the successors to Keble, Pusey, Newman and the others was Arthur Michael Ramsey (1904–1988), theologian and Bishop. In his sermon on being Enthroned as Bishop of Durham on St Luke's Day, 18 October 1952,[1] he said:

Let me charge you to serve Christ in his Church above all else with *joyfulness*. Members of the Clergy, rejoice that you are privileged to teach his truth, to celebrate the mystery of

---

[1] Michael Ramsey was later (1956) Archbishop of York, and from 1961 to 1974 the 100th Archbishop of Canterbury.

his body and blood, and to know perhaps his patience and his suffering as you serve him. Let the source and spring of your joy come ... from him. Members of the Laity, rejoice that you are privileged to worship a Creator who made you for himself, to enjoy all the gifts of Christ in his Church, to do all you can in the building up of the common fellowship and the worship of the Church in days of trial, to bear the reproach of Christ. Rejoice that he asks the whole of your allegiance, that he honours you with the most complete demand upon you.

Near to us always is the constraining love of Christ, Enthroned as the Prince of Peace, of Life, and the Bishop of our souls.

Bibliography

Primary Sources

Keble College Oxford Archives
Guildhall Library/London Metropolitan Archives Gibbs Collection
National Trust Tyntesfield Collection
Lord Aldenham's Journal, Holwell Manor, Dorset
Butterfield Mss: Starey Chest, Bursea Chest
Manchester Public Library, Heywood texts
Mander and Mitchenson Theatre Collection
Royal Naval College
Bristol University Theatre Collection, OVLB Section
Finsbury Park Public Library
Sadler's Wells Collection

Unpublished Theses/Dissertations

Garnett, E. Jane, *Aspects of the Relationship Between Protestant Ethics and Economic Activity in Victorian England*, DPhil Thesis, University of Oxford, 1987.

Evershed, William Anthony, *Party and Patronage in the Church of England, 1800–1945*, DPhil Thesis, Oxford, 1985.

Horsley, Alan Avery, *The Crawleys*, PhD Thesis, Pacific Western University, USA, 1985.

Heale, Rosemary, *New Status, Old Structures: Problems and Progress*

213

at St Alban's Cathedral, 1877–1914, MTh Dissertation, University of Wales, Lampeter, 2006.

McPherson, Albert Bayne, *That Uncomfortable Genius: The Building of Melbourne Cathedral,* MA Thesis, University of Melbourne, Australia, 1984.

Sheen, H.E., *The Oxford Movement in a Manchester Parish – The Miles Platting Case,* MA Dissertation, University of Manchester, 1941.

Memoirs Printed for Private Distribution

In Memoriam: William Gibbs, 1875.

The Reminiscences of John Lomas Gibbs, 1875.

The Diary of George Henry Gibbs, 1842.

The Pedigree of the Family of Gibbs, Rachel Gibbs, 1981.

A Memoir of Benjamin Heywood, Thomas Heywood, 1885.

Reminiscences of Thomas Percival Heywood, by his daughter Isabel Mary Heywood, 1899.

Nobody's Friends Club: History and Autobiographical List of Members, 1885.

Printed Sources: Primary

Records of Meeting of Church Congress, 1861–1938.

Parish Magazines.

Letters to *The Times* newspaper.

Periodicals:

Architectural Review

Building News

Contemporary Review, Volume VIII

Listener Supplement VIII

New Statesman and Nation

Saturday Review of Literature

The Builder
The Era
The Listener
The Stage
Gladstone, W.E.: Diaries, Ed. H.C.G. Matthew.
Keble, John, *Sermons Occasional and Parochial.*
Fiske, George, Lectures, *The Moral Influence of the Commercial Spirit of the Day.* Parliamentary Papers
Parliamentary Debates: Hansard
Three Banks Review, Vol 3 (1949) Bank of Scotland.

Printed Sources, Secondary: Books

Aristotle, *Nichomachean Ethics*, (Tr. David Ross), Oxford, 1986
Arthur, William, *The Successful Merchant: Samuel Budgitt*, Bennet, 1894
Bamford, T.W., *The Rise of the Public Schools*, Nelson, 1967
Battiscombe, Georgina, *John Keble*, Constable, 1963
Beauchamp, Tom L. and Bowrie, Norman E., *Ethical Theory and Business Practice*, New Jersey, 2004
Bebbington, D.W., *Unitarian Members of Parliament in the 19th Century*, Internet, 2009
Bentley, James, *Ritualism and Politics in Britain*, Oxford University Press, 1978
Binyon, Gilbert Clive, *The Christian Socialist Movement in England*, SPCK, 1931
Blair, Kirstie (Ed.), *John Keble in Context*, Anthem, 2004
Bradley, Ian Campbell: *Enlightened Entrepreneurs*, Weidenfeld and Nicolson, 1987
Braham, Ernest G, *Ourselves and Reality*, Epworth, 1929
Brillioth, Ingve, *The Anglican Revival*, Longmans, Green, 1925
Brogan, Hugh, *Alexis de Tocqueville*, London, 2006
Brookes, Chris, and Saint, Andrew, *The Victorian Church, Architecture and Society*, Manchester University Press, 1995

Bruce, F.F., *Tradition Old and New*, Paternoster, 1970

Butler, Bishop, *Analogy of Religion, Natural and Revealed*, 1733

Butler, Percy, *Gladstone, Church and the Tractarians*, Oxford, 1982

Button, E.P., *Christian Economics*, Washington D.C., 1888

Carlsson, P. Allan, *Butler's Ethics*, Mouton, 1964

Carrick, John, *Evangelicals and the Oxford Movement*, Wales, 1984

Chadwick, Owen, *From Bossuet to Newman*, Oxford, 1957

Chadwick, Owen, *The Spirit of the Oxford Movement*, Cambridge, 1990

Chadwick, Owen, *The Victorian Church*, A. and C. Black, 1966

Chapman, Raymond, *Faith and Revolt*, Weidenfeld and Nicolson, 1970

Chapman, Raymond (Ed.), *Firmly I Believe*, Canterbury, 2006

Childs, James E. Jnr, *Ethics in Business: Faith at Work*, Minneapolis, 1995

Christiansen, Thorben, *The Origins of Christian Socialism*, Aarhus, 1962

Clark, Kenneth, *The Gothic Revival*, John Murray, 1995

Clark and Linzey (Eds), *Dictionary of Ethics, Theology and Society*, Routledge, 1996

Clarke, Basil F., *Church Building in the Nineteenth Century*, SPCK, 1938

Clarke, Basil F., *Anglican Cathedrals Outside the British Isles*, SPCK, 1958

Cockshutt, A.O.J., *Anglican Attitudes*, Collins, 1959

Coleridge, Ernest Hartley, *Life and Correspondence of John Duke Lord Coleridge*, Heinemann, 1904

Coleridge, J.T., *Memoir of the Revd John Keble*, James Parker, 1869

Cowton, Christopher and Crisp, Roger (Eds.), *Business Ethics*, Oxford, 1998

Dale, R.W., *The Old Evangelicalism and the New*, Hodder, 1889

Daniel, Evan, *The Prayer Book, its History, Language, and Contents*, Wills, Gardner and Darton, 1894

Darley, Gillian, *Octavia Hill*, Constable, 1990

Dearmer, Percy, *Art and Religion*, SCM Press, 1924

Dearmer, Percy, *Everyman's History of the Prayer Book*, Mowbray, 1912

Dearmer, Percy, *The Necessity of Art*, SCM Press, 1924

De-La-Noy, Michael, *The Church of England*, Simon and Schuster, 1998

Dent, Edward Joseph, *A Theatre for Everybody*, Boardman, 1945

Diggle, John W., *The Lancashire Life of Bishop Fraser*, London: Sampson, Low, Marsden, Beale and Rivington Ltd, 1890

Dixon, Roger and Muthesius, Stefan, *Victorian Architecture*, Thames and Hudson, 1978

Donovan, Marcus, *After the Tractarians*, Philip Allan, 1933

Duffield, A.J., *The Prospects of Peru*, London, 1881

Eastlake, Charles Lock, *A History of the Gothic Revival*, 1872/Leicester University Press Reprint, 1970

Elliott, John and Pritchard, John, *Henry Woodyer, Gentleman Architect*, Oxford, 2002

Faber, Geoffrey, *Oxford Apostles*, Penguin, 1954

Ferguson, David, *Faith and its Critics*, Oxford, 2009

Ferrey, A. Benjamin, *Recollections of A. Welby Pugin and his Father Augustin Pugin*, Stanford, 1861

Findlater, Richard, *Lilian Baylis, the Lady of the Old Vic*, Allen Lane, 1975

Ford, Chris, et al, (Eds), *The Church in Cottonopoli*, Lancashire and Cheshire Antiquarian Society, 1997

Gilbert, Susie, *Opera for Everybody*, Faber, 2009

Girouard, Mark, *The Victorian Country House*, Yale, 1979

Gladstone, W.E., (Edited D.C. Lathbury), *Letters on Church and Religion*, London, John Murray, 1910

Gore, Charles (Ed.), *Lux Mundi*, Murray, 1889

Gray, Donald, *Percy Dearmer*, Canterbury, 2000

Green, T.H., (Edited A.C. Bradley), *Prolegomena to Ethics*, Oxford, 1906

Green, T.H., (Edited Maria Derova-Cookson and W.T. Mander), *Ethics, Metaphysics and Political Philosophy*, Oxford, 2006

217

Hadas, Edward, *Human Goods, Economic Evils*, Delaware, 2007

Haliday, Stephen, *The Making of the Metropolis*, Breedon, 2003

Hamilton, Cicely and Baylis, L.M., *The Old Vic*, Jonathan Cape, 1926

Hebert, A.G., *Liturgy and Society*, Faber, 1935

Heeney, Brian, *Mission to the Middle Classes*, SPCK, 1969

Hegel, G.W.F. (Tr. K.T.M. Knox), *Philosophy of Right*, Oxford, 1952

Hegel, G.W.F. (Tr. Allan W. Wood), *Ethics*, Cambridge University Press, 1993

Hennell, Michael M., *John Venn and the Clapham Sect*, Lutterworth, 1958

Hill, Rosemary, *God's Architect*, Penguin, 2007

Hilton, Boyd, *The Age of Atonement*, Oxford, 1991

Hinchcliff, Peter, *God and History ... 1875–1914*, Oxford, 1992

Hobsbawm, C.J., *The Age of Capital, 1848–1875*, London, 1977

Hogg, David J. (Ed.), *Diaries of Tyntesfield*, David Hogg, 2009

Hope, J.B., *Rugby Since Arnold*, Macmillan, 1867

Hubbard, John Gillibrand, *The History of Taxation*, Longmans, 1852/1999

Hughes, Thomas, *James Fraser, Second Bishop of Manchester*, Macmillan, 1889

Illingworth, Agnes Louisa, *The Life and Work of John Richardson Illingworth*, Murray, 1917

Ingram, Kenneth, *John Keble*, Philip Allen, 1933

Jacob, W.M., *The Clerical Profession in the Long Eighteenth Century*, Oxford, 2007

Jay, Elizabeth, *The Evangelical and Oxford Movements*, Oxford, 1983

Jones, Dominic, *Victorian Revolution*, Oxford, 2009

Jones, Owen, *The Grammar of Ornament*, Day, 1888, 1914 and 1986

Jordan, Robert Furneaux, *Victorian Architecture*, Pelican, 1966

Kirk, K.E., *The Story of the Woodard Schools*, Hodder, 1937

Kitsch, M.J., *Capitalism and the Reformation*, Longmans, 1967

Lea, Garth, *God's Politician: William Wilberforce*, Darton, Longman and Todd, 2007

Lock, Walter, *John Keble; A Biography*, Methuen, 1893

McIntyre, Alasdair, *After Virtue*, Duckworth, 1994

McQueen, C.A., *Peruvian Public Finance*, Washington DC, 1926

Mascall, E.L., *The Importance of Being Human*, Oxford, 1959

Maritain, Jacques, *Art and Scholasticism*, Sheed and Ward, 1933

Mathew, W.M., *The House of Gibbs and the Peruvian Monopoly*, The Royal Historical Society, 1981

Maude, Wilfred, *Antony Gibbs and Sons, 1808–1958*, London, 1958

Maurice, F.D., *The Kingdom of Christ*, Dent, 1838

May, J. Lewis, *The Oxford Movement*, Bodley Head, 1933

Mill, John Stuart, *Autobiography*, 1873

Miller, James, *Fertile Fortune*, The National Trust, 2006

Moorman, J.R.H., *A History of the English Church*, A. and C. Black, 1953

Neill, Elizabeth, *Fragile Fortune*, Halsgrove/Ryelands, 2008

Niebuhr, Reinhold, *Moral Man and Immoral Society*, Continuum, 2005

O'Connell, Jean, *John Venn and the Friends of the Hereford Poor*, Logaston, 2007

Ollard, S.L., *A Short History of the Oxford Movement*, Mowbray, 1932

Palmer, Bernard, *Reverend Rebels*, Darton, Longman and Todd, 1993

Periero, James, *Cardinal Manning*, Oxford, 1998

Periero, James, *Ethics and the Oxford Movement*, Oxford, 2008

Phillips, Catherine, *Gerard Manley Hopkins and the Victorian Visual World*, Oxford, 2007

Platt, D.C.M. (Ed.), *Business Imperialism*, Oxford, 1977

Pollock, John, *Wilberforce*, Constable, 1977

Pugin, A.W.N., *Contrasts*, Leicester University Press, 1836/1969

Purcell, Edmund Sheridan, *The Life of Cardinal Manning*, Macmillan, 1896

Reckitt, Maurice B., *Faith and Society*, Longmans, Green, 1933

Rowell, Geoffrey, *The Vision Glorious*, Oxford, 1983

Rowell, Geoffrey (Ed.), *Tradition Renewed*, Darton, Longman and Todd, 1986

Sandford. E.G., *Memoirs of Archbishop Temple, 1821–1896*, Macmillan, 1906

Schafer, Elizabeth, *Lilian Baylis – a Biography*, University of Hertfordshire, 2006

Shaw, Jane and Krieder, Alan (Eds), *Culture and Nonconformist Tradition*, Cardiff, 1999

Skinner, S.A., *Tractarians and the Condition of England*, Oxford, 2004

Summerson, John, *Heavenly Mansions*, Cresser Press, 1949

Tannich, Robert, *Olivier*, Thames and Hudson, 1985

Thorndike, Sybil and Russell, *Lilian Baylis as I Knew Her*, Chapman Hall, 1938

Toon, Peter, *Evangelical Theology, 1833–1856*, Marshall, Morgan and Scott, 1979

Warburton, Brian, *John Keble, Priest, Professor and Poet*, Croom Helm, 1976

Waterman, A.M.C., *Revolution, Economic and Religious, 1798–1833*, Cambridge University Press, 1991

Watkin, David, *The Life and Work of C.R. Cockerell*, Zemmar, 1974

Webster, Christopher, and Elliott, John, 'A Church as it Should Be' – The Cambridge Society and its Influence, Shaun Tyas, 2000

Webster, George, *Hunstanton and its Neighbourhood*, Simpkin, Marshall, 1978

Williams, E.G. Harcourt (Ed.), *Vic-Wells – The Work of Lilian Baylis*, Cobden Sanderson, 1938

Yates, *Anglican Ritualism in Victorian Britain*, Oxford University Press, 1999.

Index

226